The Reflective Educator's Guide to Classroom Research

The Reflective Educator's Guide to Classroom Research

Learning to Teach and Teaching to Learn Through Practitioner Inquiry

Third Edition

Nancy Fichtman Dana
Diane Yendol-Hoppey

CORWIN
A SAGE Company

FOR INFORMATION:

Corwin

A SAGE Company

2455 Teller Road

Thousand Oaks, California 91320

(800) 233-9936

www.corwin.com

SAGE Publications Ltd.

1 Oliver's Yard

55 City Road

London EC1Y 1SP

United Kingdom

SAGE Publications India Pvt. Ltd.

B 1/I 1 Mohan Cooperative Industrial Area

Mathura Road, New Delhi 110 044

India

SAGE Publications Asia-Pacific Pte. Ltd.

3 Church Street

#10-04 Samsung Hub

Singapore 049483

Printed in the United States of America

A catalog record of this book can be found at the Library of Congress.

ISBN 978-1-4833-3198-0

This book is printed on acid-free paper.

Acquisitions Editor: Dan Alpert

Associate Editor: Kimberly Greenberg

Editorial Assistant: Cesar Reyes

Production Editor: Amy Schroller

Copy Editor: Mark Bast

Typesetter: C&M Digitals (P) Ltd.

Proofreader: Dennis W. Webb

Indexer: Maria Sosnowski

Cover Designer: Scott Van Atta

14 15 16 17 18 10 9 8 7 6 5 4 3 2 1

Contents

Additional materials and resources related to
The Reflective Educator's Guide to Classroom Research
can be found at http://www.corwin.com/
Thereflectiveeducatorsguide

Companion Website Contents

To access this website, please visit
http://corwin.com/Thereflectiveeducatorsguide

Foreword to the Second Edition

I used to shy away from anything that looked like inquiry. Where would I find the time? What did I know about data? How was it different, really, from what I did naturally as an educator—asking myself questions, reflecting on my practice, paying attention to the challenges of my craft, even going public in my critical friends group and asking my colleagues for feedback?

And then I participated in a collaborative inquiry institute and, in preparation, read the first edition of Nancy Dana and Diane Yendol-Hoppey's book, *The Reflective Educator's Guide to Classroom Research.* I was hooked. Now, I can't imagine *not* having a question that guides my thinking, a question that helps me determine what kind of data I need and how to gather it, a question that helps me look at my assumptions and helps me open up possibilities. I am a better educator because I have begun to explore questions about my practice in a systematic way.

This second edition is an even richer compendium. There are more stories told in the voices of teachers at all stages of their inquiries, and their authenticity is palpable. These teachers' stories and musings are interspersed with practical exercises and strategies. And while the authors add their assurances throughout the book that it really is just fine to find your own comfort level as you begin, the voices of the teachers—who sound just like colleagues—make you think it would be possible for you to do what they are doing, too, if only you could find your own question.

Certainly, according to Dana and Yendol-Hoppey, questions propel the inquiry. But before the question, the authors suggest, educators often begin with something else. It may be a wondering, a sense of "what if?" Or they may decide to reconnect to a passion—the reason they became a teacher in the first place. Sometimes a dilemma, or a critical incident, or a sense of not knowing sets the stage for the inquiry—or they notice that something is working and decide they need to know why. And for some, it is reading someone else's research that causes them to want to explore their own practice.

Dana and Yendol-Hoppey legitimize and give voice to all of these possible starting points—and they make it seem easy not only to begin, but to continue on through the process—finding people with whom you can collaborate, developing a plan and integrating inquiry into your practice, collecting and generating the data that will provide the most insight into your question, analyzing your data, writing up your conclusions and going public by sharing your work with others, and assessing the quality of your inquiry. At no point does it feel impossible or even overwhelming; they effortlessly convey that this next step is simply the next logical thing to do.

The dictionary defines inquiry as 1. *The act of exploration and discovery.* 2. *To ask questions; to be open to seeing new potentials and possibilities.* Indeed, the act of teacher inquiry involves searching, exploring, studying children, examining one's own practice, and discovering and rediscovering new possibilities. It demands working collaboratively with colleagues to guard against, in Peter Senge's words, "counting as 'real' the data which confirms what we already believe." Colleagues provide perspectives and insights we can't possibly have on our own, because wherever we go, there we are, looking at the world through our own lenses.

All of this, of course, requires certain dispositions. It means we must, at times, slow down and be reflective. We must develop the intellectual side of ourselves—the place where we can open up to others with curiosity and interest, where we can consider options or ideas we hadn't thought of before. We have to develop the capacity to identify and explicitly work on the questions that matter most to our students—the questions or aspects of our practice that perhaps make *us* the most uncomfortable. When we engage in collaborative inquiry, we become students of teaching and learning for one another, so we have to learn to frame good questions and develop the habit of taking an inquiry stance toward all that we do. We must become comfortable being uncomfortable—and get used to being in the place of not knowing more often, with a greater capacity for ambiguity. In fact, as Dana and Yendol-Hoppey point out, one of the reasons we engage in teacher inquiry is that it honors the complexity inherent in all teaching. Inquiry insists that we routinely unearth our assumptions—our assumptions about our students and their families, our assumptions about our colleagues and ourselves, our assumptions about achievement and what constitutes a meaningful education—and to examine these assumptions with others—because we believe that the most effective schools have adults in them who are the least satisfied with their practice. We must be willing to collect and make public the evidence from our practice—the data and the student work. We can't be afraid of hard work or of saying, "I was wrong." And we must find courage in community, as we hold each other accountable for acting on what we learn.

At one point, a teacher in *The Reflective Educator's Guide to Classroom Research* declares, "Had I not posed the question, I never would have noticed what was actually occurring!" And so, as we ask and explore questions such as, "What supports and experiences for teachers new to our district make a positive difference in their lives as educators?," "What aspects of the school do families of color experience as supportive and effective, and how can we build on what works?," "How can I make each ELL student's story visible in the organizational culture of our school?," "How does kindergarten writing impact literacy in Grade 1?," and "How can my students be cultural resources to the curriculum?," we set off on a journey to "make the familiar strange." In so doing, we echo T. S. Eliot when he says, "And the end of all our exploring, will be to arrive where we started, and know the place for the first time."

—*Gene Thompson-Grove*

Cofounder, National School Reform
Faculty Director, Professional Development and
Special Initiatives, Public Schools of Brookline, MA

Foreword to the First Edition

The Reflective Educator's Guide to Classroom Research is more than a book about how to do teacher research or action research in your own classroom. Certainly it is that, but it is much more than that. Building on the awareness that teachers have accumulated an enormous amount of knowledge through their years of teaching, the authors show how this knowledge can be mined by teachers studying their own practice, making visible the complexities of teaching. It is work that is enriched by sharing with other teachers who can learn from it, expand it, critique it, and build on it. By learning about their practice in this way, teachers not only build their capacity to better understand their own teaching, but also help to build a collaborative culture in their school.

This kind of practitioner inquiry requires teachers to have access to some kind of a group, either inside or outside their school, so that an "inquiry stance" toward teaching becomes a way of life. There is increasing evidence that some teachers who study their practice, go public with their teaching, and share what they are learning with colleagues not only develop greater confidence and understanding about their own teaching and student learning, but also begin to think differently about what it means to be a "lifelong learner" (Lieberman & Wood, 2002).

A special quality of this book is that it makes us feel like Nancy Dana and Diane Yendol-Hoppey are two friends by our side, helping us to develop a process for thinking about teaching and learning in our own classrooms. Numerous authors have attempted to write "how to" books about teacher research, but this one recognizes that doing research is a process and that the role of the authors is to engage the reader in moving through that process: how you get from a *focus* on a particular student who keeps you awake at night, or something in the curriculum, or the interaction of students, to the development of a way of studying the problem that eventually illuminates its complexities and often leads to ways of thinking that suggest actions, strategies, and solutions. It is apparent that the authors have facilitated classroom research involving many teachers, as the processes we read about are rooted in the reality of teachers' struggles to know more about their teaching and to get better at understanding their own as well as their students' motivations to learn.

The Reflective Educator's Guide to Classroom Research helps us learn that collaborating with peers helps not only one's own research quest, but that it can be the source of better group understanding as well. Do we want to do a *shared* inquiry; a *parallel* inquiry where we do our own research, as others do theirs by looking at the same topic; or an *intersecting* inquiry where people have different questions on the same topic? How can we learn to do research as a part of teaching work and not an add-on? What strategies can we develop to collect data? And once data are collected, there is the common question, "What do I do with all this information?" The authors are right there: teaching, facilitating, supporting, and moving us through a variety of ways to look at data, always grounded in teacher examples and always explicated by conceptual understandings of how to think through each of these steps.

Readers experience not only what it is like to do classroom research, but perhaps as important, gain an understanding of how teachers can become scholars of their own practice. These "scholars" become colleagues capable of developing their own means of holding themselves accountable within the context of a professional learning community; a community of teachers (as well as their students) excited about learning and stimulated by their continuous inquiries into their own practice.

—*Ann Lieberman*

Senior Scholar, The Carnegie Foundation for the Advancement of Teaching Visiting Professor, Stanford University

Preface

Since we first began working with practicing and prospective teachers engaged in inquiry in the late 1980s, we have been passionate about the process and the promise it holds to raise teachers' voices in the profession we love. While much has changed on the educational landscape since we began our work with teacher inquiry, the process of inquiry itself has endured and remains a powerful vehicle for teacher professional development as well as initial teacher preparation. Indeed, Cochran-Smith and Lytle (2009) report that "teacher inquiry and the larger practitioner research movement appear to be flourishing in the United States and in many other parts of the world" (p. 11).

While the core of our inquiry work has remained constant, with each passing year and each teacher inquirer we work with, we learn more and more about the process and how to facilitate it. In the third edition of this book, we both respond to the changing times and capture what we've learned about facilitation since authoring the first and second editions of this text.

Two of the most pressing educational issues facing teachers today are teacher evaluation and the Common Core State Standards. In this edition, we have sections that discuss the role of inquiry in both, as well as added examples of the ways the process of inquiry can help teachers unpack the Common Core and what these standards will mean to their practice. Additionally, since the second edition, the concept of teacher leadership has continued to gain momentum. In this edition, we provide a more pointed discussion on the relationship between teacher leadership and teacher inquiry.

As we teach about inquiry at the university and coach teachers in the process, we continue to learn much from our students and the wonderful teacher researchers we have worked with across the nation and abroad. In the experiences we have had since writing the second edition, we have learned about the use of iPads as a tool for teacher research, how to make interviewing a part of teaching practice, and the importance of structuring journal entries. We've updated our discussion of data collection strategies to include these lessons learned. Furthermore, we've expanded our coverage of how and when to use literature to inform a teacher researcher's work.

In addition to updates in the chapter that focuses on data collection, in previous editions, we mentioned the iterative nature of data collection and data analysis but then proceeded to mainly focus on the summative data analysis process in the chapter on this subject. In this edition, we add a discussion of formative data analysis and provide examples of what this might look like in practice. We hope with this addition, readers will better understand what is meant by the "iterative" nature of data collection and analysis and the ways these two components of the inquiry process go hand in hand.

Our passion for the process of inquiry has helped us build bridges between K–12 and higher education contexts and experience powerful school-university partnerships. As teacher inquiry spans both these contexts, we have learned the importance of celebrating commonalities as well as understanding and appreciating differences. In this edition, we sharpen our discussion of the differences between academic research and teacher inquiry as well as discuss ethical issues related to engaging in the process of inquiry whether you are doing it as part of school-based work, university-based work, or a combination of both.

Finally, shortly after our second edition was published in 2009, we published a separate facilitator's guide with ideas and tips for using the book in district professional development endeavors and/or college coursework. In this third edition, we seamlessly meld activities and ideas for teaching or facilitating professional development using this text by including a substantial accompanying website for professional development providers and course instructors.

This third edition emerges from our understanding of the literature in the areas of professional development, action research, teacher research, qualitative research, quantitative research, and the process of change as well as our collective experience working with practicing and prospective teachers engaged in inquiry for over 20 years. What we have learned from these teachers about how and why they inquire provides insights into the power teacher inquiry holds to transform classrooms and schools to places where teachers' voices contribute to the knowledge generated about teaching and learning.

ABOUT THIS BOOK

Using a journey metaphor, in this text we take you through the process of inquiry step by step. You begin your journey with a brief introduction to teacher inquiry in Chapter 1 and then move to Chapter 2 to define your first inquiry. This chapter, appropriately entitled "The Start of Your Journey: Finding a Wondering," gets you started on an inquiry by engaging you in a series of exercises designed to help you cut through all of the intricacies and complexities of teaching to "focus in" on one area that you are passionate about studying. We define eight passions as places where you may locate your wondering. The passions we cover are inquiring into an individual child's academic, social, and/or emotional needs; a desire to improve curriculum; a desire to enhance content knowledge; a desire to improve or experiment with teaching strategies and teaching techniques; a desire to explore the relationship between your beliefs and your classroom practice; an investigation of the intersection between your personal and professional identities; issues of social justice; and understanding the learning context. As we explore each passion, we use examples from teacher-inquirers we have worked with to illustrate the ways their wonderings emerged from the intersection of their real-world classroom experiences and one of the particular passions defined in Chapter 2.

In Chapter 3, we explore the importance of collaboration with other educators and define four possible structures for inquiry collaboration that might support your inquiry work. At the close of this chapter, you will be ready to begin data collection, a process explored in Chapter 4. In this chapter, we discuss a dozen common strategies for data collection used by teacher-inquirers (literature, field notes, document analysis, interviews, focus groups, digital pictures, video, reflective journals, blogs, surveys, standardized test scores and other assessment measures, critical friend group feedback). Throughout our discussion, we point to the ways each of these strategies connects to what you already do in your life and work as a teacher. We do this because we want you to see how teacher inquiry is *a part of*, not *apart from*, the work you do as a teacher.

In Chapter 5, we provide important guidelines for you to consider in relationship to the ethical dimensions of teaching and inquiry. Key questions are raised to help you assure that the work you are doing as a teacher and inquirer is ethical and will do no harm to the students you teach.

In Chapter 6, we explore what we have found to be one of the most difficult steps for teacher-inquirers—data analysis. We discuss and illustrate the ways you analyze data *as* you are collecting it as well as *after* collection is complete. If you enjoy jigsaw puzzles you will particularly enjoy your journey through this chapter, as we fully develop this metaphor to describe the summative data analysis process step by step. In addition, we use the work of one teacher-inquirer to illustrate what data analysis might actually look like in practice.

In Chapter 7, we look closely at the "writing it up" process as a way to extend the learning that has occurred during data analysis. One teacher-inquirer's work is shared in its entirety to illustrate four basic components of any teacher's inquiry write-up.

In Chapter 8, we discuss the ways engagement in inquiry is connected to every individual teacher becoming the best he or she can be! One part of becoming the best you can be is reflecting on the quality of the teacher research you produce. Chapter 8 offers five quality indicators and questions you can ask yourself as you reflect on your own and your colleagues' research.

Finally, in Chapter 9, we bring closure to your first inquiry journey by discussing the importance of sharing your inquiry with others and helping you identify outlets for your work.

Across the nation, prospective and practicing teachers vary greatly in their experience with teacher inquiry. Perhaps you are brand new to teacher inquiry. Perhaps you have been engaged in inquiry for years and wish to further the development of teacher inquiry in your school. Perhaps you wish to make teacher inquiry a more visible or meaningful part of your teacher education program. Perhaps you seek to mentor other professionals in their first inquiries. Wherever you may be in your inquiry journey, we hope this text provides the impetus for you to take the next steps along the pathway of simultaneous renewal and reform. Happy inquiring!

Acknowledgments

We have had the honor and privilege to work with many tremendous teachers throughout our careers, and it is through these teachers' work that we have witnessed the process of inquiry and the power of inquiry as a tool for professional learning. Throughout our careers, we have also always been passionate about raising the voices of teachers in educational reform, teaching, and teacher education. In an effort to raise teacher voices, we weave within this text many rich examples of these teachers' inquiries as we describe the process step by step. Hence, this book would not have been possible without the inquiries that only prospective and practicing teachers can provide. We are grateful to all of the practicing and prospective teachers with whom we have worked. Their time, dedication, and contribution to teacher inquiry and the education profession are immeasurable. We continue to admire their devotion and are grateful for their dedication to the profession of teaching and their support in writing this book.

We are also grateful for numerous colleagues who helped us conceptualize and enact our work with inquiry and have pushed our thinking about the process over time. While in past editions we have attempted to name all the wonderful colleagues who have supported our work, the list is becoming quite long. Therefore, in this edition we name those who have provided feedback specifically on the third edition—Susan Ariew, Jamey Bolton Burns, Mary Klehr, Jennifer Thulin Jacobs, Gail Ritchie, Jason Jude Smith, Sarah van Ingen, and Rachel Wolkenhauer. We are grateful for these and all of our colleagues named in previous editions who have supported our work throughout the years. We also thank the great people at Corwin, specifically Dan Alpert, Kim Greenberg, and Cesar Reyes, for their support of the third edition.

Finally, we wish to thank our husbands. In his roles as supervisor of curriculum and staff development, inclusion specialist, and special education faculty at the University of South Florida, David Hoppey has spent the last decade helping practitioners understand how to enact an inquiry stance that can transform the experiences of struggling learners. His work serves as an example to all interested in high-quality special education teacher education and job-embedded professional learning. And Tom Dana, the University of Florida's College of Education associate dean for academic affairs, continues to lay the foundation for the spread of teacher inquiry that we began at Penn State with his unselfish support and encouragement in the early stages of our work. The many conversations we had as all three editions of this book were taking shape were invaluable to each book's completion. He served as our computer consultant, editor, idea bouncer, and friend. We are grateful for and admire his dedication to rethinking teacher education and building an inquiry stance toward teaching, as well as his awesome administrative talent that makes these things happen.

Publisher's Acknowledgments

Corwin Press gratefully acknowledges the contributions of the following reviewers:

Emily Bonner
Assistant Professor, Curriculum and Instruction
University of Texas at San Antonio
San Antonio, TX

Carole English, Ed.D.
Director of Teacher Education and Assessment
Lipscomb University
Nashville, TN

Rita Hagevik
Graduate Director of Science Education
University of North Carolina at Pembroke
Pembroke, NC

Virginia Harder
Professor
Eastern Michigan University
Ypsilanti, MI

Kimberly Livengood
Assistant Professor in Curriculum and Instruction
Angelo State University
San Angelo, TX

About the Authors

Nancy Fichtman Dana is currently professor of education in the School of Teaching and Learning at the University of Florida, Gainesville. She began her career in education as an elementary school teacher in Hannibal Central Schools, New York. Since earning her PhD from Florida State University in 1991, she has been a passionate advocate for teacher inquiry and has worked with numerous schools and districts across the nation and abroad to develop programs of inquiry as well as conducted extensive research on the process. She has published nine books and over 50 articles in professional journals and edited books focused on teacher and principal professional development and practitioner inquiry. Dana has received many honors, including the Association of Teacher Educator's Distinguished Research in Teacher Education Award and the National Staff Development Council (NSDC) Book of the Year Award, both honoring Dana and Yendol-Hoppey's work related to practitioner inquiry.

Diane Yendol-Hoppey is a professor of education and associate dean in the College of Education at the University of South Florida. Prior to her appointment at the University of South Florida, she served as the director of the Benedum Collaborative at West Virginia University and taught for many years at the University of Florida where she was the evaluator of numerous district, state, and national professional development efforts. Before beginning her work in higher education, Diane spent 13 years as an elementary school teacher in Pennsylvania and Maryland. She holds a PhD in curriculum and instruction from The Pennsylvania State University. Diane's current work explores national and international research in clinically rich teacher education, job-embedded professional learning, and teacher leadership. Diane received the AERA Division K Early Career Research Award for her ongoing commitment to researching innovative approaches to professional development. She has published three books and over 50 articles in professional journals.

For our children, who keep our passion for reforming teaching and teacher education alive—Greg, Kirsten, Caran, Billy, and Kevin

Introduction to The Reflective Educator's Guide to Classroom Research

WEBSITE FOR PROFESSIONAL DEVELOPMENT FACILITATORS AND COURSE INSTRUCTORS

As discussed in the Preface, after the second edition of this book was published in 2009, we published a separate facilitator's guide with ideas and tips for using the book in district professional development endeavors and/or college coursework. As we authored the third edition, we wished to seamlessly meld activities and ideas for teaching or facilitating professional development using this text into the book itself. We did so by creating an accompanying website for use by professional development providers and college course instructors, based largely on the facilitator's guide previously published for use with the previous edition. On this website, you will find numerous ideas for facilitating discussion, learning, and the process of inquiry itself using this book.

The accompanying website contains a chapter-by-chapter guide to the use of this book. Click on the link for each individual chapter to find a chapter summary, discussion questions, activities, journal writing prompts, and resources for extended learning. You may also access handouts for use with the activities described in each chapter. Finally, you'll find a series of two- to three-hour workshop agendas distributed over an entire school year (September—May) to be a powerful way to guide teachers through the inquiry process step by step. Note that the suggested time frame of these workshops can be condensed to start at any time in the school year or to fit within a typical 16-week semester, if you are using this book as a required text for a college course on action research.

Over the years, we have learned that the quality of a teacher's experience with the process of inquiry is directly related to the coaching that teacher receives in the process. This website was designed to support the work of inquiry coaches, whether one is coaching inquiry as a part of a district professional development effort, college course, student-teaching supervision, or professional development school work. To access this website go to http://www.corwin.com/Thereflectiveeducatorsguide.

HOW TO USE THE INQUIRY BOOKS

This table summarizes the books we have authored or coauthored related to inquiry and describes their focus, differentiating the texts and delineating their use.

Book	Authors	Focus
The Reflective Educator's Guide to Classroom Research: Learning to Teach and Teaching to Learn Through Practitioner Inquiry, 3rd edition (2014)	Nancy Fichtman Dana Diane Yendol-Hoppey	This book provides an in-depth introduction to teacher inquiry for both prospective and practicing teachers, taking the reader step by step through the process, including developing a wondering, collaborating with others, collecting data, analyzing data, writing up one's work, assessing the quality of inquiry, and sharing one's work with others. A great first book on teacher inquiry.
The Reflective Educator's Guide to Professional Development: Coaching Inquiry-Oriented Learning Communities (2008)	Nancy Fichtman Dana Diane Yendol-Hoppey	This book focuses on coaching the inquiry process within professional learning communities. In addition to tips on the establishment of healthy learning communities, it contains numerous coaching resources to take teachers through each stage of the inquiry process.

Book	Authors	Focus
Leading With Passion and Knowledge: The Principal as Action Researcher (2009)	Nancy Fichtman Dana	This book takes administrators through the process of inquiry step by step, offering rich examples of principals engaged in each step of the process. A perfect resource for districts to provide powerful professional development for principals as well as university professors to help their students enrolled in educational leadership programs write an action research thesis or dissertation.
Powerful Professional Development: Building Expertise Within the Four Walls of Your School (2010)	Diane Yendol-Hoppey Nancy Fichtman Dana	This book provides a bird's-eye view of numerous job-embedded professional development strategies. In addition to a chapter on inquiry, chapters focus on book studies, webinars and podcasts, coteaching, conversation tools, lesson study, culturally responsive and content-focused coaching, and professional learning communities.
Inquiry: A Districtwide Approach to Staff and Student Learning (2011)	Nancy Fichtman Dana Carol Thomas Sylvia Boynton	This book describes the ways engagement in inquiry fits together for all constituencies within a district— principals, teachers, students, and coaches. This systems overview of inquiry and the ways the process can connect improved practice to student achievement enables the reader to enhance learning for adults and students across an entire district.
Digging Deeper Into Action Research: A Teacher Inquirer's Field Guide (2013)	Nancy Fichtman Dana	This book takes off where other introductory texts on action research leave the reader, providing teacher-inquirers tips for each part of the inquiry process as they are in the midst of doing it (i.e., developing a wondering, developing an inquiry plan, analyzing data, and presenting one's work). A perfect complement to

(Continued)

(Continued)

Book	Authors	Focus
		The Reflective Educator's Guide to Classroom Research, this book can also be used as a short, succinct, stand-alone text to guide teachers through the inquiry process in a very targeted and specific way. It may also be used as a text in any university course (whether or not the course focuses on action research) to help students complete a required inquiry-based assignment.
Inquiring Into the Common Core	Nancy Fichtman Dana Jamey Bolton Burns Rachel Wolkenhauer	This book tells the story of Woodson Elementary School and the ways the teachers and administrators in this building used the process of inquiry to better understand their implementation of the Common Core State Standards (CCSS). In addition, teachers engaged their students in inquiry to actualize the CCSS in classroom practice. Examples of teacher inquiry and student inquiry provide insights for the reader into their own pathway to accelerating achievement with the CCSS as their guide.

1

Teacher Inquiry Defined

Teaching involves a search for meaning in the world. Teaching is a life project, a calling, a vocation that is an organizing center of all other activities. Teaching is past and future as well as present, it is background as well as foreground, it is depth as well as surface. Teaching is pain and humor, joy and anger, dreariness and epiphany. Teaching is world building, it is architecture and design, it is purpose and moral enterprise. Teaching is a way of being in the world that breaks through the boundaries of the traditional job and in the process redefines all life and teaching itself.

—William Ayers (1989, p. 130)

Whether you are a beginning or veteran teacher, an administrator, or a teacher educator, when you think of teaching, learning to teach, and continuing one's growth as a teacher, you cannot help but be struck by the enormous complexities, paradoxes, and tensions inherent in the simple act of teaching itself, captured so eloquently in the quote from William Ayers. With all of these complexities, paradoxes, and tensions, a teacher's work shapes the daily life of his or her classroom. In addition to responding to the needs of the children within the classroom, a teacher is expected to implement endless changes advocated by those outside the four walls of the classroom—administrators, politicians, and researchers. While teachers have gained insights into their educational practice from these three groups, teachers' voices have typically been absent from larger discussions about educational change and reform. Historically, teachers have not had access to tools that could have brought their knowledge to the table and raised their voices to a high-enough level to be heard in these larger conversations. Teacher inquiry is a vehicle that can be used by teachers to untangle some of the complexities that occur in the profession, raise teachers' voices in discussions of educational reform, and ultimately transform assumptions about the teaching profession itself. Transforming the profession is really the capstone of the teacher inquiry experience. Let's begin our journey into the what, why, and how of teacher inquiry with an overview of the evolution of the teacher inquiry movement and a simple definition of this very complex, rewarding, transformative, provocative, and productive process.

WHAT IS TEACHER INQUIRY?

Understanding the history of teacher inquiry will help you recognize how today, as a current or future educator, you find yourself investigating a new paradigm of learning that can lead to educational renewal and reform. This history lesson begins by looking closely at three educational research traditions: process-product research, qualitative or interpretive research, and teacher inquiry (see Table 1.1).

Two paradigms have dominated educational research on schooling, teaching, and learning in the past. In the first paradigm, the underlying conception of "process-product research" (Shulman, 1986) portrays teaching as a primarily linear activity and depicts teachers as technicians. The teacher's role is to implement the research findings of "outside" experts, almost exclusively university researchers, who are considered alien to the everyday happenings in classrooms. In this transmissive mode teachers are not expected to be problem posers or problem solvers. Rather, teachers negotiate dilemmas framed by outside experts and are asked to implement with fidelity a curriculum designed by those outside of the classroom. Based on this paradigm, many teachers have learned that it is sometimes best not to problematize their classroom experiences and firsthand observations because to do so may mean an admittance of failure to implement curriculum as directed. In fact, the transmissive culture of many schools has demonstrated that teachers can suffer punitive repercussions from highlighting areas that teachers themselves identify as problematic. The consequences of pointing out problems have often resulted in traditional top-down "retraining" or remediation. In the transmissive view, our educational community does not encourage solution-seeking behavior on the part of classroom teachers.

In the second paradigm—educational research drawn from qualitative or interpretative studies—teaching is portrayed as a highly complex,

Table 1.1   Competing Paradigms: The Multiple Voices of Research

	Research Paradigms		
	Process-Product	*Qualitative or Interpretive*	*Teacher Inquiry*
Teacher	Teacher as technician	Teacher as story character	Teacher as storyteller
Researcher	Outsider	Outsider	Insider
Process	Linear	Discursive	Cyclical
Source of research question	Researcher	Researcher	Teacher
Type of research question	Focused on control, prediction, or impact	Focused on explaining a process or phenomenon	Focused on providing insight into a teacher's classroom practice in an effort to make change
Example of research question	Which management strategy is most successful?	How do children experience bullying in the classroom?	How can I accommodate ESL students at the kindergarten writing table?

context-specific, interactive activity. In addition, this qualitative or interpretive paradigm captures differences across classrooms, schools, and communities that are critically important. Chris Clark (1995) identifies the complexity inherent in a teacher's job and the importance of understanding and acknowledging contextual differences as follows: "Description becomes prescription, often with less and less regard for the contextual matters that make the description meaningful in the first place" (p. 20).

Although qualitative or interpretive work attends to issues of context, most of the studies emerging from this research paradigm are conducted by university researchers and are intended for academic audiences. Such school-university research provides valuable insights into the connections between theory and practice, but, like the process-product research, the qualitative or interpretive approach limits teachers' roles in the research process. In fact, the knowledge about teaching and learning generated through university study of theory and practice is still defined and generated by "outsiders" to the school and classroom. While both the process-product and qualitative research paradigms have generated valuable insights into the teaching and learning process, they have not included the voices of the people closest to the children—classroom teachers.

Hence, a third research tradition emerges highlighting the role classroom teachers play as knowledge generators. This tradition is often referred to as "teacher research," "teacher inquiry," "classroom research," "action research," or "practitioner inquiry." In general, the teacher inquiry movement focuses on the concerns of teachers (not outside researchers) and engages teachers in the design, data collection, and interpretation of data around a question. Termed "action research" by Carr and Kemmis (1986), this approach to educational research has many benefits: (1) Theories and knowledge are generated from research grounded in the realities of educational practice, (2) teachers become collaborators in educational research by investigating their own problems, and (3) teachers play a part in the research process, which makes them more likely to facilitate change based on the knowledge they create.

Elliot (1988) describes action research as a continual set of spirals consisting of reflection and action. Each spiral involves (1) clarifying and diagnosing a practical situation that needs to be improved or a practical problem that needs to be resolved; (2) formulating action strategies to improve the situation or resolve the problem; (3) implementing the action strategies and evaluating their effectiveness; and (4) clarifying the situation, resulting in new definitions of problems or areas for improvement, and so on, to the next spiral of reflection and action.

Note that in our description of this third research tradition we have used a number of terms synonymously—teacher research, action research, classroom research, practitioner inquiry, and teacher inquiry. While these phrases have been used interchangeably, they do have somewhat different emphases and histories (Cochran-Smith & Lytle, 2009). Action research, for instance, usually refers to research intended to bring about change of some kind, usually with a social justice focus, whereas teacher research quite often has the goal only of examining a teacher's classroom practice in order to improve it or to better understand what works. For the purposes of this text and to streamline our discussion of research traditions, we have grouped all of these related processes together to represent teachers' systematic study of their own practice. Yet we use the term *inquiry* most often as, in our own coaching of teachers' systematic study of their own practice, we became discouraged by the baggage that the word *research* in the term *action research* carried with it when the concept was first introduced to teachers. The images that the word *research* conjures up come mostly from the process-product paradigm and include a "controlled setting," "an experiment with control and treatment groups," "an objective scientist removed from the subjects of study so as not to contaminate findings," "long hours in the library," and "crunching numbers." Teachers, in general, weren't overly enthused by these images, and it took a good deal of time for us to deconstruct these images and help teachers see that those images were antithetical to what teacher/action research was all about. So, over time, we began replacing the terms *action research* and *teacher research* with one simple word that carried much less baggage with it—*inquiry*—and we will continue this tradition both in this section on research traditions and throughout the remainder of this text.

To help unpack some of the baggage the word *research* carries with it, it is important to further explore the difference between research conducted in a university setting (stemming from the process-product and interpretive paradigms) and inquiry conducted by classroom teachers. First and foremost, in general, the purpose of research conducted by academics and classroom teachers is quite different. The general focus of university-based research is to advance a field. Professors are required to publish their work in journals read by other academics and present their work at national and international venues to their peers at other institutions as evidence of their ability to impact the field broadly. In fact, professors' value within an institution is measured largely by their publication record and the number of times their publications are cited by others. In contrast, the purpose of engagement in inquiry by classroom teachers is to improve classroom practice. The point of doing inquiry is for implementation and change, not for academic impact (although this can happen too).

The focus of university-based researchers and teacher inquirers is also different. In general, university-based researchers working in the process-product paradigm focus their efforts on control, prediction, and impact, and university-based researchers working in the interpretive paradigm focus their efforts on description, explanation, and understanding of various teaching phenomena. In contrast, teacher-inquirers focus on providing insights into teaching in an effort to make change, working tirelessly to unpack all of the complexities inherent in the act of teaching to become the very best teachers they can be for every individual student.

A final difference between research conducted at the university and inquiry conducted by classroom teachers into their own practice is ownership. While the research generated by university researchers is critically important to teachers, it is university researchers who make the decisions about what is important to study and how to go about studying it based on a careful and critical analysis of a broad and extensive body of literature related to the topic of study. In contrast, teacher-inquirers make decisions about what is important to study and how to go about studying it based on a careful and critical analysis of what is happening at a local level in their own classrooms, schools, and districts. The work of university-based researchers informs the inquiries of teachers, but ownership of the classroom-based investigation resides with the classroom teacher herself.

To help distinguish between research produced at a university and inquiry done in classrooms and schools (summarized in Table 1.2), we often invoke the words of Lawrence Stenhouse, who noted "that the difference between a teacher-researcher and the large-scale education researcher is like the difference between a farmer with a huge agricultural business to maintain and the 'careful gardener' tending a backyard plot" (Hubbard & Power, 1999, p. 5).

> In agriculture the equation of invested input against gross yield is all: it does not matter if individual plants fail to thrive or die so long as the cost of saving them is greater than the cost of losing them. . . . This does not apply to the careful gardener whose labour is not costed, but a labour of love. He wants each of his plants to thrive, and he can treat each one individually. Indeed he can grow a hundred different plants in his garden and differentiate his treatment of each, pruning his roses, but not his sweet peas. Gardening rather than agriculture is the analogy for education. (Ruddock & Hopkins, 1985, p. 26)

This image of the university-based researcher as a farmer with a huge agricultural business and the teacher-inquirer as a gardener helps to encapsulate the differences between the university-based research you are likely most familiar with and the research you can generate from within the four walls of your own classroom. It is of value to note that the work of both farmers and gardeners is important and somewhat related but also quite different. Such is the case with university-based researchers and teacher-inquirers. The work of both is important and somewhat related but quite different. As we discuss each component of the inquiry process in depth throughout this book, you will continue to uncover the importance of both types of research, including the relationship between them and the differences.

Now that we have explored three educational research traditions, acknowledged the limitations of the first two traditions, introduced teacher inquiry, and explicated the differences between university-based research and teacher inquiry, our brief history lesson might suggest that teacher inquiry is just another educational fad. However, although the terms *teacher research*, *action research*, and *teacher inquiry* are comparatively

Table 1.2 University-based research and teacher inquiry comparison

	University Research	*Teacher Research (Inquiry)*
PURPOSE	Advance a field	Improve classroom practice
FOCUS	Control/Prediction/Impact/ Explanation	Provide insight into teaching in an effort to make change
OWNERSHIP	Outsider	Insider
IMPACT	Broad	Local

new, the underlying conceptions of teaching as inquiry and the role of teachers as inquirers are not. Early in the 20th century, John Dewey (1933) called for teachers to engage in "reflective action" that would transition them into inquiry-oriented classroom practitioners. Similarly, noted teacher educator Ken Zeichner (1996) traces and summarizes more than 30 years of research, calling for cultivating an informed practice as illustrated in such descriptors as "teachers as action researchers," "teacher scholars," "teacher innovators," and "teachers as participant observers" (p. 3). Similarly, distinguished scholar Donald Schon (1983, 1987) also depicts teacher professional practice as a cognitive process of posing and exploring problems or dilemmas identified by the teachers themselves. In doing so, teachers ask questions that other researchers may not perceive or deem relevant. In addition, teachers often discern patterns that "outsiders" may not be able to see.

Given today's political context, where much of the decision making and discussion regarding teachers occur outside the walls of the classroom (Darling-Hammond, 1994; Cochran-Smith & Lytle, 2006), the time seems ripe to create a movement where teachers are armed with the tools of inquiry and committed to educational change. In the words of Joan Thate, one teacher researcher we have worked with:

> Teachers have for so long had perfunctory or no influence on school policy, on curriculum frameworks, on time use, on professional standards—or pretty much anything involving their work experience—EXCEPT in the privacy of their own classrooms. I think this is why the deadly and stifling isolation has become such an intractable monolith. We're all trying to preserve the one area in which we have some choice. But I have long known—gut knowledge eventually found words—that in preserving isolation we were doomed to forever have the locus of power stay in other hands than ours. And real power could only come when we could justifiably say: we know what's best because we have tested the possibilities and have found what works. Inquiry is exciting because it allows for the testing of ideas in real life, and begins to give us the concrete support for insisting attention be paid to what we have to say. (Thate, 2007a)

If that is our goal, we now need to understand how teacher inquiry can serve as a tool for professional growth and educational reform. We believe that the best stated definitions of teacher research come from teacher-inquirers themselves. We end this section with a few from teachers we have collaborated with on inquiry:

> Very simply put, inquiry is a way for me to continue growing as a teacher. Before I became involved in inquiry I'd gotten to the point where I'd go to an inservice and shut off my brain. Most of the

teachers I know have been at the same place. If you have been around at all you know that most inservices are the same cheese— just repackaged. Inquiry lets me choose my own growth and gives me tools to validate or jettison my ideas. (Kreinbihl, 2007)

You know that nagging that wakes you in the early hours, then reemerges during your morning preparation time so you cannot remember if you already applied the deodorant, later on the drive to school pushing out of mind those important tasks you needed to accomplish prior to the first bell, and again as the students are entering your class and sharing all the important things happening in their lives. Well, teacher inquiry is the formal stating of that nagging, developing a plan of action to do something about it, putting the plan into action, collecting data, analyzing the collected works, making meaning of your collection, sharing your findings, then repeating the cycle with the new nagging(s) that sprouted up. (Hughes, 2007)

Teacher inquiry is not something I do; it is more a part of the way I think. Inquiry involves exciting and meaningful discussions with colleagues about the passions we embrace in our profession. It has become the gratifying response to formalizing the questions that enter my mind as I teach. It is a learning process that keeps me passionate about teaching. (Hubbell, 2007)

WHAT IS THE RELATIONSHIP BETWEEN TEACHER INQUIRY AND TEACHER PROFESSIONAL GROWTH?

Simply stated, teacher inquiry is defined as systematic, intentional study of one's own professional practice (see, e.g., Cochran-Smith & Lytle, 1993; Dana, Gimbert, & Silva, 1999; Hubbard & Power, 1993). Inquiring professionals seek out change by reflecting on their practice. They do this by posing questions or "wonderings," collecting data to gain insights into their wonderings, analyzing the data along with reading relevant literature, making changes in practice based on new understandings developed during inquiry, and sharing findings with others. Hence, whether you are a prospective teacher at the dawn of your teaching career or a veteran teacher with years of experience facing new educational challenges every day, teacher inquiry becomes a powerful vehicle for learning and reform.

As a teacher-inquirer in charge of your own learning, you become a part of a larger struggle in education—the struggle to better understand, inform, shape, reshape, and reform standard school practice (Cochran-Smith, 1991).

Teacher inquiry differs from traditional professional development for teachers, which has typically focused on the knowledge of an outside "expert" being shared with a group of teachers. This traditional model of professional growth, usually delivered as a part of traditional staff development, may appear an efficient method of disseminating information but often does not result in real and meaningful change in the classroom.

Those dissatisfied with the traditional model of professional development suggest a need for new approaches that enhance professional growth and lead to real change. For example, over 40 years ago, Goldhammer (1969) emphasized the need for supervision to become an opportunity to help teachers understand what they are doing and why, by changing schools from places where teachers just act out "age-old rituals" to places where teachers participate fully in the supervision process and their own professional growth. Nolan and Huber (1989) described teacher reflection, a key component of inquiry, as the "driving force" behind successful professional development programs. They described successful professional development programs as "making a difference in the lives and instruction of teachers who participate in them, as well as the lives of the students they teach" (p. 143). More recently, in the *Journal of Staff Development*, educators from across the country put forth their vision for "The Road Ahead" for professional learning. These ideas included the importance of creating activities, tools, and contexts that blend theory and practice (Darling-Hammond, 2007); supporting collaborative learning structures that deepen innovation implementation efforts (DuFour & DuFour, 2007); strengthening professionalism by recognizing the complexity and importance of teacher professional knowledge (Elmore, 2007; Hord, 2007; Schlechty, 2007); and making professional learning a part of the everyday work of each teacher in every classroom (Fullan, 2007).

Consonant with the movement to change traditional professional development practices is the teacher inquiry movement. This movement toward a new model of professional growth based on inquiry into one's own practice can be powerfully developed by school districts and building administrators as a form of professional development. By participating in teacher inquiry, the teacher develops a sense of ownership in the knowledge constructed, and this sense of ownership heavily contributes to the possibilities for real change to take place in the classroom.

The ultimate goal is to create an inquiry stance toward teaching (Cochran-Smith & Lytle, 2009). This stance becomes a professional positioning, owned by the teacher, where questioning one's own practice becomes part of the teacher's work and eventually a part of the teaching culture. By cultivating this inquiry stance toward teaching, teachers play a critical role in enhancing their own professional growth and, ultimately, the experience of schooling for children. Thus, an inquiry stance is synonymous with professional growth and provides a nontraditional approach to staff development that can lead to meaningful change for children.

WHAT EVIDENCE EXISTS THAT TEACHER INQUIRY IS WORTH DOING?

At this point in the chapter, you may be thinking that this process called teacher inquiry sounds okay in theory, but you have developed a healthy skepticism. The everyday work of teaching is challenging, and teachers are constantly asked to do more and more with less and less. If teachers are to incorporate inquiry into their very full days, it's important to know what evidence exists that it is truly worth doing.

Fortunately, evidence abounds that teachers' engagement in inquiry is indeed worth the effort. The first set of evidence comes from teachers themselves who have published their work. There are numerous collections of teacher research, and from reading and analyzing the work of actual teacher researchers that appear in these collections, it is clear that engagement in inquiry can have a powerful impact on the professional learning of teachers and the lives of the students in their classrooms. Some of our favorite collections of teacher research include the following:

- *Creating Equitable Classrooms Through Action Research* (Caro-Bruce, Flessner, Klehr & Zeichner, 2007). This book shares the research of 10 educators from the Madison Wisconsin Metropolitan School District, whose inquiries focused on making their school district a more equitable place for all learners.
- *Taking Action With Teacher Research* (Meyers & Rust, 2003). This book shares the research of six teacher researchers from the Teacher Network Leadership Institute in New York, whose inquiries focused on political action.
- *Empowering the Voice of the Teacher Researcher: Achieving Success Through a Culture of Inquiry* (Brindley & Crocco, 2009). This book shares the research of six teacher researchers from a single school in Florida, whose inquiries focus on better meeting the needs of middle school children.
- *Our Inquiry, Our Practice: Undertaking, Supporting, and Learning From Early Childhood Teacher Research(ers)* (Perry, Henderson, & Meier, 2012). This book shares the research of six early childhood professionals, working in both primary grades and preschool, as well as reviews some of the finer points of the inquiry process and how it is particularly suited for early childhood contexts.
- *Teachers Engaged in Research* (Langrall, 2006; Masingila, 2006; Smith & Smith, 2006; Van Zoest, 2006). This four-volume series published by the National Council of Teachers of Mathmatics (NCTM) shares the inquiries of several teachers into their mathematics teaching in Grades K–2, 3–5, 6–8, and 9–12, respectively.

The second set of evidence that teacher inquiry is worth doing comes from university-based researchers. There is a large body of university-based research conducted on both preservice and practicing teachers engaged in the inquiry process to better understand the impact of their work. While it is beyond the scope of this book to review all of the empirical studies completed by academics focused on teachers' engagement in inquiry, many of these studies are reviewed and referenced in Marilyn Cochran-Smith and Susan Lytle's book *Inquiry as Stance: Practitioner Research for the Next Generation* (2009). It is clear in this text from the extensive review of research on teacher inquiry that engaging in the inquiry process results in several benefits for both perservice teachers who conduct inquiry as a part of their studies in teaching at the university and practicing teachers who conduct inquiry as part of their everyday work in schools.

The publications by teachers of their own inquiries as well as publications by university-based researchers that report research efforts to understand the impact of teachers' engagement in the process attest to the important role inquiry can play in the lives of teachers and the children they teach. An additional source of evidence of the value inherent in engagement in inquiry comes from the ways inquiry can interface with many current initiatives and processes underway in schools. Some of these current initiatives and processes include differentiated instruction, data-driven decision making, progress monitoring, Response to Intervention, lesson study, teacher evaluation, and the Common Core State Standards.

WHAT IS THE RELATIONSHIP BETWEEN TEACHER INQUIRY AND DIFFERENTIATED INSTRUCTION?

The most important benefactors of taking an inquiry stance toward teaching and actualizing that stance by engaging in action research are the students you teach. Just as teaching is complex, so is the makeup of each individual student that walks through your classroom door. Each student enters your classroom with unique life experiences as well as differing social, emotional, and academic needs. Each student who enters your classroom varies in background knowledge, readiness, language, preferences in learning, and interests. Yet, in the ways traditional school structures are set up, individual needs can easily become lost.

One current emphasis in the field of education targeted at making visible individual student needs that can become lost in traditional school structures is differentiated instruction (Sousa & Tomlinson, 2010; Tomlinson, 2001, 1999; Tomlinson & Imbeau, 2010). According to Hall (2002),

> Differentiated instruction applies an approach to teaching and learning so that students have multiple options for taking in information and

making sense of ideas. The model of differentiated instruction requires teachers to be flexible in their approach to teaching and adjusting the curriculum and presentation of information to learners rather than expecting students to modify themselves for the curriculum. (n.p.)

Through engaging in action research, teachers can generate valuable knowledge about their learners' readiness, interest, learning styles, and more! With this knowledge, teachers make adaptations to instruction, increasing the probability that the needs of *all* learners will be met within one single class period or lesson.

For example, through engaging in action research to better understand the reading habits of his high school seniors, Tom Beyer (2007) adjusted his summer reading list and built in choice for his students, accommodating the vast differences in their interests his research uncovered. Engaging in action research to ascertain better ways to structure chemistry extra-help sessions, Steve Burgin (2007a) adjusted his approach to these sessions to accommodate both his general-chemistry students, who benefited from an enriched repeat version of a lesson on a particular chemistry concept taught during the regular school day, and his honors students who benefited from independently working though more challenging chemistry problems based on particular concepts to be tested in an upcoming exam. Through engaging in action research to better understand student anxiety associated with the upcoming probability and statistics unit, Kristin Weller (2007) rewrote her lessons that strictly followed the adopted mathematics text book to introduce the same concepts through studying the upcoming NCAA basketball tournament and the odds of each team reaching the Final Four. Action research is a wonderful tool teachers can use to differentiate instruction, ultimately making schools a better place for all students, regardless of their interests, abilities, background, and learning styles.

WHAT IS THE RELATIONSHIP BETWEEN TEACHER INQUIRY, DATA-DRIVEN DECISION MAKING, AND PROGRESS MONITORING?

In line with the goals of teacher research, data-driven decision making (DDDM) and progress monitoring are two professional activities that school reformers suggest will lead to improved student learning. According to Scott McLeod (2007), DDDM is a system of teaching and management practices that places information about students into practitioners' hands. Data-driven decision making is embedded in teacher inquiry as teachers use assessment data and background information to inform decisions related to planning and implementing instructional strategies at the school, classroom, or individual student levels.

Similarly, the National Center of Student Progress Monitoring (2007) defines progress monitoring as "a scientifically based practice that is used to assess students' academic performance and evaluate the effectiveness of instruction." Teachers engaged in progress monitoring follow a series of stages embedded in the teacher research process, including identifying students' current level of performance, establishing learning goals that will be targeted during the inquiry, monitoring students' academic performance on a regular basis, comparing expected and actual rates of learning, and adjusting instruction based on these data.

Given these definitions, DDDM is used to inform decisions prior to instruction, and progress monitoring is used to assess the effectiveness of the instruction. In combination, data-driven decision making and progress monitoring share the same basic steps underlying the "cycle of inquiry." For example, when teacher-inquirer Debbi Hubbell reviewed multiple sources of reading data, including student performance on her state's assessment test, DIBELS (Dynamic Indicators of Basic Early Literacy Skills) test scores, and informal assessments, she decided that a subset of her students struggled with reading fluency. In response, she selected instructional interventions that targeted fluency and then used progress monitoring to understand the degree of student growth after the intervention. Her teacher research work integrated both data-driven decision making and progress monitoring.

Central to the success of data-driven decision making, progress monitoring, and teacher research is the degree of teacher "data literacy." Data literacy refers to the teacher's basic understanding of how data can be used to inform instruction, which assessment is a valid and reliable measure of what is being taught, and what types of assessments are appropriate for district-, classroom-, or individual student–level decision making. In returning to Debbi Hubbel's teacher research, Debbi had a sophisticated ability to interpret the high-stakes scores as well as identify valid and reliable tools that could measure her students' fluency development. Teacher researchers, data-driven decision makers, and progress monitors are aware of the problems associated with an overreliance on high-stakes testing. As described, Debbi Hubbell used multiple types of data (e.g., DIBELS, running records, informal observation) to study her students and discovered what worked within her specific classroom. Teachers who effectively use data within the teacher-research process find that identifying the right kind of data to use in their work can improve their instructional interventions, reenergize their enthusiasm for teaching, and increase their feelings of professional fulfillment and job satisfaction.

McLeod (2007) explains that "data-driven decision making requires an important paradigm shift for teachers—a shift from day-to-day instruction that emphasizes process and delivery in the classroom to pedagogy that is dedicated to the achievement of results" (p. 1). Fundamental to teacher research, data-driven decision making, and progress monitoring is the importance of helping practitioners develop the inclination to wonder, "Is there a better way?" and "How can I do things differently?" This inclination is essential to the teacher-research movement. By embracing an inquiry approach, teachers expand their idea of what data are and how using data can inform their teaching and enhance student learning. The inquiry stance embraced by teacher researchers supports both data-driven decision making and progress monitoring.

WHAT IS THE RELATIONSHIP BETWEEN TEACHER INQUIRY AND RESPONSE TO INTERVENTION (RTI)?

Another approach that shares similarities with teacher inquiry and is receiving current attention from educators across the United States is referred to as Response to Intervention or RtI. Response to Intervention is an intervention approach that is a part of the eligibility process for emotional behavior disorders (EBD) and specific learning disabilities (SLD) and is strongly supported by both the Individuals with Disabilities Education Act (IDEA) and No Child Left Behind (NCLB). However, the application of RtI is much broader than a screening process to determine special education eligibility. The goal of RtI is to prevent unnecessary student assignment to special education by offering low-performing students intense, individualized academic intervention paired with systematic study of the intervention. According to Jim Wright (2007), a school psychologist and administrator from central New York, RtI gives a student with delays one or more research-validated interventions. As the intervention is used, the student's learning is systematically studied or monitored to identify whether the interventions will allow the student to catch up with his or her peers.

The RtI process follows the inquiry process described in this book as the intervention is systematically studied. The process begins with problem analysis that identifies the desired change for the student experiencing academic or behavioral difficulty. Next, educators design and implement an evidence-based intervention. Finally, the effectiveness of the intervention is determined by synthesizing and analyzing the data collected. This step is termed Response to Intervention because during this step a student's response to the implemented intervention is measured to evaluate the effectiveness of the instruction. Just as inquiry focuses on the systematic and intentional collection of data focused on a wondering, in RtI, educators focus on systematically and intentionally collecting data to understand if the response to the intervention results in adequate academic and/or behavioral growth. According to Jim Wright (2007), to implement RtI effectively,

schools must develop a specialized set of tools and competencies, including a structured format for problem-solving, knowledge of a range of scientifically based interventions that address common reasons for school failure, and the ability to use various methods of assessment to monitor student progress in academic and behavioral areas.

Given the sophistication that educators need in each step of the inquiry process as well as the importance of adequate knowledge of powerful interventions, the success of RtI will likely depend on whether the process is appropriately implemented and whether an inquiry stance is embraced by highly skilled professionals. The inquiry process illustrated within this book can offer support to those engaged in RtI. In fact, RtI can literally become one form of inquiry occurring in a school or across a district.

WHAT IS THE RELATIONSHIP BETWEEN TEACHER INQUIRY AND LESSON STUDY?

Inquiry is often tied directly to curriculum and its implementation. When curriculum and its implementation is the focus of inquiry, inquiry shares all of the same core features of the popular professional development strategy termed *lesson study*. As a professional development strategy, lesson study allows teachers to systematically and collaboratively examine and improve their teaching practice through "studying" lessons. Teachers create study lessons together by planning, teaching, observing, critiquing, and revising the lessons as a group. This spiraling process is driven by an overarching goal and a research question shaped by the group. The end result is not only a better developed lesson, but typically teachers also develop a stronger understanding of the content, enhanced observation skills, stronger collegial networks, and a tighter connection between daily practice and long-term goals (Lewis, Perry, & Hurd, 2004). In essence, lesson study becomes a specialized form of the inquiry process focused on the planning and teaching of one lesson and the ways that lesson plays out for multiple teachers and learners in a school or across multiple schools in a district. Like RtI, described in the previous section, lesson study can literally become one form of inquiry occurring in a school and/or across a district.

WHAT IS THE RELATIONSHIP BETWEEN TEACHER INQUIRY AND TEACHER EVALUATION?

Teacher evaluation has gained increasing attention in the last decade as policymakers and school district officials work in tandem to assure that every child has a qualified teacher. These evaluation efforts are designed to provide the pressure that when coupled with support (Fullan, 2009) can lead to improved teaching practices. Too often school districts identify evaluation techniques that provide pressure for teachers to improve without dedicating adequate attention and resources to the supports teachers need to be successful. Teacher inquiry is one of the support structures that school districts can pair with evaluation to enhance teaching and learning.

Many school districts have identified frameworks that they believe make explicit performance expectations for educators. These frameworks include, but are not limited to, the work of Charlotte Danielson (2006) and Robert Marzano (2007). For example, Danielson's framework is comprised of research-based instructional components grounded in a constructivist view of learning and teaching while Marzano's framework is comprised of 41 strategies that he believes a comprehensive language of instruction should include. Teacher inquiry provides a process for educators to systematically and intentionally investigate components of frameworks, like these, that they themselves identify as areas of need or that others have identified as challenges to their teaching effectiveness. The process of inquiry can empower the educator to set important goals related to the evaluation frameworks, study his or her own practice in an identified area of weakness, and reflect on ways to continually improve performance. In many ways, districts that do not provide this kind of support are engaged in their own special version of educational malpractice. Teacher inquiry is a tool for supporting teachers as they seek to improve instruction.

Illustrating the ways inquiry can fit appropriately within a teacher evaluation system, the Anacortes School District in the state of Washington has embedded the inquiry cycle into their teacher evaluation process (see www.asd103.org/pages/Anacortes_School_District/Staff/Teacher_Principal_Evaluation). Anacortes School District Teacher Association president Jennie Beltramini describes their teacher evaluation system as follows:

> In Anacortes, we set out to develop a new teacher and principal evaluation model for the purpose of fostering professional growth. While we acknowledge that the traditional purpose of evaluation is accountability and making employment decisions, accountability and employment decisions only serve a small minority of teachers and principals. In order to leverage the evaluation system to promote professional growth among all satisfactory performing teachers and principals, we needed a new system comprised of feedback on research-based instructional and leadership frameworks and student growth, as well as a structured, supported, job-embedded professional growth model to ensure growth.
>
> In Anacortes, we chose to use the Cycle of Inquiry to support teacher and principal professional growth within the evaluation system. Armed with detailed, specific data about their teaching and student growth via the evaluation system, teachers were ready to ask relevant inquiry questions about challenges they were facing

with their practice. All teachers develop an inquiry plan of action trying new teaching strategies informed by the evaluation rubric, carry out a Cycle of Inquiry, and collect data on their students and their own teacher practices to measure the impact of their actions. Principals also carry out a Cycle of Inquiry based on their leadership practices each year. With the support of inquiry facilitators/ teacher leaders in each school building, as well as inquiry-oriented PLCs, teachers and principals have a structure and the support they need to make lasting improvements to their practice. (Beltramini, personal communication, 9/15/13)

By coupling teacher inquiry and teacher evaluation, this district has integrated both pressure and support to improve teaching performance.

WHAT IS THE RELATIONSHIP BETWEEN TEACHER INQUIRY AND THE COMMON CORE STATE STANDARDS?

The Common Cores State Standards, designed "to provide a clear and consistent framework to prepare our children for college and the workforce" (NGA & CCS, 2012a), are everywhere! Forty-five states, the District of Columbia, four territories, and the Department of Defense Education Activity have adopted them. Common Core workshops, websites, conferences, webinars, and in-service days abound as teachers work to figure out what difference the Common Core will make to their everyday teaching practice.

Perhaps the most important difference the Common Core will make to teachers and the students they teach is that teachers "are not merely the recipients of standards, but the architects of their implementation" (Dunkle, 2012, p. x). During the era of high-stakes testing that preceded the Common Core, teachers were often handed teacher editions to textbooks and pacing guides that determined every minute detail of when, how, and what they would teach their students. Teachers lost the ability to be creative with their students, to enact "teachable moments," to respond to their students' needs, and to make instructional decisions in the best interest of the children they teach. Subsequently, in many cases the rigidity of the high-stakes testing regime resulted in students who were not engaged or excited about learning. The joy of teaching and the love of learning were literally sucked out of many classrooms across the nation.

In contrast to rigid adherence to a long list of standards that mandate what, how, and when to teach, the Common Core gives teachers and schools a lot of flexibility. If implemented as intended, the CCSS will be used as a *guide* rather than a *bible*. The standards are not a curriculum that tells teachers *how* they will teach but rather where they need to go with their students (NGA & CCSS, 2012b). And, most importantly, it is teachers themselves that make the decisions regarding how to get their students where they need to go! This creates the potential for a much more dynamic and engaging curriculum for both teachers and students.

The potential for a much more dynamic and engaging curriculum is good reason to learn more about the Common Core and how it can be actualized in practice. While it will be important for teachers to read about the standards and attend workshops and webinars to develop content knowledge about the Common Core, these professional development mechanisms alone are not enough to help teachers become architects of the Common Core's implementation.

This is where teacher inquiry enters the Common Core picture. Engagement in inquiry is a logical mechanism with which teachers and administrators can gain insights into the CCSS, what the Common Core means for teachers and students, and how the Common Core can be actualized within the reality of teachers' everyday work with students in the classroom. The inquiry process can help teachers gain insights into the Common Core as teachers try out new techniques and strategies related to Common Core implementation in their classrooms (Dana, Burns, & Wolkenhauer, 2013).

HOW IS TEACHER INQUIRY DIFFERENT FROM WHAT I ALREADY DO AS A REFLECTIVE TEACHER?

All teachers reflect. They reflect on what happened during previously taught lessons as they plan lessons for the future. They reflect on their students' performance as they assess their work. They reflect on the content and the best pedagogy available to teach that content to their learners. They reflect on interactions they observed students having, as well as on their own interactions with students and the ways these inter-actions contribute to learning. Teachers reflect all day, every day, *on* the act of teaching while *in* the act of teaching and long after the school day is over.

Reflection is important and critical to good teaching (Schon, 1987; Zeichner & Liston, 1996). In addition, reflection is a key component of teacher inquiry. Yet teacher inquiry is different from daily reflection in and on practice in two important ways. First, teacher inquiry is less happen-stance. The very definition of teacher inquiry includes the word *intentional*. We do not mean to suggest that reflection is never intentional, but in the busy, complex life of teaching, reflection is something that occurs most often in an unplanned way, for example, on the way to the teachers' room for lunch, during a chat with a colleague during a special, when students are engaged in an independent activity, on the drive home, in the shower, or during dinner—wherever and whenever a moment arises. Unfortunately, few teachers have a planned reflection time. Teacher inquiry invites intentional, planned reflection, heightening your focus on problem posing. Second, teacher inquiry is more visible. The daily reflection teachers engage in is not observable by others unless it is given some form (perhaps through talk or journaling). As teachers engage in the process of inquiry, their thinking and reflection are made public for discussion, sharing, debate, and purposeful educative conversation, and teaching becomes less isolated and overwhelming. Gail Ritchie, veteran teacher researcher from Fairfax County Schools, Virginia, notes that the goal of being a teacher researcher is to facilitate teaching and learning and maximize student potential. As a teacher researcher engages in reflection, she intentionally asks questions about teaching and learning, organizes and collects information, focuses on a specific area of inquiry, and benefits from ongoing collaboration and support of critical friends (Lassonde, Ritchie, & Fox, 2008).

WHAT ARE SOME CONTEXTS RIPE FOR TEACHER INQUIRY?

With an understanding of what teacher inquiry is; how it contributes to professional growth; how it relates to differentiating instruction, data-driven decision making, progress monitoring, RtI, lesson study, teacher evaluation, and the Common Core State Standards; and how it differs from natural, daily reflection, let us consider the kinds of contexts that support teacher inquiry. As previously discussed, teaching is full of enormous complexities, paradoxes, and tensions, and hence, teaching itself invites inquiry. However, even as inquiry beckons each and every teacher, becoming a "lone inquirer" is difficult! For this reason, we explore three particularly ripe contexts for facilitating the development of an inquiry stance in practicing and prospective teachers: professional learning communities, student teaching and/or other clinical experiences, and professional development schools. You may currently be a part of one of these three contexts or you may wish to seek these contexts out as you begin or continue your teaching career.

Professional Learning Communities

Professional learning communities (PLCs) serve to connect and network groups of professionals to do just what their name entails—*learn* from practice. Professional learning communities meet on a regular basis, and their time together is often structured by the use of protocols to ensure focused, deliberate conversation and dialogue by teachers about student work and student learning. Protocols for educators provide a script or series of timed steps for how a conversation among teachers on a chosen topic will develop.

A variety of protocols have been developed for use in professional learning communities by a number of noteworthy organizations such as the National Staff Development Council (see, for example, Lois Brown Easton's *Powerful Designs for Professional Learning*, 2004), the Southern Maine Partnership (http://usm.maine.edu/smp/about/index), School Reform Initiative (www.schoolreforminitiative.org) and the National School Reform Faculty (www.nsrfharmony.org), which developed one version of a professional learning community called Critical Friends Groups (CFGs). In their work conceptualizing CFGs, the National School Reform Faculty laid much of the groundwork for shifting the nature of the dialogue between and among teachers about their practice in schools and is responsible for training thousands of teachers to focus on developing collegial relationships, encouraging reflective practice, and rethinking leadership in restructuring schools. The CFGs provide deliberate time and structures dedicated to promoting adult professional growth that is directly linked to student learning.

By their own nature, then, PLCs enhance the possibilities for conducting an inquiry and cultivating a community of inquirers. In fact, in our companion book to this text, *The Reflective Educator's Guide to Professional Development* (Dana & Yendol-Hoppey, 2008a), we describe a model for school-based professional development that combines some of the best of what we know about action research and professional learning communities and, in the process, address a weakness that has been defined in traditional professional development practices. We name this new entity the "inquiry-oriented professional learning community" and define it as a group of six to twelve professionals who meet on a regular basis to learn from practice through structured dialogue and engage in continuous cycles through the process of action research (articulating a wondering, collecting data to gain insights into the wondering, analyzing data, making improvements in practice based on what is learned, and sharing learning with others). The book *Inquiry: A Districtwide Approach to Staff and Student Learning* illustrates inquiry-oriented learning communities of teachers and principals and how they can be set up across an entire district (Dana, Thomas, & Boynton, 2011).

Student Teaching and/or Other Clinical Experiences

If you are a veteran teacher, you likely reminisce about your own student teaching experience as an important feature of your preservice education. Similarly, if you are a prospective teacher, you have likely looked forward to your field experience and student teaching with great anticipation. According to a report prepared by the National Council for the Accreditation of Teacher Education (2010), a paradigmatic shift in teacher preparation is needed that places a greater emphasis on the clinical experience and learning within the field. According to the report, to prepare effective teachers for 21st century classrooms, teacher education must shift away from a norm which emphasizes academic preparation and course work loosely linked to school-based experiences. Rather, it must move to programs that are fully grounded in clinical practice and interwoven with academic content and professional courses. (p. ii)

Within the report, teacher inquiry is highlighted as an important tool for strengthening clinical practice, and an inquiry stance is an orientation believed to strengthen teacher preparation. Mounting evidence suggests that field experiences that include engagement in teacher inquiry enhance the quality of teacher preparation (see, e.g., Dana & Silva, 2001; Wilson, Floden, & Ferrini-Mundy, 2001). The reason for this is quite logical. Given that the act of teaching is an enormously complex endeavor, "learning to teach" in any brief, simple, and step-by-step way is impossible. As a preservice teacher, you are immersed in the complexities of teaching for the first time in clinical experiences. Immersion in this complexity naturally encourages engagement in inquiry, as questions about teaching, schools, and schooling abound. As you student teach, inquiry can help you learn to identify the complexities and problems inherent in teaching and tease these complexities apart to gain insights into your work with children. Given the comprehensive nature of teaching, identifying complexities and striving to understand them is a process that lasts an entire career. Engagement in teacher inquiry as an integral component of field preparation enhances the power of the field experience. As you simultaneously learn to teach and to inquire into teaching, these two processes become intricately intertwined. When teaching and inquiry become synonymous, you have cultivated an inquiry stance toward teaching that will serve you, your students, and the field of education well for the duration of your career!

Professional Development Schools and Other Networks

Since the late 1980s, a specialized setting for student teaching and other field experiences has emerged—professional development schools (PDS). According to Darling-Hammond (1994), professional development schools

aim to provide new models of teacher education and development by serving as exemplars of practice, builders of knowledge, and vehicles for communicating professional understanding among teacher educators, novices, and veteran teachers. They support the learning of prospective and beginning teachers by creating settings in which novices enter professional practice by working with expert practitioners, enabling veteran teachers to renew their own professional development and assume new roles as mentors, university adjuncts, and teacher leaders. They allow school and university educators to engage jointly in research and rethinking of practice, thus creating an opportunity for the profession to expand its knowledge base by putting research into practice—and practice into research. (p. 1)

In a PDS then, teacher inquiry is a central part of the professional practice of all members—practicing teachers, prospective teachers, administrators, and university teacher educators. This transition to inquiry is the mechanism for reinventing schools as "learning" organizations. Hence, a PDS culture supports and celebrates the engagement of teachers and other PDS professionals in constructing knowledge through intentional, systematic inquiry and using that knowledge to continually reform, refine, and change the practice of teaching (Dana, Smith & Yendol-Hoppey, 2011; Yendol-Hoppey & Dana, 2008).

Professional development schools have organized themselves through a national network, the National Association of Professional Development Schools (NAPDS). The vision of this organization is to serve as an advocate for those dedicated to promoting the continuous development of collaborative P–12 school and higher education relationships. The work of teacher inquiry remains a vital component of the NAPDS, and teacher-inquirers regularly share their work at the NAPDS conference

In addition to NAPDS, a variety of other educational networks support the teacher inquiry movement. For example, the National Network for Educational Renewal (NNER) embraces the work of inquiry as a central component to school improvement. The network's goal is to improve the quality of P–12 education for thoughtful and informed participation in a democracy. One way this improvement occurs is through developing programs that encourage teachers to inquire into the nature of teaching and schooling, with the intention that practitioners will make inquiry a natural aspect of their professional lives. These are just a few of the larger national networks that support teacher inquiry.

HOW DOES MY ENGAGING IN TEACHER INQUIRY HELP SHAPE THE PROFESSION OF TEACHING?

Regardless of your method of inquiry, the subject of your inquiry, or the context of your inquiry, what is most important is that you do inquire! According to numerous leading scholars on teaching and teacher education, such as Aronowitz and Giroux (1985), Greene (1986), and Zeichner (1986), "teachers are decision makers and collaborators who must reclaim their roles in the shaping of practice by taking a stand as both educators and activists" (Cochran-Smith, 1991, p. 280). Inquiry is a core tool teachers evoke when making informed and systematic decisions. Through the inquiry process, teachers can support with evidence the decisions they make as educators and, subsequently, advocate for particular children, changes in curriculum, and/or changes in pedagogy. Inquiry ultimately emerges as action and results in change.

As a prospective teacher, practicing teacher, or mentor-teacher interested in problematizing your professional practice, you have committed to simultaneous renewal and reform of the teaching profession and teacher education! Teacher inquiry is the ticket to enact this reform! Cochran-Smith and Lytle (1993) claim that in any classroom where teacher inquiry is occurring, "there is a radical, but quiet kind of educational reform in process" (p. 101). Your individual engagement in teacher inquiry is a contribution to larger educational reform, a transformation of the teaching profession . . . so let us begin the journey!

CHAPTER 1 EXERCISES

1. Look at some examples of teacher research published in some of the collections we mentioned in this chapter. or that you may find in journals such as *Voices of Practitioners*, *Action Research*, and *Networks: An Online Journal for Teacher Research*. What are some things you notice about the process of inquiry you will explore in this book from looking at actual examples of teachers' research?

2. Start a journal to trace your own inquiry journey as you proceed through this book. For your first entry, capture both the excitement and enthusiasm you may be feeling for the inquiry process after reading Chapter 1, as well as any apprehension or trepidation you feel about the process. Use these sentence starters as your journal prompts:

   • My greatest hopes for engaging in the inquiry process include ...
   • My greatest fears for engaging in the inquiry process include ...

   Discuss your responses with colleagues and continue to use your journal throughout the text to respond to the exercises provided in each chapter. When you actually begin your own inquiry, your journal can evolve into a way to collect data (covered in Chapter 4).

2

The Start of Your Journey

Finding a Wondering

WHERE DO I BEGIN?

In Chapter 1, we welcomed you to teacher inquiry by defining the process, discussing inquiry as professional development, and exploring the relationship between inquiry and educational reform. This welcome to inquiry places you, as prospective and practicing teachers, in charge of your own professional growth and development. Leading your own learning is likely quite different from many of your past experiences in preservice and inservice teacher education. If you are a prospective teacher, up to this point you have likely engaged in coursework at college, where professors define learning objectives for you in course syllabi, choose your education texts, and define assignments that must be completed for graduation and initial certification. If you are a veteran teacher, you have likely attended inservice sessions covering topics selected for you by administrators or curriculum specialists in your district or perhaps topics mandated by your state. Hence, by taking charge of your own learning, you are beginning your journey into uncharted territory! Charting new territory, when you are unfamiliar with both the terrain and your final destination, can be exciting but also quite frightening. Beginning your journey becomes less daunting after you do some initial preparation and take your first steps.

Just as hikers gather certain equipment before proceeding with a hike, as a teacher-inquirer you will need maps and a compass before you embark on your first inquiry journey. The map for this journey is what Charles Kettering refers to as the welcoming attitude toward, and active seeking of, change: "Essentially research is nothing but a state of mind . . . a friendly, welcoming attitude toward change . . . going out to look for change instead of waiting for it to come" (Kettering, in Boyd, 1961). This welcoming attitude provides the foundation for mapping your inquiry journey. The compass that provides the direction or question for your inquiry comes from critical reflection in and on your own teaching practice.

As teachers seek out change and reflect on practice, the first step of their journey begins with brainstorming questions or wonderings for exploration. One teacher-inquirer describes the new stance she assumed toward her teaching as she prepared to begin her inquiry journey as follows:

> A teacher-inquirer is someone who searches for questions as well as answers. I am learning that saying, "I don't know" is not an admittance of failure, but a precursor of positive change. I have become comfortable with the expressions: "I wonder . . . ," "I think . . . ," and "What if . . . ?" (Stiles, 1999)

WHERE DO I FIND MY WONDERINGS AND QUESTIONS?

A teacher's completion of the expressions "I wonder . . . ," "I think . . . ," and "What if . . . ?" do not materialize out of thin air. According to Hubbard and Power (1993), teachers' wonderings and questions come from their "real world observations and dilemmas" (p. 2). After working with hundreds of teacher researchers, we believe that a teacher's wonderings materialize as professional passions at the nexus of a teacher's work—his or her teaching dilemmas or "felt difficulties" (see Figure 2.1).

The complex nature of teaching makes the profession an especially ripe context for cultivating an inquiry question. Teaching requires teachers to make sense of the interaction among the following five elements simultaneously: the context, the content, the children, the teacher's own beliefs or dispositions, and the acts of teaching. So how do teachers think about the five elements of teacher work? In any teaching event, teachers consider the context in which they teach. For instance, they may ponder, "What resources are available?," "What are the state standards or system objectives?," "What support is provided for this innovation?," or "How will the broader community react?" In conjunction with thinking about context, teachers also make sure they understand the key content knowledge that must be constructed. Teachers ask, "What misinformation or misunderstandings often occur as children construct knowledge in this area?," and "What are the multiple perspectives that must be shared in order to capture the complexity of the content?"

In addition to recognizing the impact of the context and the key underpinnings of the content that must be taught, teachers consider the children whom they will need to teach. They raise questions such as, "Who will need more scaffolding?," "How can I make this content relevant to my students?," and "How can I accommodate the diverse learners within my classroom?" All of these areas and questions influence the acts of teaching. For example, as teachers determine which curriculum and content are relevant, they plan, select, and use instructional strategies. They also identify assessment tools that will support student learning. Teacher decision making is even further complicated by the presence of a teacher's beliefs and professional identity. Teachers may wonder, "How do my own attitudes toward writing influence my teaching?," or "How do my beliefs about learning influence the way I accommodate diverse learners?" These five elements are central to teachers' thinking and provide the foundation for identifying felt difficulties or teaching dilemmas that prompt the development of inquiry questions.

Qualitative researcher Robert Sherman (Sherman & Webb, 1997) argues that powerful research questions emerge from "felt difficulties." Teachers are constantly faced with felt difficulties or dilemmas as they reflect in and on their acts of teaching. As a result, these felt difficulties are direct concerns that emerge from one's own teaching experiences. Figure 2.1 presents how these five elements representing the complexity of teaching and the resulting dilemmas, or felt difficulties of teaching, merge to form eight passions.

In this chapter, we map out the eight passions that emerged from our analysis of over 100 teacher inquiries (Dana, Yendol-Hoppey, & Snow-Gerono, 2006). In some ways, the eight passions overlap with each other, but we present them as distinct entities in order to help you view an array of possibilities for finding and defining your first wondering. Each passion is illustrated with the work of one or more teacher-inquirers. As we share excerpts from the work of these prospective and practicing teachers, we analyze the thought processes they used to derive their first wondering. In so doing, we offer you practical suggestions and guidance as you progress through a similar process. Finally, we end each section with exercises designed to help you explore areas ripe for the development of your wonderings. You may wish to pause at the end of each section to complete these exercises before reading further. By the end of this chapter, we hope you will have defined a question to get you started and you can celebrate the completion of what is often the most difficult component of teacher inquiry—defining your question and getting started.

As you interact with this chapter to define a question that will get you started on your inquiry journey, it is important to note that the passions we present in this chapter (A Child, Curriculum, Content Knowledge, Teaching Strategies/Techniques, Beliefs About Practice, Personal/ Professional Identity, Social Justice, and Context) are not meant to be "topics" or "categories" for inquiry questions but rather triggers for you to explore dilemmas that may be surfacing in your teaching practice from which questions worthy of study may emerge. As triggers rather than topics or categories, the exercises you engage in related to one passion might lead you to develop a question that seems to "fit" within another. It matters not what "passion" your inquiry seems to "fit" within. In fact, a single inquiry question may overlap with several passions. Rather, what matters is that you use the passions to conduct a careful and critical analysis of your teaching and explore many possibilities for great wonderings you might choose to pursue.

Figure 2.1   Developing Your Research Question

FINDING YOUR WONDERING

Eight Passions

- A Child
- Curriculum
- Content Knowledge
- Teaching Strategies/ Techniques
- Beliefs about Practice
- Personal/Professional Identity
- Social Justice
- Context

Complexity of Teachers' Work in the Classroom

Felt Difficulties and Real- World Dilemmas

Passion 1: Helping an Individual Child

You are likely familiar with a very common saying proudly displayed by many teachers:

> *A hundred years from now, it will not matter what my bank account was, the sort of house I lived in, or the kind of car I drove. But the world may be different because I was important in the life of a child.*

In fact, you may have very well entered the teaching profession on the basis of your passion for children, your talent for connecting with them, and your willingness to commit yourself to touching children's lives.

Each year, classroom teachers encounter particular learners who stand out from the rest for a variety of reasons—perhaps a learner is struggling with a particular concept in the curriculum, is experiencing difficulty in social interactions, has progressed far beyond the expectations for your particular grade level and is in need of enrichment, or behaves in ways that are not conducive to your classroom learning environment. These learners are like puzzles that teachers try to understand as they strive to make a difference in a particular child's life.

A puzzling child can be a wonderful source for sparking your first wondering. If you are a beginning teacher, this is a common, comfortable, and developmentally appropriate place to develop your inquiry stance toward teaching. If you are a practicing teacher, you may also find that studying a particular student can contribute to and facilitate the child's experience in your classroom and the individualized education plan (IEP) or staffing process within your school. This process also informs your own ability to accommodate individual differences and track student growth. Each year, we work with numerous prospective and practicing teachers who use the process of inquiry to gain insights into learners who stand out to them in their classrooms. A few examples follow.

Amy Ruth, an intern in a kindergarten classroom, did not have a difficult time generating a large number of curiosities and wonderings for her first inquiry project. In fact, Amy ended each of her professional journal entries with questions that emerged from her daily practice. As she brainstormed, she came to the realization that many of her wonderings focused on student growth, and she eventually narrowed her inquiry to focus on an English as a Second Language (ESL) learner in her classroom. As you read the following excerpt from Amy's inquiry, note how she describes the process of finding her wondering:

> It was not hard for me to come up with a huge number of curiosities or wonderings that I have within my classroom. As I began to narrow down the wonderings, I began noticing that many of them centered around topics that held things in common, particularly the following areas: peer interactions, peer influence, ESL students,

and the kindergarten writing center. Out of the list that I narrowed down, I asked myself, "What is it that really fascinates me?," "What am I passionate about?," and "Why am I a teacher?" The answer to all three of these questions for me is *student growth*. It fascinates me to see the enormous growth students have over a period of time. I am passionate about setting up a learning environment that fosters growth. I am a teacher because it is the challenge of finding ways to help a child grow, the excitement in the student growth as it is taking place, and the joy I feel of seeing that growth has and is taking place within my classroom that excite me!

My inquiry project became more apparent as I began to take over at the writing center during Language Arts time. Since the beginning of the year, I had watched one ESL student's language develop and grow right before my eyes. His forceful nature, strong personality, and undying energy had at times exhausted me, while at the same time empowered me. He instilled a challenge in me to find ways to facilitate his entrance into our school, our classroom community, and our language. For being a child who came to school knowing very little of the English language, he is extremely outgoing and eager to be accepted by his teachers and his peers.

It was not long after I began working with the students at the writing center that I decided that my inquiry would focus on this ESL student, who I will refer to as Adam. As an intern in a kindergarten classroom, from the beginning of the year I had been amazed by the growth students show in their illustrating and drawing. I am always full of wonder and amazement as children's one-page illustrations develop into seven- or eight-page detailed stories.

The first time that Adam's group came to the writing center, I was "blown away" to see how he interacted with his peers. Immediately after sitting down with his writing folder, he handed a new sheet of paper to a peer, Kevin, and told him to draw a fish. "Fish!" he said. "Big Fish!" I was amazed at the request. The thought that Adam would ask Kevin, a well-known artist in our room, seemed so clever to me. Where would this request lead Adam in his writing? Was this interaction/request going to be typical of Adam at the writing center? Would this help Adam's written language develop, as his spoken language had recently?

Now I had found my initial inquiry wondering: How does peer interaction facilitate Adam's writing at the kindergarten writing center? (Ruth, 1999)

To find her first wondering, Amy began by raising questions as she journaled about her classroom each day. Then, she began listing broad categories of areas that fascinated her—peer interactions, ESL students, the writing process. She found a common theme that connected all of her current fascinations in her teaching—student growth. Finally, an observation of an interaction between two of her learners during a writers' workshop triggered the final focus of her inquiry wondering. This incident provides a fine illustration of what Hubbard and Power (1993) refer to as inquiry resulting from "real-world observations." Wonderings also come from "dilemmas" or "felt difficulties." In the next example, note how Quinn Garman encountered a very common dilemma faced by many beginning teachers—she actually began to fear a student who challenged her directions:

Imagine that you are a prestudent teacher in a kindergarten room during the third day of your experience. At her request, all of the students join your cooperating teacher on the rug for a story . . . all except one child, "Suzy." After I remind Suzy several times that it is time to stop her project and join the others on the rug, she continues to color using just one more marker, to sprinkle glitter in just one more place, and to put on just one more piece of sequin. Then, instead of quietly joining the group, she decides it would be more exciting to also sprinkle glitter on the work table, pour glue on the carpet, and use marker wherever there is room on the floor, the table, and even her hands. The more she ignores my reminders, the more frustrated and agitated I become. Finally, with a stern face and voice, I stoop down to Suzy's eye level and give her a choice: Either she can quietly meet Mrs. Brown and the others at the rug or she can have a time-out. Just as those seemingly harmless words spill off the tip of my tongue, Suzy raises her right hand and with all her might, grazes my cheek with a mixture of pure anger and fear while yelling, "no!" Her unexpected reaction immediately stuns my words and freezes me like a popsicle. My numb legs can barely hold my paralyzed body up straight. Unaware of the situation, Mrs. Brown gently reminds Suzy that her place is at the rug. Immediately, Suzy bolts from the scene and finds a cozy spot right in front of the story, as if there from the start. For a few minutes afterwards, I can't move or think. I stand in a daze wondering what has just happened. Is this how this innocent five-year-old usually reacts to situations? Or is this just her way of reaching out?

Unfortunately, this was not just an imagined scenario for me, but rather a serious "slap in the face." As absurd as this may sound, I actually began to fear Suzy. She was the first person I thought of in the morning and the last person I thought of at night. In fact, I found myself trying to avoid contact with her whenever possible. As horrible as this may sound, I sometimes felt more comfortable working with someone who I knew would not hurt me rather than risk having a confrontation with Suzy. With all of this happening, I knew that I needed to develop a better relationship with Suzy during my student-teaching experience.

During this time, I began attending seminars on teacher inquiry and reading books on teacher research during my student teaching. This led me to question my own teaching beliefs and practices. This skepticism about my teaching, coupled with Suzy's slap, led me to complete a systematic study of our relationship. Therefore, the purpose of my study was to understand the behavioral patterns of one student, Suzy, in relation to my behavior as the teacher.

The following research question guided my inquiry, "How do the structure and management of my classroom encourage or deter a particular student's behavior?" (Garman, 1997, pp. 1–4)

Like Amy's, Quinn's question was triggered by a specific incident in the classroom that led her to focus on a particular child. In contrast to Amy's critical incident, where she observed two learners interacting with each other, Quinn's critical incident was characterized by her own interaction with a learner. Out of this particular interaction a dilemma developed—a desire to avoid a five-year-old whom she was responsible for teaching each day. Her wondering or "felt difficulty" was born out of the combination of her own interaction with a learner, subsequent reflection on that interaction, and desire to confront the dilemma she faced.

While you, like Amy and Quinn, note observations of particular learners and interact with individual learners hundreds of times each teaching day, sometimes a wondering about a particular child is not spawned by one observation or critical incident but emerges from what you notice and are learning about a particular child over time. In the following example, note how Jenn Thulin's (1999) interest in a particular first-grade child emerged after many months of discussion and observation between Jenn and her mentor-teacher:

Meg is an imaginative child who stood out to my mentor-teacher and I from the beginning of the year when she told us her stories of castles, princesses, and dogs that talk. She told these stories with the enthusiasm and excitement of an actress who was "on stage." We knew that she was very creative, but did not know the extent of her talent until she sang to us one day. Meg sang with the most incredible voice and perfect pitch. She not only enjoyed singing songs but also making up her own songs as well.

While it was clear from the first day of school that Meg was a very talented and creative young girl, she also stood out in the classroom because of extreme language difficulties. At first we noticed problems with her speech. Many of her syllables were reversed and she would often substitute incorrect sounds. For example, she would say "bery" instead of "very." She also had a hard time processing auditory information such as questions and directions. From the beginning of the year Meg also struggled with all subjects, but was especially discouraged and falling behind in reading.

In contrast to most of her peers, she did not know many sounds and confused many letters of the alphabet. We struggled for many months to help her learn the alphabet and sounds. She would make progress, but it was inconsistent. Just because Meg knew a sound one day did not automatically guarantee she would know it the next day. To help her achieve consistency, it was necessary to give Meg a great deal of individual instruction.

Therefore, Meg was recommended as a candidate for Instructional Support, which led to observation and testing by a team of educators. Through this process, we discovered that Meg had very poor auditory processing skills and auditory memory. It was very hard for her to comprehend and remember things that were told to her orally. Meg scored extremely low on auditory processing; however, she scored exceptionally high in visual processing. If Meg saw a picture or a visual representation it was easy for her to understand. Because of the processing and memory difficulties, reading was a challenge for Meg. If you read Meg a passage from a book, she may not understand a word of it. However, if you showed her an illustration associated with that passage, she could tell you what the passage was about.

After witnessing the Instructional Support Process and observing Meg struggle throughout the year with reading, I wanted to find a way to help her. The first thing that came to my mind was music. I noticed not only that Meg was a wonderful singer but also that she remembered songs very easily, so I hoped that music might work well with her auditory memory and processing difficulties. I hoped there was some way I could connect music to reading. I wondered, "In what ways could I utilize music to help Meg become a better reader?" and "How might music help her combat some frustrations when reading and boost her self esteem?" (Thulin, 1999)

Jenn's long-term commitment to understanding and supporting an individual child provides a fertile foundation for the cultivation of this inquiry.

As you can see by looking across these three examples of inquiry into a particular child, inquiry questions emerge in a variety of ways.

PASSION I EXERCISES

1. Create a list of all the children in your class (elementary teachers) or a list of all the students in one period you teach each day (middle and high school teachers). As you add each student's name to the list, think about what makes that particular individual unique. Focus on attributes that your students exhibit and observations

(Continued)

(Continued)

of students rather than judgments or critiques about student performance or personality. Jot down one question next to each student's name that would provide you with insights into this particular learner. A few examples from Gary Meegan (2007), a high school theology teacher and department chair at an all-boys Catholic school, follow:

I have 108 students in four sections. Below is a listing of the students who most intrigue me because of their background, performance, or personality.

Tyler: In the Academic Resource Center, verbally doing well, but difficulty in writing, larger concepts are difficult to comprehend and bring to real life situations; How can I help him to process the ideas and apply them to his situation?

Arthur: Bright, very quiet, demanding parents, soccer is his outlet, kind, gets upset when he does not do well; What are ways I can help Arthur to understand that learning is a process and not a product, that not being perfect is OK?

Brad: Low performing, but no learning differences, extremely quiet, meek to the point of being painful; How can I construct the classroom atmosphere so that Brad can feel more free to contribute?

Adam: A joy, smiles all the time, messy, notebook is completely out of order, difficult for him to keep track of things, father concerned about this; Should I take time to work with Adam on structuring his assignments and notebook? Are there easy ways to do this so that I can empower him to be this way?

Bill: Extremely quiet and kind, has turned almost nothing in since the beginning of the semester, grade in the class is 11, yes 11, mother does not know what to do about him, many meetings with counselor and administration, kind young man, procrastinates, failing in other classes also; How can I be there for him when obviously there are deep psychological issues at play here? This is the one student I agonize over.

Miller: Sincere, honest, caring, slower than the rest of the students, not afraid to raise his hand in class, not afraid to be wrong in class, takes many rewrites to get papers up to where they need to be, hard worker; How can I keep Miller motivated and make sure that he does not get frustrated throughout the entire year because he needs to work much harder than the rest of the students?

Troy: Troy has missed fourteen of the first 32 days of classes this semester. The handbook says that a teacher can lower a student's grade after missing eight classes in the semester. He has a history of coming into school late and not much has been done about it from his teachers. Headaches are blamed for his missing the first couple of periods, but this doesn't seem right, and the attendance secretary senses that his mother is merely covering for him not wanting to come to school. He is very intelligent and well spoken, but there is a problem when he cannot be in class for discussions. I'm wondering how I can reach Troy, not that I need to know exactly what is going on, but this seems like a symptom of something larger.

Myles: A sullen boy, I have seen him smile only twice, he produces good work, but has never volunteered information to the class and rarely to his small group of three. What sort of activities would get Myles to participate and become a member of the group?

Craig: Gregarious and outgoing, enjoys the class and discussing with others, very verbal and not afraid to admit when he is wrong, enjoys a good conversation and has an excellent vocabulary, but his writing is always terse and to the point, he rarely goes beyond the obvious in print where he would go deep in conversation; How can I help Craig to do the same in his writing as he does in conversation? How can what he says with his mouth be transferred to what he puts down on paper?

2. Thinking back over the course of the school year, create a "Top 10" list of critical incidents or intriguing observations that have occurred with particular learners in your classroom. Create a chart by generating a column next to each critical incident or observation that notes the student or students who were involved. Finally, in a third column, add a few words that describe the essence of the experience or observation. After you have completed your chart, look for themes across incidents, such as, "Does one student appear on my chart consistently?," and "What are the commonalities between each of the incidents or observations I listed?"

Passion 2: Desire to Improve or Enrich Curriculum

Just as you are involved in interacting with and observing children each day, each day of teaching you interact with the required curriculum you are expected to teach. You work diligently to develop lessons and units of study that engage your students with meaningful content designed to actualize your objectives. Sometimes, for different reasons, teachers become dissatisfied with a curriculum unit and particular lessons they have delivered in the past.

Locating your inquiry within the development or enrichment of curriculum is a ripe area for the development of your first wondering. A curriculum development inquiry is popular for veteran teachers, as they often emerge from a dissatisfaction of "what was" the last time the unit was taught. In addition, veterans can reap the benefits of revising and enriching curriculum when they return to the same units or lessons each year. Inquiry into student learning as a result of teaching a particular "chunk" of curriculum can also provide the point of entry for inquiry for prospective teachers. This kind of inquiry allows prospective teachers to systematically explore and critique existing curriculum that can lead to changes in their own use or conception of curriculum. Prospective teachers often teach curriculum for the first time in their field and experience and study what student learning occurred as a result of the curriculum.

We now share two excerpts of veteran teacher inquiries motivated by the desire to improve curriculum. Judi Kur, a first-grade teacher, finds her initial wondering in the tension between the required teaching of an outdated dinosaur curriculum unit, focused on the acquisition of facts, and the specific topic that is highly motivating for her primary school–aged children:

I first thought about my inquiry project about the same time I began contemplating my upcoming responsibilities as the Chair of a unit entitled: Prehistoric Life and Fossils. In my district, teachers are organized into teams that collaborate to teach four thematic, literature-based units each school year. As the Unit Chair, it was my responsibility to organize activities, orchestrate the sharing of books and materials among the teachers on my team, and lead the development of a culminating activity at the close of the unit.

I had been dissatisfied with most of the science units in the primary curriculum since I began teaching first grade in 1996. I enjoy science and am fascinated with teaching science. However, to me science curriculum should focus on topics that children can experiment with, topics where the students can use the scientific process to ask and answer questions. This had not been my experience with the dinosaur unit. Yes, the children love the topic and they are motivated to learn, but I didn't feel that I was taking advantage of the children's and my enthusiasm. This unit as it was written didn't help me. In addition, a survey of the primary teachers in the district showed that most teachers thought the unit was extremely outdated. The science curriculum focuses on fossils, and the objectives can be covered in about a week, and to top it off, we were being told that we cannot use the word "theories" in our teaching of the unit, due to concerns expressed by parents that the dinosaur unit was teaching evolution and this was contrary to their religious beliefs.

Is it any wonder that when I last taught the dinosaur unit, the learning the children did was reading about other people's discoveries, not making their own? My students, as those mentioned by Craig Munsart in his book *Investigating Science with Dinosaurs* (1993), "easily memorized names and dimensions of dinosaurs but learned little about the science that surrounds them." And yet I agreed with a statement that I read by Don Lessem in an article in the *New York Times* (1991): "Dinosaurs are often a child's first introduction to science. As such, they could be the key to engendering a lifelong interest in all science."

And so, I wondered, "How can I take a science unit that is heavy on content, and make it more science inquiry based?" After reading the book *Organizing Wonder: Making Inquiry Science Work in the Elementary School* (1998) by Jody Hall and talking with Carla Zembal-Saul, a professor in science education at the university, I embarked on developing lessons for this unit framed around the question, "How do scientists know so much about dinosaurs?" Once my lessons were developed and implemented, I pondered an additional research question: "What evidence exists that my newly developed inquiry based lessons on dinosaurs help children develop the abilities advocated by the National Science Standards in the section that discusses science as inquiry?" (Kur, 2000)

In sum, Judi's inquiry question emerges from her dissatisfaction with existing curriculum and her own commitment to providing primary-grade students the opportunity to experience scientific inquiry. As a result of these interacting conditions (students, curriculum, and teacher beliefs), Judi seeks outside support in the form of human and other resources to further refine her question. Like Judi, fourth-grade teaching colleagues Amy Jones and Diane Reed collaborated on an inquiry, finding their first wondering in a social studies unit on explorers. As you read the excerpt from Amy and Diane's inquiry, note that, once again, they articulate a dilemma or felt difficulty in the curriculum's existing approach to teaching. In this case, the unit covers Columbus:

"In 1492, Columbus sailed the ocean blue." Most elementary students early in their education learn this traditional verse. A less familiar verse, which comes to us from native peoples, is "In 1493, Columbus stole all that he could see." This striking difference between the two quotes offers a glimpse at the task that we, as educators, are trying to accomplish by meshing two different perspectives in the teaching of the "true discovery" of America. This idea led to our collaboration, as two fourth-grade teachers, to investigate other possibilities for teaching a unit on explorers in our district.

Teaching the explorer unit presented several dilemmas that needed to be addressed prior to the implementation of the unit. First, we struggled with the fact that we had four weeks to instruct the children with the material. The question was raised, "Should we spend the four weeks highlighting several explorers, or should we focus on Columbus and do an in-depth study of his encounter with the native people?"

After reviewing the materials and discussing the time limitations together, we felt that our time and our students' time were better served by focusing on Columbus's encounter. With that decided, the next dilemma revolved around the concern of whether fourth-grade students are able to look at multiple perspectives and accuracy of historical events? This question initiated our frame work for our inquiry.

When we began working on this project, we first had to find our focal point. In *Rethinking Columbus* (Bigelow & Peterson, 1998), we found the following quote that would navigate our curriculum writing:

> Our goal is not to idealize native people, demonize Europeans, or present a depressing litany of victimization. We hope to encourage a deeper understanding of the European invasion's consequences, to honor the rich legacy of resistance to the injustices it created, to convey some appreciation for the diverse indigenous cultures of the hemisphere, and to reflect on what this all means for us today. (p. 11)

We also needed to enhance our own background knowledge of this historical event. *Lies My Teacher Told Me: Everything Your American History Textbook Got Wrong* (Loewen, 1995) presented a more historically accurate account of Columbus's arrival. *The Tainos: The People Who Welcomed Columbus* (Jacobs, 1992) provided specific information on the lifestyle of the Tainos, both before and after the arrival of Columbus. Both resources were not developmentally appropriate for fourth graders; however, they provided us with the essential background knowledge needed to teach this unit.

As we began to review the literature for the unit, as well as additional resources, several questions emerged that became the basis for our inquiry project: "How can the story of the 'true discovery' of America be taught to fourth graders in a developmentally appropriate way?" and "What changes occur in students' knowledge/ understanding of the 'true discovery' of America as a result of the lessons we constructed?"

Subquestions targeted at change emerged and included "What changes occur in students' knowledge/understanding of Columbus?," "What changes occur in students' knowledge/ understanding of the Taino people?," "What changes occur in students' knowledge/understanding of authors' bias regarding the depiction of this historical event?," and "What changes occur in students' knowledge/understanding of the meaning of 'discovery'?" (Jones & Reed, 2000)

Often, when teachers engage in inquiry around curriculum, they start with a "How can I?" phrased question. In Judi's case, she began with, "How can I take a science unit that is heavy on content and make it more inquiry based?" Similarly, in Amy and Diane's case, they began with, "How can we teach the story of the 'true discovery' of America to fourth graders in a developmentally appropriate way?" While "How can I . . . " phrased questions are wonderful starting points for curriculum development inquiries, if a teacher-inquirer stops here, his or her work may become purely the development of lesson plans without systematic study. While the development of new lesson plans and implementing these plans is important work, focusing on what is learned as a result of the curriculum development makes the work teacher inquiry. Hence, if you begin with a "How can I . . . " wondering, also formulate a companion wondering that leads you beyond the lessons you developed to what you have learned about children, curriculum, and/or yourself as a teacher as a result of developing and implementing these new lessons. These companion questions are often generated by engaging in adult-level research about the content as well as the teaching strategies you are about to use. In the earlier examples, Judi turned to Hall's (1998) *Organizing Wonder: Making Inquiry Science Work in the Elementary School*, whereas Amy and Diane read *Lies My Teacher Told Me: Everything Your American History Textbook Got Wrong* (Loewen, 1995) and *The Tainos: The People Who Welcomed Columbus* (Jacobs, 1992). In these cases, content area reading becomes an essential component of wondering development.

PASSION 2 EXERCISES

1. Browse through your textbooks, your district's curriculum documents, and your old plan books. As you browse, generate a list of the topics you teach each school year that you felt uncomfortable teaching in the past or wished to enrich in some way. Next to each entry on your list, jot down a few words that describe your dissatisfaction with this unit and/or the ways the unit might be enhanced. Select one item from your list on which to focus a potential inquiry and begin the process of brainstorming questions related to the teaching of this curriculum.

2. Visit the websites of the leading national organizations for teaching of specific subject matter, such as the National Council for Teachers of Mathematics (www.nctm.org), National Science Teachers Association (www.nsta.org), National Council for the Social Studies (www.ncss.org), and National Council for Teachers of English (www.ncte.org). View each organization's standards for best practice in that field. How does the delivery of your curriculum mesh with best teaching practice as advocated by these associations?

3. Meet with the curriculum specialist or administrator in your building. Find out what changes they are anticipating in the curriculum. Identify an interest area and question connected to these changes. By studying the new implementation or change process, you are likely to have some influence regarding what develops!

Passion 3: Focus on Developing Content Knowledge

In Passion 2, inquiry focused on developing curriculum with new alternative instructional approaches and objectives to shape curriculum. As indicated in both inquiries, a precursor to this kind of curriculum development was a focus on developing deeper teacher content knowledge and then identifying the developmentally appropriate content knowledge for the children within each teacher's classroom. In this case, the inquiry wondering emerges as teachers identify areas of the curriculum they teach that provoke a content-related felt difficulty. For example, Diane and Amy's inquiry into "How can we teach the story of the 'true discovery' of America to fourth graders in a developmentally appropriate way?" provoked them to inquire into the underlying content of the curriculum they were planning. They needed to understand the voices represented in alternative stories. This required substantive adult-level content reading and research.

Inquiry or research into content requires multiple phases of teacher activity. First, the inquiry begins as teachers pose a question about the content they are teaching, for example, "What do I know about the 'true discovery' of America?," "What do I know about the Holocaust?," or "How do airplanes fly?" Next, teachers obtain multiple resources and perspectives that can help them respond to that inquiry. For example, teachers may explore reference materials, review primary documents, conduct an oral history, or delve into artifacts that inform their inquiry question. One teacher shared the following:

> You know, as an elementary teacher, I really don't have the time to be an expert on anything. I felt really fortunate to have the time to investigate one content area in depth and figure out a way to make sense of it for my young students. The Holocaust is a particularly sensitive issue. I am always wondering what my first through fourth graders should know about it and what I can teach them that is really at their level of understanding. After spending a good month reading everything that I could about the Holocaust and really trying to get an adult-level understanding of the events and atrocities that happened, I finally felt prepared to teach. (Field notes, SBAC teacher)

By exploring multiple sources, the teacher constructs a stronger understanding of the various perspectives on the content she needs to teach.

Once the adult-level content knowledge has been developed, teachers begin the third step of the inquiry, which focuses on defining what is believed to be the developmentally appropriate content for the students within the classroom. This is a "teacher activity," as it requires teachers to investigate their own students' cognitive, physical, social, and emotional levels regarding the content area investigated. One example of this emerged as elementary teachers considered the students' readiness for the content of the Holocaust as follows:

> We talked to a lot of people about how to share the Holocaust with young children. We spoke to our administrator, guidance counselor, and a slew of parents. We met with the media specialist, too, and some local experts on the Holocaust. We even talked to members of the Jewish community within our town. I think the most important information came from interviews with our students. Although most of them knew nothing about the Holocaust themselves, which wasn't surprising to us, we realized through analyzing our data that certain content specific to the Holocaust should be incorporated into the elementary curriculum and that, in addition, certain democratic dispositions or underpinnings for addressing and understanding issues of the Holocaust were missing from our current curriculum. (Field notes, SBAC teacher)

After a great deal of background research, this elementary teacher and her inquiry partner decided that it was more developmentally appropriate to structure the elementary students' learning around key ideas underpinning the Holocaust as follows:

> By the time we finished digging into our own understanding of the Holocaust, we realized that our students needed to understand some fundamental ideas. We focused on helping our students develop themselves in moral and responsible ways by promoting a caring and accepting nature toward others. We taught them the importance of helping others seek better conditions and the difference between being a "bystander" and a "rescuer." We focused on teaching them about "random acts of kindness," developing good habits, and respecting "otherness." We also worked on helping our students understand that change is necessary in the world if we are to survive and that prejudice, discrimination, and stereotyping are unproductive activities if we strive to reach these goal. (Field notes, SBAC teacher)

Interestingly, these teachers decided that these were the important concepts for their students to learn in regard to the content of the Holocaust.

Because the teacher is key to student learning, spending your time constructing content knowledge and transforming that knowledge into developmentally appropriate content for children is a legitimate and worthy task. You will not only become much more familiar with the content, but you will also become clearer about what you do not know. Exploring content and determining its relevance to the students within your classroom is a powerful way to enhance your teaching and the learning process.

PASSION 3 EXERCISES

1. Make a list of topics you teach for which deeper content knowledge would enhance your classroom practice. On this list, circle the topics that you believe require substantive transformation or adaptation if you are to teach the content area to children.

2. Evaluate the materials you currently use to teach content within each subject area and unit you teach. Do these resources represent diversity of perspectives and multiple voices? Whose voices are present or missing?

Passion 4: Desire to Improve or Experiment With Teaching Strategies and Teaching Techniques

In Passions 2 and 3, wonderings are located around a particular topic and content area. The work of the teacher also encompasses applying generic teaching strategies (such as cooperative learning, role play, simulation, lecture, and discussion) and specific teaching techniques (such as questioning, assessing student learning, and integrating technology into instruction) throughout the teaching day. Similar to the desire to improve or enhance a particular piece of curriculum as discussed in Passion 2, you may have a desire to gain insights into, improve, and/or experiment with new or routine teaching strategies and techniques. In the following example, Nancy Sunner is intrigued with learning more about the questions she poses to students in her daily teaching:

> Questioning is an enormously powerful and important skill in productive teaching. For decades, teacher questioning has been a topic of study. Researchers had found that teachers rely on questioning as an essential element of their teaching repertoire. On an average, elementary school teachers ask 348 questions during a typical school day (Acheson & Gall, 1997). Through the process of effective questioning, teachers can stimulate thought, help students reinforce basic skills, involve shy or quiet students, draw in the attention of a student who has drifted off, and promote self-esteem and success in the classroom.
>
> The skill of effective questioning requires teachers to constantly balance several things at once. During questioning, teachers must remember their lesson goals, monitor their communication with the students, assess the students' verbal and nonverbal responses (nods, raised hands, shrugs, and downcast eyes), and think about the next question. This impressive and sometimes overwhelming aspect of teaching sparked my curiosity about my own questioning techniques in the classroom.
>
> As a beginning teacher, I have experienced great satisfaction when I asked a student a question and I got a correct response. I

feel as though the students "get it" and I am somehow responsible for this accomplishment. On the other hand, I have had experiences this year when a lesson is falling apart and it seems that no matter what questions are asked, the students cannot follow my line of questioning. This is the ultimate frustrating experience for everyone.

Therefore, the focus of my inquiry is to better understand my questioning behavior as a teacher. The questions I will address through this inquiry are "What type of questions do I ask?" and "How does questioning change with the subjects I am teaching?" (Sunner, 1999)

Of the examples of teachers' wonderings we have explored thus far, note that Nancy's wonderings are perhaps the most straightforward and technical. They emerge at the intersection of her professional readings and her felt difficulty regarding her use of questioning. Straightforward and technical wonderings are often powerful in that they lead to teachers' discoveries that their beliefs, philosophies, and desires are not always congruent with their practice. For example, through scripting the questions posed throughout different lessons and sorting each question into one of five categories (higher order/thought questions, recall/narrow questions, managerial/behavioral questions, procedural questions, and probing questions) as her inquiry unfolded, Nancy discovered that the majority of her questions were fact/recall questions. This discovery was inconsistent with her desire to teach for conceptual understanding and led to keener attention to her questioning efforts as well as changes in her questioning.

There is an old proverb, "A fish would be the last creature to discover water." In teaching, generic strategies and techniques can become so routine and ingrained in our practice that we do not notice significant ways in which our routines interface with the goals of our teaching. In addition, we can become so immersed in strategies and routines that have worked in the past that we fail to try new strategies that could potentially enhance our teaching. Systematically studying teaching strategies and techniques can lead to discoveries that would not have become apparent in the absence of systematic study, and these discoveries ultimately lead to new and significant change in teaching practice.

PASSION 4 EXERCISES

1. Brainstorm a list of teaching strategies you would like to try. Next to each entry on your list, jot down a few words that describe your reasoning for wanting to try this strategy. Formulate a question that connects the strategy and your reasoning for trying to use that strategy. For example,

(Continued)

(Continued)

   a. Cooperative learning—My students are very talkative. Cooperative learning could fulfill their need to talk and focus their talking on academic learning simultaneously. How can I use my children's social skills to enhance their learning and instruction at the same time?

   b. Integrating a SMART Board into instruction—After seeing a SMART Board demonstrated at a conference I recently attended, I was intrigued by the power this technology might hold to enhance instruction but reluctant to try a SMART Board as my prior teaching experiences suggest that integrating technology into instruction can be intimidating and frustrating. How can a team of teachers work through problems together and support each other to overcome hurdles when using new technologies?

2. Brainstorm a list of the most frequent strategies and/or techniques you draw on in your teaching. After brainstorming your list, place a star next to the strategies that are most intriguing to you. Jot down a few sentences or phrases next to your starred strategies that capture why these techniques are intriguing. Then formulate a question that connects the strategy and your intrigue with it. For example,

   a. *Questioning—Sometimes students don't answer the questions I am asking. How do the ways I phrase questions contribute to how learners interpret them?

   b. *Facilitating discussions—During my literature circles, it feels like the students never talk to each other when discussing a book. The conversations feel like they resemble Ping-Pong matches as the dialogue goes back and forth between me and my students: teacher → student → teacher → student → teacher → student. I'd prefer the students to talk to each other. What are some strategies I could use to facilitate better literature discussions?

Passion 5: Desire to Explore the Relationship Between Your Beliefs and Your Classroom Practice

In the example used to illustrate Passion 4, Nancy's wondering led to her conclusion that her teaching desires and her practice were inconsistent with each other. While Nancy's inquiry *ended* with this discovery, many teachers *begin* their inquiry with the realization that the relationship between their beliefs and practice are incongruent. Exploring the relationship between your beliefs and practice provides another possibility for generating your first wondering. In the example that follows, Holly Niebauer Jones finds her first teacher inquiry wondering as she discovers that her implementation of a classroom management plan does not match her philosophy.

I was fortunate to be a part of an experimental student-teacher-as-researcher program at Penn State designed to focus on learning about and doing teacher research during the student teaching experience. Class discussions about teacher research and three books entitled *The Art of Classroom Inquiry* (1993) by Ruth Shagoury Hubbard and Brenda Miller Power, *Inside/Outside: Teacher Research and Knowledge* (1993) by Marilyn Cochran-Smith and Susan L. Lytle, and *Teachers as Researchers: Qualitative Inquiry as a Path to Empowerment* (1991) by Joe Kincheloe helped give me a strong background for pursuing research.

As I progressed through the semester, I thought of numerous projects that were possibilities for teacher research projects. The topic that consistently surfaced, however, was that I noticed inconsistencies between my philosophy of education and my actions as a teacher, particularly as they related to classroom management. The idealistic components in my philosophy were not always practiced. I pondered over this daily and wanted to find reasons for the inconsistencies.

In order to focus my data collection for research, I generated two questions: (1) In what ways do my classroom management and practices deter from my philosophy of teaching and my beliefs about how children learn? and (2) What are my underlying/suppressed beliefs about teaching and learning and children and schooling that cause/contribute to the gaps that exist between my beliefs and my actions? (Niebauer, 1997)

As you can see, Holly found her inquiry at the intersection of her espoused teaching philosophy and her ability to critically self-reflect on her own classroom management.

PASSION 5 EXERCISES

1. Write a series of philosophy statements that describe your general teaching philosophy; your philosophy of teaching science, social studies, reading/language arts, mathematics; and/or creating a classroom learning environment conducive to instruction. (If you are a preservice teacher, you may have already completed essays such as these in your prior teacher preparation coursework at the university.) Once committed to paper, share your philosophy with a colleague or friend. Discuss the ways you are and are not enacting your philosophies of teaching in your classroom practice.

2. Keep a teaching journal for one week. Each night, reflect on one happening in the classroom that you wish you had the opportunity to repeat and react to in a different way. Note what beliefs you hold that led you to react as you did, as well as how you would react differently if able to turn back time. What beliefs undergird your alternative reaction?

Passion 6: The Intersection of Your Personal and Professional Identities

Just as wonderings may be found at the intersection of your beliefs and practice, they may also be found at the intersection of your personal and professional identity. According to William Ayers (1989), who you are as a teacher and who you are as a person are intricately intertwined. In his study of six exemplary preschool teachers, he came to the conclusion that

> "teaching as identity" is the clearest theme to emerge in this inquiry, and "teaching as identity" is the frame through which each portrait makes sense. In these portraits, there is no clear line delineating the person and the teacher. Rather, there is a seamless web between teaching and being, between teacher and person. Teaching is not simply what one does, it is who one is. (p. 130)

Hence, a wonderful place to find your first wondering is by focusing on who you are as a person and a teacher and further exploring one of your own personal passions and the ways that passion plays out in your teaching.

An example of personal passion translating to teaching is found in the work of Julie Russell. In Julie's inquiry that follows, note how her personal passion for writing led to her first wonderings:

> I can still remember every detail of the moment when I became a writer. The warm August air sticks to my skin, powdery chalk dust tickles my nose, and the comforting sounds of my mother making dinner fill my ears whenever I begin to put words on a page. I found my voice as a writer the summer before second grade. I was six years old, and my older sister had suddenly decided that she was too mature to play with me. She would disappear with her friends, and I was left to fill the long, summer days without her. One afternoon, I wandered into the basement and started to draw on an old chalkboard that my sister and I used when we were "playing school." After a while, I stopped drawing and began writing poetry. When my mother called me for dinner, she saw my poems and became my first audience. She encouraged my efforts and gave me a small, yellow notebook so I could continue to write. My passion for writing grew as I continued to read quality literature and experienced the powerful ways in which expert authors manipulate language and develop engaging stories. Throughout my life, I have turned to written words to express my thoughts and ideas.
>
> As I developed a teaching philosophy, I realized that my passion for teaching is intertwined with my passion for writing. My goal as a teacher is to help children become lifelong learners who can think critically about the world around them and create and

articulate their own ideas. I hope that, by sharing my love for writing with my students, I can help them express the thoughts and opinions that are important and meaningful to them. Therefore, when I pictured my future classroom, I always seemed to arrive during writer's workshop. I assumed that I would be an effective, engaging writing teacher simply because I enjoyed writing. I imagined a classroom filled with eager students who loved writing and could not wait to commit their ideas to paper. I was thrilled to be an intern in a second-grade classroom, because I could remember the wonderful writing experiences I had during my own second-grade year.

As I began my internship experience, I helped provide writing instruction for a group of second graders with differing strengths, needs, and interests. I quickly realized that teaching writing is extremely complicated. Some children wrote independently and produced several pages of text during each workshop. Others wrote one sentence at a time and frequently approached me to ask, "Am I done yet?" I often sat with a small group of students who struggled to get their thoughts down on paper. As I tried to keep these children on task and encourage them to continue writing, I asked questions and made story maps. At the end of many writing sessions, I felt uncomfortable with the amount of support I was giving to some young writers. Several children who were quite capable of writing independently often came to me and asked, "Can I write with you?" I worried that I was allowing some children to become too dependent on my help and my influence was hindering the flow of their ideas.

As I studied children's writing development, I realized that the range of writing behaviors in my classroom was common for second graders. I felt relief when I read the experts' descriptions of second-grade writers and they mirrored my feelings about the young writers in my classroom. Some children write "fluently" and approach writing with "carefree confidence" (Calkins, 1986, p. 67). These children write long, detailed narratives with ease. Other children seem to erase more than they write. Second graders are beginning to become "aware of an audience" for their writing, and the "easy confidence" they felt as first graders often turns into their first cases of "writer's block" (Calkins, 1986, p. 68). They are concerned about approaching tasks in the "right way" and that vulnerability makes writing a difficult and painstaking process for many children (Calkins, 1986, p. 69). Therefore, writing instruction in second grade must address this wide range of writing behaviors.

During the students' goal-setting conferences in the beginning of the school year, my mentor, Linda Witmer, spoke to many of the children about working toward meeting the district's benchmark for writing by the end of the year. According to this benchmark, the students must be able to write stories with beginnings, middles, and endings. These stories should be understandable and must include characters, settings, and major events. The students are also expected to include some descriptive language, use some punctuation and capitalization, and spell the district benchmark words correctly. The students must complete the writing assessment independently. After winter break, Linda and I were both concerned about our students' writing. As I looked through the students' work, I noticed that extremely capable children were often scoring below the benchmark. Many of the children were still writing incomplete stories, and endings were particularly difficult for many students. Although our students had wonderful, creative ideas, we worried that several of them would not meet the district's benchmark for writing because they did not take the reader on a complete journey from beginning to middle to end.

My initial experiences as a writing teacher were frustrating. After years of imagining myself as an effective writing teacher, I was dismayed when I realized that my efforts were not helping my students meet their writing goals. In some cases, I worried that I was doing more harm than good because my attempts to help often became persistent prompting that drowned out the students' voices in their own writing. I was heartbroken when students resisted writing, because I was so eager to share my passion for stories and language. When I conducted a survey to collect data about the students' attitudes toward writing, I was concerned when I realized that many children thought that they were good writers because of "neat handwriting," "good spelling," or "using time wisely." Although those skills are important, I noticed that most children did not mention that they were proud of their ability to create stories. Gradually, I began to doubt my ability to provide my students with writing instruction that would help them meet the district's writing goals and that would inspire them to enjoy writing. My passion for writing, which I believed would be an asset in the classroom, actually hindered my progress as a writing teacher because I struggled to relate to and communicate with students who resisted writing. As I studied writing instruction, I learned that a teacher's personal experiences with the subject matter influence the way he or she teaches his or her students (Frank, 1979). I realized that, because I had positive writing experiences as a child, I naively assumed that all of my second graders would react to writing with similar enthusiasm.

My passion for writing and teaching, as well as my frustrations about the realities of teaching writing, led me to my wonderings. I wanted to do a project that would focus on my students' development as writers and would also help me develop as a writing teacher. Therefore, I began my project with the following wonderings: "Will my second graders write more complete stories if the elements of a story are broken down into a series of mini-lessons?," "Will my second graders become more independent writers and gain confidence in their writing abilities if my expectations for their writing are more explicit?," "Will collaborating with other learners help my students grow as writers?," "Will my students grow as writers if the lessons include opportunities to make connections between children's literature and their own stories?," and "Will these changes in writing instruction improve the way my students feel about themselves as writers and the way I feel about myself as a writing teacher?" (Russell, 2002)

As indicated, Julie's wonderings developed from her own personal interest in writing and her identity as a writer. Similarly, in the following example, Algebra I teacher Carlee Escue finds that her prior life experiences in architecture played a big role in the ways she approached the teaching of high school mathematics:

My college BA is in Architectural Design. I chose to become a teacher and I am very happy with my decision, although there are times that I feel I have an interesting background for a math teacher and I would like to share it more with my students. In my teaching experience the most common question from students is, "When am I going to use this in the real world?" For at least a handful of math concepts I teach, I am able to answer that I have actually experienced having to use these skills in the real world. I have also experienced in architectural business that we do not work alone. Every project I did consisted of more than four people contributing to the final outcome. Everyone depended on one another to do their job accurately and on time. So, over the past three years, I've been engaged in a continuous cycle of inquiry to address the question, "How can I share my love of architecture, demonstrate real-world mathematics skill application to high schoolers, and provide them with real-world experience in working together?"

My quest to explore this wondering translated into my assignment of a cooperative learning project to design a playground in the spring to my ninth-grade Algebra I students. It lasts about two months from introduction to the final group presentation. Students work in groups of four with each group member being assigned one of the following specified roles: Project Manager, Designer, Accountant, and Technician. Each group is responsible for taking site measurements and designing a playground for two different age groups (ages 2–5 and ages 5–12) with an outside classroom that can accommodate sixty seated adults. They then need to consult with real playground equipment companies to purchase the materials. Their budget is $80,000. The project culminates with presentation of their playground proposals to a fictitious investor, "Escue Enterprises." They must incorporate technology into this presentation. It is a detailed project with many "checkpoint" grading periods to keep the students on track.

Because I find this project to be very interesting, and because it relates to my background and real-world experiences, I want to improve on it constantly. I have modified my approach every year. For the past three years most of my modifications have involved organization, real-world accuracy, and ease of application and delivery on my part. I find it is time to approach the problems that have been more difficult to solve. Facilitating effective cooperative learning groups has been one of these challenges. I need to address group dynamics, positive confrontation skills, parental involvement, and understanding of the project.

Although these issues were present in the past three years, students struggling with cooperative learning were more apparent to me this year. It proved to be an issue I needed to address immediately. Although the nuts and bolts of the project were addressed and refined, I discovered the problem with collaboration when I had my first large grading cycle. I have designed the grading to have little "checkpoints" throughout the two months. The grading period that addressed the rough draft and site plan revealed to me which groups were functioning and which were "dysfunctional."

I addressed each group and discussed the expectations I had for them, as well as why their work was appropriate or unacceptable.

After these grades were posted and my group discussions were concluded, I received emails from parents who were hearing for the first time about this project. They were not pleased with what was going on in their child's group and/or with their child's grade. At first I found myself getting defensive because I had thought I had been thinking ahead. For example, I had allotted time in my class for work. Giving half the class period to work in their groups, I gave each student a job description form and a sign up sheet. I had allowed the students to pick their top two job choices, and everyone was put into a group with their top choice position. Each group had a portfolio that I reviewed with the classes when I presented my PowerPoint introduction to the project with sample drawings and models. But what seemed to support my argument most was I had groups that were working very effectively. I found myself defending my project and not addressing the concerns. I couldn't understand how there was an issue when I had done so much to prevent the issue from occurring.

After I relaxed and started to face the fact that there was a problem with "dysfunctional groups," I decided that I would pick my two most dysfunctional groups and try to figure out what went wrong. The reason I chose these two groups is they were my most "dysfunctional" in the aspect that they had the least amount of work turned in. In addition, when they met with me, they demonstrated through their comments and body language that they were miserable, confused, angry and frustrated. These groups consisted of one group from my Honors Algebra class and the other from my regular Algebra class. My inquiry questions for this year became, "What can I learn about how to group ninth graders for my yearly playground design project by closely examining the group dynamics of low-functioning groups?," and, "What action can I take as a teacher to help 'dysfunctional' cooperative learning groups ascertain the difficulties they are having in working together and become 'functional'?" (Escue, 2006)

In this example, by weaving her prior life experiences in architecture with her teaching, Carlee was able to breathe new, creative life into the Algebra I curriculum that went beyond traditional textbook coverage for her students each year. However, because teaching is so complex, it is natural and normal for issues to surface as teachers try out new pedagogy and projects with their students. While our first instinct may be to become defensive or to pretend problems don't exist, taking an inquiry stance toward teaching means we celebrate problems by naming them and systematically studying them to gain insights into practice, as Carlee did in this case. As a result of this inquiry, Carlee was able to name three main issues that she would address in the future: (1) the teaching of positive confrontation skills, (2) providing practice in cooperative learning, and (3) remaining in constant contact with parents. The exercises at the end of this section help you explore, like Carlee and Julie did, who you are as a person and teacher and serve as precursors to the development of wonderings that might emerge from your prior life experiences and intersect your personal and professional identities.

PASSION 6 EXERCISES

1. Write your own autobiography. Discuss the development of your own interests and passions. Finally, discuss the factors that led to your chosen career field as a teacher.

2. Design a time line of your growth and development as a person and a teacher, beginning with your birth and noting years and dates of critical incidents that impacted your personal and professional life.

(Continued)

(Continued)

3. Follow the guide provided to design a Teacher's Coat of Arms. In space 1, draw a real or mythical animal that best describes the teacher you want to be. In space 2, choose a real symbol, or create your own design, for an insignia that best describes the teacher you want to be. In space 3, choose one color in any shade—or a rainbow effect—that best describes the teacher you want to be. In space 4, draw one character, real or fictional, that best describes the teacher you want to be. In space 5, choose one word that best describes the teacher you want to be. How you write that word should also help to describe the teacher you want to be.

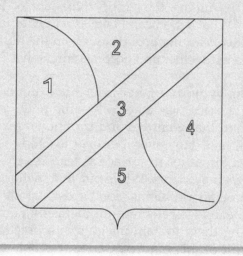

Passion 7: Advocating Social Justice

Recall from Chapter 1 the notion that engaging in inquiry is a responsibility you accept as a teacher that enables you to take a stand and effect educational change. By generating data and evidence to support the decisions and positions you take as an educator, you help reform classrooms and schools, which results in the promotion of social justice. According to Cochran-Smith and Lytle (1993),

> When teachers research their own practice . . . they begin to envision alternative configurations of human and material resources to meet the needs of culturally diverse groups of students, teachers, and administrators. And they are willing to invest more of their own resources and professional energy in larger efforts to reform classrooms and schools. (p. 80)

Your first teacher inquiry wondering may come from your desire to effect social change by exploring questions of race, class, gender, or ability. In fact, effecting social change in regard to issues of social justice may indeed become the focus for your entire teaching career. Inquiry can be a powerful vehicle that begins your journey working toward this goal. Entire school districts have used the action research process to focus on equity, race, and closing gaps in opportunity and academic achievement between groups of students. For example, as mentioned in Chapter 1, the Madison Metropolitan School District in Wisconsin has published a collection of teacher research authored by teachers within their district focused on creating equitable classrooms through action research (Caro-Bruce, Flessner, Klehr, & Zeichner, 2007). These excellent examples range in scope "from a close study of one child and how his elementary teacher adapted instructional practices to ensure school success to a study of how a high school science department changed inclusive practices in an effort to eliminate tracking" (p. 3). We highly recommend this text for all teachers interested in understanding the significance of the student and teacher learning that can occur when teachers use action research to better understand issues of social and educational equity from inside classrooms and schools.

In addition to the insightful pieces of teacher research published in this text, in this chapter, we provide three examples from elementary, middle, and high school contexts, respectively, that illustrate teachers beginning their inquiry journeys motivated by addressing the complex questions about equity that face our schools.

In the first example, teaching intern Andrea Hosfeld begins her journey toward exploring questions related to teaching for social justice by reflecting on her own childhood experiences:

> As a child growing up in the 1980s, I believed that the world was a place where anyone with an aspiration could succeed with determination. It was a time when poverty and racism were covered by a thick haze of Reaganite rhetoric. Men and women of every race and nationality need only believe that their dreams would be realized and it would be so. In high school, I began to see, for the very first time, that the world was not so fair and just as I had always assumed. I found myself experiencing feelings of powerlessness and vulnerability. As a female, in particular, I felt boxed in by society's expectations and constraints.
>
> Upon escaping from high school I began to replace my pessimism with passion. I started to conduct research and read interesting books that spoke of the hopelessness and hatred pervading our world. For the past four years, I have spent a great deal of time educating myself and grappling with difficult issues involving race, class, and gender. Part of my decision to become a teacher was influenced by my desire to introduce children to these issues. It was my hope that while portraying an honest though sometimes grim picture of humanity, I might also replace blind acceptance with a sense of empowerment and a hunger for change.

I knew very early on in the year that I wanted to engage my students in antibias activities and lessons that would build on each other throughout the year. Identifying the question I was seeking to answer, however, proved to be a very long and searching process. Although I'd read multiple theorists that suggested children were capable of engaging in lessons of this nature, I didn't really have any first hand experience. I was comforted by the words of Louis Derman-Sparks (1989), who stated: "We know enough not to underestimate the power of children to perceive the negative messages in their world or the power of those messages to harm them" (p. 10).

Initially, I had many questions: Are third graders capable of discussing difficult and controversial issues? How do I begin to engage them in this process? Which activities lend themselves to such an exploration? I answered several of these questions in the first few months of my inquiry and my original queries were replaced by more complex questions. I wanted to know the role of developmentally appropriate practice in implementing an antibias curriculum approach as well as the role of the district curriculum in determining the events and issues I could introduce. It was only in analyzing and reflecting on the data I'd collected that I realized the wondering I was pursuing. What began as a project primarily geared toward the thoughts and ideas of children became an inquiry into my own evolution as a teacher of antibias curriculum. (Hosfeld, 2000)

Andrea's commitment to issues of social justice emerged out of her own political stance and ideology demonstrating the intersection between the role of teacher beliefs and inquiry into issues of social justice.

Andrea's work presents another important lesson about finding and developing your first wondering. She notes that her questions changed and emerged over time. This is a very common occurrence in teacher research. Therefore, understand that as you work diligently to find, develop, and conduct your first inquiry question, your question(s) may change and emerge. This is a totally natural part of the inquiry process. Consequently, as you proceed with your inquiry, you may find that the question you originally developed no longer suits your work or captures the most powerful components of what you are learning. Remember, you may still be "finding" your question. Be prepared to recognize and embrace an emerging question by remaining calm and flexible. You can return to your original questions and modify or change them throughout the duration of your inquiry.

In our second example, middle school teacher and reading coach Joan Thate finds her first inquiry question by reflecting on populations that historically have not made Adequate Yearly Progress (AYP) at her school:

The achievement gap: The problem is nationally pervasive and perennially stubborn and the questions are numerous and enormous. Our school is no exception. For as many years as records have been available, our school has had two populations that have not made AYP in either reading or math: Exceptional Student Education (ESE) students and African-American students, particularly males. My concern was with black males who were not identified as ESE, and therefore shouldn't have (theoretically, at least) any physical reason why they can't read perfectly well.

We know that many of these nonperforming students come from backgrounds where reading was not modeled or materially supported. We also know that many come from circumstances where scarcity and lack of variety of parent/child verbal interactions left them linguistically well behind their peers the first day they appeared at school. Obviously, these things we cannot change. Looking into and working on some of the things we might try, things we *can* change, was where I needed to begin. We must break the cycle, and I see the middle school years as offering our last likely chance.

In such a short time span as the inquiry provided, the major questions needed to be pared down to monitoring one action that might help at least point to a direction we might take at the middle school level to begin to turn some of these students into less reluctant, more resilient, more comprehending readers—the kind of readers who cannot only survive our state's standardized reading test with some skill and confidence, but also emerge as people who pick up and read a book because they choose to, not because they must. Until a reader reads by choice, I do not believe we can accurately say they are readers, even though they may decode and comprehend adequately.

Our school storage areas are littered with the debris of unsuccessful attempts to address and remedy the problem, concrete proof that many advertised panaceas simply did not work—and in some cases, apparently aggravated the problem. I have read a considerable amount of opinion and research on this subject (see, for example, Allington, 2006; Fashola, 2005; Lesesne, 2003; and Tatum, 2005). The most consistent finding of all reading research is that the most valuable contribution schools can make to their developing readers is providing the right books and the time to read them. One of the points that many writers and researchers make is that much of what reluctant readers, most particularly adolescent black males, are asked or required to read in school is neither engaging nor culturally relevant for them.

Now, I am not a proponent of the idea that everything one reads should mirror his own experiences and life. As a matter of fact, one of the principle reasons to read is to expand the experience and understanding of people/places/times/cultures that are different from what is known. But perhaps, if virtually *no* reading matter is ever introduced that does relate to the reader's life, reading can seem dry, alien, irrelevant—a "school" thing that can't and doesn't and won't ever touch what is closest to him. And we all know that we return to and practice what brings us some joy, some satisfaction, some meaning.

Therefore, I started looking for lists of reading that featured African-American males as central characters, or had been written by African-American males, or biographical stories, books, or articles based on famous or not-so-famous African-Americans who had made significant contributions in some way. From the writings of Alfred Tatum (2005) and others came some good suggestions. We also had experienced some positive responses to a series of books from Townsend Press, the Bluford Series. This series of (currently) thirteen books is set in an urban high school named after the first black astronaut. The plots are based on the kinds of problems all kids face: peer pressure to participate in illegal activities, family problems such as divorce, difficulties with friends or girlfriend/boyfriend relationships, and school problems, including bullying. The books are thin, written on a sixth-grade level, and feature minority faces on the covers. The two sets we had brought into the school from a reading conference last year had caught on immediately with struggling readers in one class. I now had some ideas for books to start ordering.

Thus, my question became: In what ways will offering more culturally relevant materials improve the relationship of this constituency with reading? Collateral questions also emerged: Will these nonreaders read more and less reluctantly because they have such material to read? Can we provide enough books to test the theory? Is providing, presenting, and promoting culturally relevant materials a direction we should explore in more depth as a means of enticing this group of chronic underachievers to read more and therefore become better readers? And what might be some effective ways of introducing and incorporating this material? (Thate, 2007b)

Joan's work presents yet another important lesson regarding finding your wondering. Note that in framing her wonderings, Joan drew on literature in the field of reading research (Allington, 2006; Fashola, 2005; Lesesne, 2003; and Tatum, 2005). Joan's knowledge of the reading research literature helped her craft her inquiry question to target reluctant African American middle school male readers in order to get the right books to them at the right time. The core concept of Joan's inquiry (providing the right books and the time to read them) came directly from research on reading and therefore situated Joan's inquiry in the larger knowledge base on learning to read. When teacher researchers do not connect and situate their studies to what is already known, we risk powerful and meaningful teacher research becoming an unsystematic piling up of accounts of learning that have occurred in individual classrooms, and while powerful for individual teachers, such research does not contribute to the larger discussion in the educational literature. We also risk missing some important knowledge that may contribute to the way we frame our research questions and subsequently design our research. For this reason, we suggest all teacher researchers draw on literature at two critical junctures in the teacher research process: finding and framing your wondering (as illustrated by Joan in the example earlier) and data collection and analysis (as is discussed and illustrated in later chapters in this text).

In our last example, high school teacher Justin Lang uses the social justice lens to reflect on his own race, culture, and upbringing and how the ways in which he positions himself as a white male in his classroom interplay with the race, culture, and upbringing of his African American students.

> When I was an English major as an undergraduate at the University of Florida, I had a broad range of classes from which to choose for my course of study. Rather than choose the more traditional English major path of Middle English and Chaucer or Shakespeare, instead I mainly focused on modern literature, critical theory, and cultural studies. To me the beauty of writing and language is its ability to express the business of being human, from our many perspectives, both personally and culturally, and how this expression can help to deconstruct and demystify our social systems. But it was always issues of race and culture in writing that intrigued me most, and that hasn't changed. Now, as I have taken the career path as educator, I have found that it is race and culture and how they relate to my classroom and my teaching that I find myself pondering often. I have realized that as liberal as I might be, or at least see myself, the fact that I am a white male does affect my students of other races and my interactions with them, no matter how much I want to believe otherwise. Additionally, I am similarly enamored with classroom management techniques and how my own natural inclinations play into my style. Specifically, I am more likely to approach classroom management in a liberal, humanist way, expecting that my students appreciate being talked to like young adults and given requests that ask them to behave in a way that is kind and considerate. While I do become stern when necessary, and raise my voice at times, it feels wholly unnatural for me to make threats or dole out punishment as negative reinforcement.

Every day in my classroom I have to fight a battle of order and volume. Because my classroom shares two pass-through doors with adjacent classrooms, volume carries easily and directly to the classrooms next door. One of the teachers next door to me is very strict about classroom volume and will not hesitate to come into my class to make a show of power to question any volume she feels is too much, including during group work. Thus, in order to appease my colleague, volume must always be kept reasonably low. Additionally, there are tests and quizzes to consider, which certainly do require a quiet environment. We three teachers who share adjacent classrooms have to constantly make sure we are coordinating when the others are giving tests and adjust our classroom instruction and activities as necessary.

Now, I have many black students who are what many people in the school call "problematic" and have been low-achieving students since early elementary school. Most of them share the same community outside of school or other classes and are very familiar with each other socially. Regardless of seating arrangement and consistently stated expectations, these students remain very loud and interested most often in the activities of each other rather than the classwork or instruction. I have come to understand that in general, communication in some black subcultures is inherently louder than that of the typical white middle-class, which is my background. I do not dispute this and understand it is social fact and have been told as much by many black friends and acquaintances. Also, many of my black students require frequent reminders about staying on task and in their seats, rather than letting their whims take them wherever they like in the classroom. While I have an excellent rapport with most of these students and they seem to respect me in general, I wonder constantly about how my classroom management approach of asking politely for them to perform tasks or control their volume in my liberal, white man sort of way affects their learning. Am I ensuring that I validate who they are as people, both personally and culturally, while still helping to do all I can for them to succeed academically and enjoy success in our bicultural world? It is definitely a fine line to walk and that is the crux of my inquiry, how to blend my natural beliefs and personality with the need to maintain order in my classroom without causing a repressive environment that is devoid of learning and personal achievement for not only my black students, but all of my students of various races.

Because I live in a community where there is still a sharp division between the black side of town and the white, I believe this type of inquiry can help serve not only me as an educator, but the fellow teachers in my school and perhaps even the community at large. Perhaps it will allow, if nothing else, for us to open a dialogue in our school and maybe even the community about how to address our differences in race and culture, but still make sure we are all as successful as possible, that everyone has adequate opportunity to achieve their academic and life goals by working collaboratively. Rather than assigning blame or just ignoring the issue, instead this would allow the local educators to understand how to best serve all of their students rather than a select group, and perhaps the patterns of power and division in the community could be altered. I realize I may be dreaming big, but why not? At the start of my big dream, the inquiry question I wish to explore is, "What is the impact of my being a white liberal male on the behavior (loud speech and lack of engagement) of some of my black students?" A secondary question for exploration through this inquiry is: "What is the relationship between positive behavior support and secondary student behavior (regardless of race or culture)?" (Lang, 2007)

Justin's work points to an additional lesson about wondering development. Inquiry questions do not always lend themselves to neat, definitive answers, and sometimes teacher researchers realize this even as they are crafting their wonderings at the beginning of their inquiry journeys. Justin acknowledges that less important to finding the answer to his wondering is the potential exploring this wondering has to open up and extend dialogue in his school and community about issues of race, class, gender, and ability. Sometimes the most important contribution of an inquiry is not in finding the definitive answer to a research question posed by the teacher but in serving as a catalyst to uncover and discover hidden assumptions and issues about teaching and learning that pervade schools. In so doing, inquiry becomes a catalyst for social change.

PASSION 7 EXERCISES

1. Look closely at the demographics of the students you teach. Pick a subset of them (e.g., gender, race, class, or ability) and pay particular attention to them during the day. Record in a journal your general observations and emerging questions. Do these children all experience schooling in a similar way?

2. Brainstorm a list of units/topics you teach. Investigate the content of the resources you are using to teach these units. What perspectives seem to be present or missing (e.g., gender, race, class, and ability)? Then analyze each unit by asking yourself how these resources and activities support diversity, democracy, and literacy opportunities for all students.

3. Write down your philosophy of how you prepare your students to become democratic citizens. What role does teaching children about democracy play in your classroom? To what extent does your classroom encourage the development of participation and character traits central to a democratic citizen?

Passion 8: Focus on Understanding
the Teaching and Learning Context

An important feature of teacher inquiry is that inquiry occurs within a context. That context represents a particular classroom within a particular school, within a particular state, and within a particular country. Some teachers' felt difficulties actually emerge as a result of these contextual characteristics that influence their teaching.

For example, teacher Ashley Pennypacker Hill worked on a K–12 school campus that recently built a new school building for elementary students that used innovative architecture to support 21st-century teaching and learning (Fielding & Nair, 2005). Within this new, large open space, typical grade level and classroom structures were abandoned. Students and teachers in kindergarten and first grade, second and third grades, and fourth and fifth grades each occupied their own wing of the school, and students and teachers from all grade levels collaborated in all teaching and learning. The undergirding philosophy of the new organizational structure was to allow for more flexibility, increased differentiation of instruction and more student autonomy to develop the collaboration, critical thinking, and creative thinking skills students would need in the 21st century.

As the person responsible for providing Tier 3 intensive instruction in reading to fourth- and fifth-grade learners, Ashley was concerned with the ways this new architectural space would impact the students who were struggling in reading, with a particular focus on how they would function during autonomous time. Autonomous time was a 50-minute block each day when all 108 fourth- and fifth-grade students spread out across the fourth- and fifth-grade wing to work independently on achieving goals set by their teachers. Ashley knew for this time to be productive for her students, she would need to teach them how to be self-regulated learners, able to reflect on their thoughts, behaviors, and progress independently to strategically achieve their personal learning goals (Zimmerman, 2000). Ashley's school context, where her students no longer learned within a traditional classroom bound by four walls and one teacher, led her to wonder:

- In what ways do I support the self-regulation of learners receiving Tier 3 intensive instruction within a 21st-century learning space?, and
- How do learners receiving Tier 3 intensive instruction experience and use the self-regulation strategies I teach? (Hill, 2013).

While the physical space associated with Ashley's school context led to her wondering, sometimes it is the makeup of the students in a classroom or school that leads teachers to develop wonderings related to their community context. These wonderings relate to understanding the diverse cultures within the classroom and school community in order to better provide instruction, communication, or relationship development. For example, two prospective teachers, who were interning in a low–socioeconomic status school, investigated the feelings of various stakeholders around Ebonics:

> We were nervous about the topic of Ebonics. As two white novice teachers we were not sure how to respond to the speech of some of our students. We wanted to be sensitive and affirming of their identity but we also struggled with how to prepare them for citizenship responsibilities. As a result, we decided to explore the question of, "How can we respond to student use of Ebonics in an appropriate and sensitive way that allows them to gain the participative skills necessary for citizenship?" . . . We explored this question by interviewing many different school and community members—parents, counselors, veteran teachers, administrators . . . we also read a lot of literature on the subject. What we developed was a continuum of responses that we believe both honor and extend our work with these students. (Field notes, PK)

Another example of how context can be the source of an inquiry question emerges as teachers respond to state and national pressures and policy. For example, one pressure many teachers are currently feeling relates to their state's adoption of the Common Core State Standards as they try to figure out what the Common Core will mean for their teaching. Lareal Haslem, a first-grade teacher at Woodson Elementary School in Jacksonville, Florida, responded to this pressure alongside all of the teachers in her building by using the process of inquiry to unpack the standards and investigate their implementation (Dana, Burns, & Wolkenhauer, 2013). After reading Lucy Calkins, Mary Ehrenworth, and Christopher Lehmans's text *Pathways to the Common Core: Accelerating Achievement* (2012), Lareal developed a passion for integrating more nonfiction text into her first-grade classroom and creating opportunities for her students to interact with this text in meaningful ways, an emphasis in the Common Core. She wondered, "How can I effectively use nonfiction text in my first grade classroom?" Similarly, Kathy Christensen, literacy coach and specialist for Collier County Schools, responded to the pressure she felt as her state adopted the standards by developing a wondering related to the teaching of writing to English language learners. She reflects:

> In the writing section of the CCSS, under the heading of Key Design Consideration, it states that the standards for K–5
>
> > . . . set grade-specific standards but do not define the intervention methods or materials necessary to support students who are well below or well above grade-level expectations. . . . It is also beyond the scope of the Standards to define the full range of supports appropriate for English language learners and for students with special needs.

Hence, as teachers implement the Common Core State Standards in their classrooms, particular attention must be given to students in need of intervention. In my context, a specific group of learners that will need particular attention as the Common Core State Standards in Writing are implemented are English language learners (ELLs).

I teach in a Title 1 school which serves 751 students in pre-K through 6th grade. The student body is 97% economically needy, 77% speak languages other than English at home (primarily Spanish and Creole), and 44% of our families are migrant workers. While our students have performed relatively well on our state test, the Florida Comprehensive Assessment Test (FCAT), it has been increasingly difficult for students to earn a "proficient" score on the FCAT in writing. As the reading/literacy coach and teacher, I am concerned that I am not meeting the needs of English language learners in relationship to writing instruction. Meeting the needs of this population of students becomes increasingly important as we implement the Common Core State Standards at my school during the coming year and prepare for the new Common Core writing assessments. To help English language learners actualize the Common Core State Standards in writing, I will develop and enact small group support for ELLs during Writers' Workshop. I am intrigued by the use of Collaborative Writing as a part of Writers' Workshop and interested in learning more about how this strategy might work for ELLs. As I implement Collaborative Writing as a part of Writers' Workshop with a small group of ELLs, the wonderings that will guide my study are:

- What is the relationship between ELLs' engagement in Collaborative Writing and their development as writers as the CCSS are implemented in my school?
- What types of teaching moves support the development of ELLs during Collaborative Writing? (Christensen, 2013)

As Kathy's reflections allude to, before the pressures of the Common Core, many teachers faced (and continue to face) pressure associated with student performance on high-stakes testing. We have seen many wonderings emerge in response to this pressure, such as "How can we make learning relevant and motivating in a context where testing seems to dominate curriculum and scheduling?," and "How can I maintain an inclusive classroom when high-stakes testing seems to encourage noninclusive practices?" As teachers recognize the role of context and its impact on their teaching, teachers can use inquiry to identify ways to accommodate, merge, or deflect contextual influences that affect their work in the classroom. Teacher-inquirers can also use their research as an "important means through which to expose the various sources of tension between policy and teaching, as well as to elucidate the impact of education policies on teachers' practice" (Rust & Meyers, 2006, p. 69). Teacher inquiry provides context-sensitive tools to accomplish these tasks.

PASSION 8 EXERCISES

1. Make a three-column list.

Challenge Within Your Context	Felt Difficulty	Wondering

After brainstorming a list of contextual challenges, identify the frustrations that you can potentially influence at either a student, classroom, or school level.

As indicated, these eight passions are not discrete entities, and as noted early in this chapter, any single wondering one develops within the exploration of one passion can end up relating to another passion or multiple passions. We offer these eight passions not to classify wonderings but as lenses for looking at your own teaching. As you use the passions as lenses, think about each passion as a pair of glasses you try on. For example, if you try on the "social justice glasses," you analyze your classroom by looking at issues of race, class, gender, or ability. If you try on the "child glasses," you analyze your teaching from the perspective of the students you teach. It may be that as you analyze your teaching from the perspective of the children you teach, you uncover issues of race, class, gender, or ability in your classroom, and your wondering emerges related to social justice. Developing an inquiry stance toward teaching relies on teachers becoming active in problematizing each of the lenses or passions and understanding the interrelations between them. These multiple lenses provide prospective and practicing teachers with a framework for systematically examining their daily work.

WHAT HAPPENS IF I STILL CANNOT LOCATE MY WONDERING?

If you are struggling to find your question independently, the next step is to collaborate with and talk to other educators. Although the exercises and descriptions of the passions provide lenses into different aspects of teaching and learning, independently exploring each of the lenses without engaging in discussion with others may still not lead to a question. The exploration of these passions can become more provocative if you collaboratively discuss them with others. For example, if you are a veteran teacher, you might discuss the passions with your teammates, resource teachers, administrators, or university partners. If you are a prospective teacher, you might talk with other prospective teachers, your mentor or field advisor, or other university teacher educators. In the following excerpt, Lisa Malaggese's mentor-teacher, Christina Clair, offers a first inquiry question that starts Lisa's inquiry journey.

"What are you planning to do for your inquiry project?" As my mentor, Christina, asked me this question, my mind was pretty blank. It was something I had thought about numerous times before, but I had not found anything that had jumped out at me. When the inquiry project had been initially described to us, it sounded as though the topic for my inquiry would be as obvious as a blinking neon sign. For some people, I am sure that this is how they come upon the topics for their inquiries. I saw no such blinking sign. When I searched my brain, looking for possible wonderings, nothing really stood out as something that I desperately wanted to find the answers to.

So, when Christina asked me this question, I told her I honestly did not know. She mentioned that something she had always been interested in was taking a more in-depth approach to teaching first graders fractions. At first, I said that could be interesting, but that I was not sure what I wanted to do yet. Christina made it clear that it was my decision and that she would help me with whatever I decided to do. I was still waiting for my neon sign. As our classes devoted to inquiry started, with my neon sign nowhere in sight, I started thinking more about Christina's fraction idea.

"Teaching fractions to first graders could be interesting," I thought. The mathematics education course I had taken had left me with a lot of unanswered questions about how to teach mathematics. Even though there is a big focus in my mentor's classroom on the children's understanding of mathematical concepts, I still did not feel confident with my ability to teach math. I decided that the questions I had and my lack of confidence could best be addressed through the actual teaching and designing of math lessons. I hoped that the information I learned about teaching mathematics would also hold true for other subject areas. That way, I could improve my teaching, and thereby my confidence in teaching in all subject areas.

After much consideration, I decided to go ahead with exploring fractions. All right, I had a topic. Now what? What was it *really* that I was trying to find out? After brainstorming with Christina, we came up with our overall question: "Can fractions be taught conceptually to primary students?" I was very proud of that question until it was pointed out to me that it could be a question that could be easily answered with a simple "yes" or "no." I reworked the question; and my official wonderings became "How does one teach fractions conceptually, and what are the impacts of that teaching on the different learners in my classroom?"

At that point, I would not say I was exactly jumping with excitement about my topic. However, I knew it was something that would prove to be interesting and challenging. I think some of my initial lack of excitement stemmed from my disappointment that my neon sign had never come. Little did I know that it really was there; I just had not turned on the switch yet! (Malaggese, 2001)

Lisa's excerpt presents two final important lessons about the development of your initial wondering. First, note how Lisa reframed her first wondering from a dichotomous yes/no question (e.g., "Can fractions be taught conceptually to primary students?") to an open-ended "How do I?" and accompanying companion question (e.g., "How do I teach fractions conceptually, and what are the impacts of that teaching on the different learners in my classroom?"). Rarely does any teacher researcher eloquently state his or her wondering immediately. It takes time, brainstorming, and actually "playing" with your question. Based on our work with teacher-inquirers and the work of Hubbard and Power (1999, p. 28), we suggest the following core principles for finding and refining a teacher research question:

- Look at your teaching through each of the eight lenses.
- Realize that your question might change over the course of your inquiry.
- Ask only real questions. Do not do research to confirm a teaching practice you already believe is good or bad. Ask questions whose answers you do not know.
- Develop open-ended rather than yes/no questions.
- Eliminate jargon.
- Be careful to ask a question that your methods can actually explore.
- Avoid value-laden words, or talk your questions over with others as talking helps to clarify the question.
- Be patient with careful articulation of your wondering(s). By playing with the wording of your question, you often fine-tune and discover more detail about the subject you are really passionate about

understanding. It is often helpful to engage in a dialogue with a critical friend (a teaching colleague, mentor-teacher, student teacher, or university supervisor). Once you have a wondering committed to paper, ask your critical friend to question you about your inquiry topic. The dialogue that transpires will help you refine your thinking. For rich examples of such dialogue between teachers as they develop their wonderings, see Chapter 3 of our companion text to this book entitled *The Reflective Educator's Guide to Professional Development: Coaching Inquiry-Oriented Learning Communities* (Dana & Yendol-Hoppey, 2008a). The text *Digging Deeper Into Action Research* (Dana, 2013) can also help you refine your wondering by taking the "wondering litmus test," a series of questions to help you "reframe and refine your wondering until you have clearly and concisely articulated a question that generates excitement, enthusiasm, and intrigue." (p. 17)

Finally, notice in Lisa's case that sometimes a passion for your work will not independently develop from the outset of your inquiry journey. Yet, based on our years of experience helping prospective teachers and practicing teachers engage in inquiry for the first time, we are confident that, as in Lisa's case earlier, a passion for your work will develop. So, as you end this chapter, take heart from the fact that you have completed one of the most difficult parts of your journey—identifying an inquiry question. Now that you have started your travels, in the next chapter we mark possible routes for conducting your inquiry by summarizing forms inquiry may take as well as noting forms of collaboration you can establish to support your inquiry journey. These summaries may help you further refine your wondering(s) and chart the remainder of your inquiry travels.

3

To Collaborate or Not to Collaborate

That Is the Question!

Whether or not you are a Shakespeare fan, you are likely familiar with the famous soliloquy spoken by Hamlet that begins, "To be or not to be, that is the question." As teacher-inquirers begin formulating their initial wonderings, they often ponder in a similar fashion: "To collaborate or not to collaborate, that is the next teacher-inquiry question."

As is the case in much of Shakespeare's work, when characters such as Hamlet begin a soliloquy, they pose a rhetorical question. A rhetorical question is asked for effect and neither expects nor requires an answer. Shakespeare would often evoke this literary device to allow his characters to use language effectively and persuasively, resulting in the audience's "eavesdropping" on the character's thinking and gaining insight into character traits vital to the development of the story.

In the style of Shakespeare, we have used the rhetorical question, "To collaborate or not to collaborate?" in the titling of this chapter, because it is a question you need not answer. No teacher-inquirer should spend time pondering whether he or she should collaborate, because when engaging in teacher inquiry, the answer to this question is always an unequivocal yes! Rather, we pose this question to help you consider how you will collaborate. As you complete this chapter, we hope, like Shakespeare's audiences' gaining insight into his key characters, you will gain insights into how collaboration supports and enhances your teacher inquiry.

WHY IS COLLABORATION SO IMPORTANT?

> If you investigate the work of any teacher researcher who has sustained his or her work over time, you quickly see another person, or many other people, standing in the shadows. Virtually all teacher researchers depend on a partner or a group who shares their passions and provides reassurance when a project bogs down. (Hubbard & Power, 1999)

Similarly, in our work with teacher-inquirers, we have identified at least four good reasons why when you look at any single teacher-inquirer, he or she is standing in the company of others. Consider these four reasons why you should seek out support as you continue on your inquiry journey.

Reason 1: Research Is Hard Work!

Because the practitioner inquiry movement "continues to flourish in the United States and many other parts of the world" (Cochran-Smith & Lytle, 2009, p. 6) and serves as a popular professional growth tool for the initial preparation and continuing education of teachers (Somekh & Zeichner, 2009), it is easy to get caught up in the movement and forget one very basic fact: The work of a teacher is quite demanding! To date, teacher inquiry has not traditionally been a part of teachers' practice. Hence, engaging in inquiry potentially adds an additional layer into the already-crowded work life of a teacher: "Participation in teacher research requires considerable effort by innovative and dedicated teachers to stay in their classrooms and at the same time carve out opportunities to inquire and reflect on their practice" (Cochran-Smith & Lytle, 1993).

While we believe it is critical to make teacher inquiry *a part of* your teaching rather than *apart from* your teaching, the fact remains that even if you are able to seamlessly integrate teaching and inquiry (as we believe should be the case!), the work is difficult and can be quite draining at times. Through collaboration with others, teacher-inquirers find a crucial source of energy and support that keeps them going and sustains their work. In addition, through collaboration, teacher-inquirers build on each other's work, so they are not constantly reinventing the wheel when it comes to exploring a new passion through inquiry. Both the energy created and the networking provided through collaboration are apparent in many teacher-researcher communities. In our work, we have created a blogging site to connect teacher researchers to those who coach teacher research from schools across our state (Glogowski & Sessums, 2007). Figure 3.1 depicts a collaborative exchange between two members of this community that indicates the power collaboration holds for energy generation and networking.

Figure 3.1   Teacher Research Blogging Site

Deciding on one Inquiry

view | edit | track

Submitted by **debbi_hubbell** on Fri, 10/20/2006 - 6:25pm.

Every time I begin an inquiry, I find it very difficult to pick just one thing to concentrate on. This year I want to do something with the iii (intensive intervention instruction) students ... but have not narrowed it down yet.

I remember my very first "action research" back when I was a UF student in 1989. I looked at kids teaching other kids (how to use a computer program with the old Apple IIe!) ... you know the idea of if you can teach someone else you learn better ... Well, what if I could teach a few iii kids a reading strategy and they taught others ... hmmm ... sounds very exciting to me, but I'm not sure how I want to do it yet.

Anyone heard of anything like this before with iii kids?

debbi_hubbell's blog | add new comment | 24 reads

(categories: **inquiry help**)

Kids Teaching Kids

Submitted by Mickey MacDonald on Fri, 10/20/2006 - 7:21pm.

Debbie - I know that Greg C. here at P.K. has done something like this with his iii students. I know he would be happy to talk to you.

I think that he actually did something with reciprocal teaching in which the iii kids may have modeled this for the regular classes of students in language arts 7th grade.

delete | edit | reply

Wow! The power of the

Submitted by debbi_hubbell on Sat, 10/21/2006 - 7:37am.

Wow! The power of the blog! Thanks Mickey! I would like to see/hear about what he did. Maybe if he had anything to share, you could bring it to our Nov. meeting -or - I can email you with personal info ... I keep forgetting we are not in a private situation on a blog. Anyone else hear of iii kids teaching kids?

delete | edit | reply

SOURCE: Used with permission of Debbi Hubbell and Mickey MacDonald.

Reason 2: Teacher Talk Is Important!

Teachers talk all the time! They talk with their students by posing questions, delivering information, giving directions, and facilitating discussions each day. They talk with their colleagues, "swapping classroom stories, sharing specific ideas, seeking one another's advice, and trading opinions about issues and problems in their own schools and the larger educational arena" (Cochran-Smith & Lytle, 1993, p. 94). They talk with administrators to solve problems and identify support necessary for success in the classroom. They talk with parents about expectations, their child's progress, and ways to work together to facilitate a child's growth. Talk consumes almost every moment of a teacher's day.

Similarly, the talk of teacher inquiry also becomes "a part of" each teacher's day. In Chapter 2 you learned the importance of talking with another person as you defined and refined your first questions and the focus of your inquiry. Similarly, as you continue on in the teacher research journey, engaging in dialogue with another professional will heighten your awareness of knowledge you've generated about teaching that you now take for granted, making what you know more visible to yourself and to others. Making your tacit knowledge more visible can often lead to significant discoveries when you are individually or collaboratively analyzing and interpreting your data.

In addition, talking with another professional may help you call into question assumptions or "givens" about a teaching practice, a process critical to making your teaching problematic through the process of inquiry. According to Cochran-Smith and Lytle (1993), "The givens of schooling compose a long list, including reading groups, rostering, inservicing, tracking, abilities, disabilities, mastery, retention, promotion, giftedness, disadvantage, special needs, departmentalization, 47-minute periods, coverage, standards, detention, teacher-proof materials, and homework" (p. 96). Teacher talk enables teachers to examine and critique these "givens" in education. In talking with others, you are able to generate possible alternatives to practice as well as consider different interpretations that help every teacher gain perspective as his or her inquiry unfolds.

Reason 3: There's Safety in Numbers!

Knowledge is power. Through teacher inquiry, you are taking charge of your own professional growth and generating knowledge that can be supported with evidence. While this is one of the most exciting components of teacher inquiry, it can also become extremely stressful, as it is quite probable that the new knowledge you construct from your study may threaten the status quo and become threatening to others' assumptions about professional practice.

For example, perhaps you complete a curriculum piece that generates new practices that many of your colleagues are anxious to incorporate, but the principal who selected and designed the original unit for your district feels that his or her personal authority and position as an educator are threatened by your findings. You face a litany of obstacles thrown out by your administrator and a long list of reasons why you can't teach the unit in the way that your evidence shows is most effective. If an inquiry leads to controversy, collaboration with other teachers can provide you personal and professional support as you share your findings and combat others who are resistant to change: Remember, change requires a critical mass.

Reason 4: There's Strength in Numbers!

Just as there is safety in numbers, there is also strength in numbers. While it *is* possible for one person's inquiry to lead to large-scale and schoolwide change, it is often not probable when resistance to change is present (as noted in the example presented in the previous paragraph).

However, when communities of teacher-inquirers begin to build on each other's work, findings become more difficult to ignore or resist.

Communities of teacher researchers can play an essential role in school reform. Not only does their work add to the knowledge base on teaching, but their collective power as knowledge-generating communities also influences broader school policies regarding curriculum, assessment, school organization, and home-school linkages. Through teacher-research communities, teachers' voices play a more prominent part in the dialogue of school reform. (Cochran-Smith & Lytle, 1993, p. 103)

Hence, any inquiry you engage in becomes stronger when connected to a collection of related inquiries generated by other teacher researchers. This strength is made possible through your collaboration with others.

In addition, sometimes, when inquiries do not go as planned, you garner strength by continuing to work with colleagues. For example, Larry Rotz, Mary Robert, Judi Kur, and Marcia Heitzmann collaborated on an inquiry that focused on effectively integrating SMART Board technology into their curriculum. When confronted with the tremendous time necessary to troubleshoot and problem-solve the SMART Board technology, they made little progress on the initial wondering: "How can we effectively integrate SMART Board technology into our curriculum?" Working in isolation, they might have easily "called it quits" when faced with so many technical difficulties. Together, though, they found the strength to forge ahead and changed their initial wondering from focusing on the integration of the SMART Board into the curriculum to focusing on how collaboration can be used to provide support for teachers interested in taking risks and experimenting with the SMART Board. At the close of their project, they reflected as follows:

How many teachers does it take to plug in a SMART Board? With all of the technology difficulties we experienced at the start of our project, the answer to this question was all four of us! Through the process of collaborating in this inquiry, however, we were able to schedule time to work together, become risk takers, and experiment with new technology. Because of this positive experience, we will look for ways to continue to collaborate not only with technology and inquiry, but in other areas of curriculum. We plan to continue to use the SMART Board to increase our comfort level and confidence in using this technology. As we gain more confidence and experience, we are excited to begin sharing what we have learned with other teachers in our building. We are all ready, willing, and eager to help other teachers use this new technology in their classrooms. We have even returned to our original wondering and have begun to enhance our curriculum by developing lessons using the SMART Board. . . . We are excited about being on the cutting edge of this new technology and the possibilities it holds for improving instruction. We are just as excited about the opportunities to continue our collaboration. It still may take four teachers to plug in a SMART Board, but only because we realize the benefits of working together. (Rotz, Kur, Robert, & Heitzmann, 2002)

These four teachers' collaboration and reframing of their question enabled their continued exploration of classroom uses of SMART Board technology.

WHAT ARE THE POSSIBILITIES FOR HOW I MIGHT COLLABORATE?

Schools are often structured in ways that promote teacher isolation rather than collaboration (Lortie, 1975). Teachers spend the majority of their day working within the four walls of their classrooms. Yet every teacher's classroom is located within a building that contains many other classrooms. Consequently, as they work within the four walls of their rooms, right beside them or across the hall are other teachers who engage in the same work each day. Hence, the work of teachers is literally a side-by-side endeavor, offering many potential colleagues who can join with one another to inquire into practice.

In addition to the side-by-side work of teachers within the same school building, side-by-side work may occur in a single classroom. For example, spurred by the inclusion movement, many general education classroom teachers are now coteaching with special education teachers to provide appropriate instruction for all students within an entire class (Bauwens & Hourcade, 1995; Friend & Cook, 2000). Similarly, as efforts are made to reduce class size, teachers are often paired with full-time paraprofessionals to provide more individual attention to each student. Another example of side-by-side work of teachers occurs when schools and universities partner in the preparation of new teachers by integrating student teachers or interns into the room to complete fieldwork. The side-by-side nature of the work of both veteran and beginning teachers within one school building or within one classroom can provide natural opportunities for collaboration in the systematic study of their own teaching practice. The following four logical structures, for veterans and/or beginning teachers to partner in inquiry, can provide the support necessary for encouraging inquiry (Dana, 2001).

Collaborative Structure 1: Shared Inquiry

Having an interest, or many, in common with another professional lays the foundation for the first configuration for collaboration—shared inquiry. Shared inquiry occurs when two or more practicing teachers, two or more prospective teachers, or a prospective and a practicing teacher pair or group define and conduct a single teacher research project together.

An imperative component of any teacher inquiry is that it must evoke passion from the teacher-inquirer. Thus, a prerequisite for engaging in shared inquiry is a shared passion across two or more individuals for the same topic. One example of shared inquiry is the work of Amy Jones and Diane Reed, introduced in Chapter 2. Recall that Amy and Diane shared a passion for finding ways to teach about Columbus in a developmentally appropriate way. As two fourth-grade teachers within the same building, they discovered during an afterschool grade-level meeting that they both shared "felt difficulties" about the upcoming unit on explorers. Diane noted that she was disturbed that the encounter between Columbus and the Taino people was not developed in the unit. Amy echoed this concern and also noted that she was unsure which components of the unit to emphasize given the constraint that the unit needed to fit within a four-week time period. Each teacher was committed to resolving her dilemma. Their shared dilemma and passion for this topic led to their collaborative completion of an inquiry in this area (Jones & Reed, 2000).

Similarly, eighth-grade general mathematics teacher Stephanie Harrell and middle school ESE teacher Kathryn Albrecht shared a concern for students who were transitioning from their school's intervention mathematics class into Stephanie's general math class. In their school, students who perform poorly on the Florida Comprehensive Achievement Test (FCAT) are placed in an intervention mathematics class to review basic, foundational skills and develop confidence as learners of mathematics. These students often make significant gains in their mathematical abilities in one school year. Consequently, they increase their math FCAT scores and, after one school year, "test out" of the intervention math class.

These students were making the transition from the intervention math class into the general math class without the support they might need. As the general mathematics class instructor, Stephanie noticed that many of these students were having difficulty coping with the curriculum and expectations of a general education math course. Many of these students were also being served for specific learning disabilities, and Kathryn's job was to provide consultation support for these students in the general education classroom. Hence, Kathryn and Stephanie shared the same passion—to ensure the success of every eighth-grade math student—and collaborated on an inquiry in which they explored their students' experience with the transition, as well as the creation and implementation of a collaborative plan that would better support students transitioning from the seventh-grade intervention mathematics course into the general education eighth-grade mathematics class (Albrecht & Harrell, 2007).

Amy and Diane's inquiry into the teaching of the explorer unit and Stephanie and Kathryn's inquiry into their students' mathematical learning exemplify two practicing teachers working together. An example of shared inquiry by a prospective and a practicing teacher pair is found in the work of Sheila Abruzzo, a 12-year veteran and mentor-teacher in a professional development school, and her intern, Missy Koziak (Koziak & Abruzzo, 2000). As Missy interned with Sheila in her first-grade classroom, both were intrigued by technology and the possibilities technology might hold for enhancing parent communication. Together, they explored, compared, and contrasted newsletters, home/school journals, and websites, as well as other strategies that enhance the teaching partnership between home and school. Each teacher had different areas of strength to contribute to their shared inquiry. Missy had learned a great deal about creating websites as part of her PDS methods coursework in the fall, and Sheila, with 12 years of teaching experience, had extensive experience in talking with, and providing written materials for, parents. Through their inquiry, they created a symbiotic relationship where they met, discussed, created, pondered, and analyzed different modes and varieties of parent communication that neither intern nor mentor could undertake on her own. Sheila shared that the most outstanding component of engaging in shared inquiry was the ability to lead and learn from each other.

In a similar fashion, mentor-teacher Darice Hampton and her intern Beth Schickel decided to conduct a joint inquiry project when Darice was enrolled in a graduate teacher-inquiry course at the university and Beth was completing a teacher-inquiry requirement for student teaching at the same time. They recall the process that led them to engage in shared inquiry as well as the benefits they reaped from conducting a single teacher-inquiry project together as follows:

> As a mentor and intern, we observe our students daily and subconsciously are participating in informal inquiry all the time. Each day, we discuss happenings in the classroom, not only to bounce ideas off of each other but also to gain a different perspective. When we decided to begin formal inquiry, we naturally began bouncing ideas off one another. When our wonderings seemed to mesh, we decided to complete our inquiry project together.
>
> When we began to map out our journey, the first step of developing phonemic awareness activities for two children in our class was one benefit from our collaboration. By working together, we doubled the number of creative ideas for activity development. From this step forward, our daily discussion led us to alter our activities based on student response, as well as discover our learnings and follow our new wonderings. Without the collaboration involved in the project, our phonemic awareness work with two students may have taken a different, less-informed direction, as it

was through our discussions that we were able to process our field notes in a way that allowed us to see different perspectives and interpretations of what was occurring. Many times, the sharing of our differing perspectives led each of us to new insights and subsequent changes in the phonemic strategies we were using with the children that we would not have discovered had we been working alone. It has been the partnership we have created through the PDS that has allowed for our wondering to be addressed and our learnings to be publicly shared. Being coauthors of this inquiry has given us the opportunity to become teacher researchers and to take our wonderings to a new level through our teamwork. (Hampton & Schickel, 2002)

A final example of shared inquiry indicates the ways two prospective teachers might work together. After being classmates in a science methods course in the fall semester, Rebecca Roberts and Lindsay Elliot discovered that the commitment they had made to teach science through inquiry in that course was easier said than done when they began their student-teaching semester. Rebecca and Lindsay's shared experience in the science methods course and subsequent desire to implement what they had learned about teaching science as inquiry led them to complete one joint inquiry project. Working together, their goal was to analyze their questioning, reflect on their students' responses, and decide whether the questions they posed were promoting science as inquiry.

With a full dose of SCIED 458 under our belt, we were walking away from our methods classes last December all pumped up and ready to teach science through inquiry. What we didn't realize, however, was the fact that we couldn't reach the top of that mountain without first grabbing on to some stepping-stones to make our way up. We understood the perks of teaching science through inquiry but we didn't understand that every single topic within science would not necessarily lend itself to inquiry. We didn't realize that we couldn't just jump into science and expect to change our methods of teaching by throwing in a few experiments and—*poof*—inquiry would magically appear.

After watching previous videos of our teaching from our science ed course and comparing them to the lessons we recently taught during our student-teaching semester, it became clear that some areas of science are just more difficult to teach through inquiry than others. This became particularly evident as we watched our sink-and-float lessons completed in October. It was simple. We were not even aware of our questioning and we were automatically asking questions such as, "How could we turn this sinker into a floater?" and "What made the boat that held more marbles a better floater than others?" It was plain to see that these questions really did ignite the students' thinking and probe them to further consider each of the factors going into the creation of their clay boats.

On the other hand, while both being fully aware of the questions we were to be asking during the first couple of lessons of our Wonderful World of Nature unit in March, we were stumbling upon questions such as, what is a beak? Do we have them? Do you think birds have better vision than us? And do all birds fly? Fortunately we can laugh with each other about these questions now, but at the time, even though we knew that every word out of our mouth was leading to a very unproductive question, it was not clear to us as to how we should go about turning them into productive ones. As mentioned before, after a lot of experimenting with different kinds of questions and analyzing the effectiveness of each of the types we were asking, we were successful in turning this unit into an inquiry-based one despite the fact that it was initially a very difficult task for us to accomplish. (Roberts & Elliot, 2002, pp. 13–14)

Through collaborating on one joint inquiry project, Lindsay and Rebecca provided support for each other as they discovered inherent difficulties of teaching science as inquiry. In addition, they provided "comic relief" for each other ("Fortunately, we can laugh with each other about these questions now . . . ") as they viewed their videos during data analysis. One benefit of shared inquiry is being able to find humor in your work with a colleague, especially when your inquiry leads to some unsettling realizations about your teaching.

Collaborative Structure 2: Parallel Inquiry

A shared passion for a single topic between two or more prospective and practicing teachers does not always emerge, as all teachers are unique individuals who share different interests and passions. In addition, collaborations between prospective and practicing teachers such as those noted earlier are not often practical, as veterans and novices are at very different places developmentally, which may naturally lead to completely different passions for teacher inquiry. If teachers in the same building or classroom hold different passions, then they may choose to engage in parallel inquiry.

Parallel inquiry occurs when teacher pairs (prospective teacher pairs, practicing teacher pairs, or a prospective and a practicing teacher pair) conduct two parallel but individual teacher-research projects, working collectively to support each other's individual endeavors. Parallel inquiry comes from the "parallel play" concept discussed in the early childhood literature. In parallel play, two toddlers may sit in a sandbox, just inches apart from each other, and be enthralled with their individual exploration of the sand. They are each individually immersed in their own activity within the same physical space. Likewise, when you engage in parallel inquiry, your playmate is a fellow teacher, your sand is the complexities inherent in teaching, and your sandbox is the same school or classroom. Unlike parallel play, however, where the two toddlers are often oblivious of each other and rarely interact as they play, when engaging in parallel inquiry, teachers support each other's individual endeavors by engaging in such activities as collecting data for each other, discussing data analysis and findings, and teaching for each other to provide the time necessary for each individual to engage in his or her own individual inquiry.

For example, recall from Chapter 2 that Judi Kur was passionate about making her delivery of a prehistoric life-forms unit more inquiry oriented. At the time of this inquiry, Judi was working with an intern, Corinne Almquist. Although supportive of and interested in Judi's work, Corinne was not passionate about participating in the curriculum revision of that particular unit. As a result, Judi's intern completed a separate inquiry project that she was passionate about (Almquist, 2000). Although their inquiries were separate, both intern and mentor supported each other's work by collecting data for each other, discussing data analysis and findings, and teaching for each other to provide the time necessary for each individual to engage in her inquiries.

Similarly, recall intern Andrea Hosfeld's passion for teaching social justice and her quest to gain insights into implementing an antibias curriculum through her inquiry project presented in Chapter 2. Andrea's mentor-teacher, Kimber Mitchell, was also interested in defining and conducting a teacher inquiry project at the time of Andrea's inquiry and was an accomplished teacher of social studies with expertise and interest in Andrea's topic. A logical deduction might be that Kimber and Andrea would engage in shared inquiry, collaborating on a single inquiry project. Yet, realizing that teaching social studies was already one of her areas of strength, Kimber supported her intern but focused her own inquiry energies on further developing another area of her teaching—the effective teaching of science through a unit on air and aviation (Mitchell, 2000). While individually inquiring into different subject areas simultaneously, Kimber and Andrea supported and learned from each other in much the same ways as Judi and Corinne. In this classroom, parallel inquiry also became a mechanism for exploring the teaching of two different subject matters. Imagine the benefit to the children in this classroom that year as science and social studies teaching were being investigated simultaneously through inquiry!

Collaborative Structure 3: Intersecting Inquiry

In parallel inquiry, two or more teachers are engaging in inquiry on completely different topics. Sometimes teachers engage in individual inquiry projects that focus on the same topic but explore different questions and wonderings about that topic. When this happens, inquiries potentially intersect and collaboration can occur at the juncture of that intersection.

We return to teacher-inquirer Judi Kur to illustrate intersecting inquiries. The year after she completed her inquiry on teaching dinosaurs, Judi and longtime first-grade teaching partner and friend Marsha Heitzmann were both interested in using peer coaching to help them gain insights into their teaching of reading. They decided to engage in a shared teacher-inquiry project to develop and explore their peer-coaching relationship and the ways this relationship could contribute to their own understandings of who they were as teachers of reading.

At this time, they made an appointment to meet with their principal, Deirdre Bauer, to share with her their upcoming plans for inquiry. Deirdre met their inquiry idea with enthusiasm and support and shared that she had been interested in the notion of peer coaching for years as well. Furthermore, intrigued by witnessing the ways teacher inquiry can lead to powerful learning, Deirdre wished to conduct her own teacher-inquiry project that year. Ironically, she wanted to explore the role principals can play in facilitating professional development through peer coaching. What transpired was the development of two separate inquiries that crossed one another. Judi and Marsha focused on developing a peer-coaching relationship and using that relationship to gain insights into the ways reading instruction played out in their classroom. Deirdre focused on studying the peer-coaching relationship as it developed in two of her teaching staff (Judi and Marsha) and subsequently was able to generate lessons learned for administrators about facilitating the peer-coaching process.

Collaborative Structure 4: Inquiry Support

If shared inquiry, parallel inquiry, or intersecting inquiry does not suit your style or emerge in relation to the topic you are interested in studying, one final option for collaboration exists. Prospective or practicing teacher-inquirers can take full ownership of their inquiry project but invite one or more professionals who are not currently engaging in inquiry to support their work; we term this option inquiry support. In this case, the invited person serves as a critical friend to help the teacher-inquirer formulate meaningful wonderings and project design, as well as aid in the collection and analysis of data. This particular structure can be extremely beneficial to both parties and has the potential to have great impact on teaching.

For example, you may know of colleagues who have completed teacher inquiry projects in the past but have decided that current life circumstances do not afford them the time to complete their own inquiries. If you invite these colleagues to provide support for your work, everyone wins! They stay connected to the systematic study of practice and you have critical friends to help you through the process.

Or you may know of a colleague who does not know much about this "thing called inquiry" and may be reluctant to try it but whose professional knowledge and teaching you greatly admire. Inviting this colleague to support you as your inquiry unfolds not only provides help for you but also allows your colleague to be introduced to inquiry in a comfortable way. Metaphorically, through supporting your work, your colleague can "test out inquiry" by putting one toe in to feel the water before jumping in.

A comfortable "testing of the water" often results in that teacher jumping in and conducting his or her own inquiry project in the future. In our work, we have found this happens most often when cooperating or mentor-teachers support the work of student teachers and interns (Dana & Silva, 2002). Often, these veteran teachers begin by supporting the work of their interns, and as they support their intern through their project, they learn the processes for engaging in inquiry and witness the power inquiry holds for meaningful learning. Simply put, they get hooked! In this way, we continue to enlarge and build the teacher-researcher community.

When prospective teachers become potential introducers of teacher inquiry into a classroom or school, the teacher educators with whom you work at the university are likely to contemplate the question, "How might we go about preparing teachers to both survive the system of school as it currently exists and contribute to reforming it at the same time?" (Richert, 1997, p. 74). If you are using this book, your teacher educators believe the answer to this question, at least in part, is in preparing prospective teachers to be critical inquirers of their own practice. As they prepare you, they may also be simultaneously introducing inquiry to veteran teachers through your work. Hence, you have an awesome responsibility: As you learn to teach and enter the profession as a new teacher, you have a responsibility to contribute to reforming the profession you are about to enter. You become a teacher leader, and it is through you that the teacher-researcher community continues to grow (Snow, Dana, & Silva, 2001)!

Remember the phrase, "There's strength in numbers"? With each teacher-inquirer we add to the teacher-researcher community, the work of teaching becomes better informed, teachers gain a louder voice in the politics of education, and teaching becomes a more respected profession. Collaborative inquiry structures hasten this process!

CHAPTER 3 EXERCISES

1. Consider the following chart that summarizes the four collaborative inquiry structures presented in this chapter.

Structure	Description
Shared inquiry	Two or more practicing teachers, two or more prospective teachers, or a prospective and a practicing teacher pair or group define and conduct a single teacher research project together.
Parallel inquiry	Teacher pairs (prospective teacher pairs, practicing teacher pairs, or a prospective and a practicing teacher pair) conduct two different teacher-research projects but work collectively to support each other's individual endeavors.
Intersecting inquiry	Teachers conduct inquiries on the same topic but explore different wonderings related to the topic.
Inquiry support	Rather than conduct their own inquiries, teachers serve as critical friends helping colleagues engaged in the process to formulate meaningful wonderings and study design, as well as aid in the collection and analysis of data.

Circle the kind of collaboration that is best for you at this moment. Create a plan for seeking out this collaborative structure to support your work.

Developing a Research Plan

Making Inquiry a Part of Your Teaching Practice

Once a teacher-inquirer has selected a focus for his or her work, defined a wondering to pursue, and located himself or herself within one of the inquiry support structures, the next step in the journey is learning about data collection and developing a plan for the study. Meaningful teacher inquiry should not depart from the daily work of classroom teachers but become a part of their daily work. Hence, selecting the data collection strategies you will use for your study simply means thinking about life in the classroom/school and the ways life in the classroom/school can be naturally "captured" as data.

WHAT DO DATA LOOK LIKE, HOW DO I COLLECT THEM, AND HOW DO THEY FIT INTO MY WORK AS A TEACHER?

In this section, we share one dozen common strategies teacher researchers use for capturing "the data of" life in schools. Each strategy is demonstrated through the work of one or more teacher-inquirers. Some examples come from teachers you have already met in previous chapters, while others introduce new teachers and their inquiry projects as examples for illustrating particular types of data collection. Once again, as we share excerpts from these teachers' work, we point to lessons learned about data collection so as to offer you practical suggestions and guidance about this component of the inquiry process.

Strategy 1: Literature as Data

The first data collection strategy we introduce may seem a bit perplexing at first glance as it is not likely something you were expecting to see as a data collection strategy. Although we often do not think of literature as data, literature offers an opportunity to think about how your work as a teacher-inquirer is informed by, and connected to, the work of others. Many researchers (both teacher and academic) have likely pondered, studied, and written about the topic of your inquiry before you, and you can benefit from their learning on the topic. In essence, their learning becomes a source of data (information you collect) to inform your personal wondering.

No one teaches or inquires in a vacuum. When we engage in the act of teaching, we are situated within a context (our particular classroom, grade level, school, district, state, country), and our context mediates much of what we do and understand as teachers. Similarly, when teachers inquire, their work is situated within a large, rich, preexisting knowledge base that is captured in such things as books, journal articles, newspaper articles, conference papers, and websites. Looking at this preexisting knowledge base on teaching informs your study, and therefore, it is one form of "data" that *every* teacher researcher should collect and use, no matter what your topic of study, no matter what your wondering, and no matter what other forms of data you collect! To emphasize the importance of literature as data, we placed this as the first strategy in this chapter.

So, if literature is a form of data every teacher inquirer should collect, the first question that needs to be addressed is "When do I collect it?" Recall one of the lessons that surfaced in Chapter 2 related to the development of your wonderings through the work of Joan Thate, who studied the impact of offering more culturally relevant reading materials to African American students, particularly males:

> Joan's work presents yet another important lesson regarding finding your wondering. Note that in framing her wonderings, Joan drew on literature in the field of reading research (Allington, 2006; Fashola, 2005; Lesesne, 2003; and Tatum, 2005). Joan's knowledge of the reading research literature helped her craft her inquiry question to target reluctant African American middle school male readers in order to get the right books to them at the right time. The core concept of Joan's inquiry (providing the right books and the time

to read them) came directly from research on reading and therefore situated Joan's inquiry in the larger knowledge base on learning to read. When teacher researchers do not connect and situate their studies to what is already known, we risk powerful and meaningful teacher research becoming an unsystematic piling up of accounts of learning that have occurred in individual classrooms, and while powerful for individual teachers, such research does not contribute to the larger discussion in the educational literature. We also risk missing some important knowledge that may contribute to the way we frame our research questions and subsequently design our research.

As indicated in Chapter 2, a great time to begin to collect and consult literature is during the formation of your wondering, as literature can help you both define and refine questions about your practice in new and interesting ways. As your study continues and you begin to collect other forms of data described in this chapter, your collection of literature can also continue, as readings on your inquiry topic continue to inform your research. Even after you have finished collecting all other forms of data, you may continue to consult the literature as your study leads you to new findings and new wonderings. In sum, use the literature throughout your inquiry to become well informed on the current knowledge in the field on your topic and as one important source of data to gain insights into your wondering.

The second question that needs to be addressed is "How do I collect it?" The fields of social work, medicine, and psychology have long recognized the importance of developing practitioners' ability to use existing research to enhance practice. In her research, Sarah van Ingen (2013), a mathematics teacher educator at the University of South Florida, notes that while practitioners in other professions often use a multistep process for integrating research with their practice, too little effort has been made to support educators in using research to inform their practice. Indeed, there has been a long history of divide between research and practice in education. Teacher inquiry is a tool that integrates the power of research done by others with the potential of research done by practicing educators themselves.

Together, Sarah and USF education librarian Susan Ariew are helping educators develop the skills needed to access and use the research literature to inform their practice (Ariew & Powers, 2012). In helping educators, Sarah and Susan have identified some important steps to streamline the process for identifying relevant research that can inform inquiry work. The textbox that appears at the end of this section creates an outline of these steps and will provide you a powerful guide for exploring the literature.

As you refer to the textbox to look for and locate literature related to your topic, a final question that needs to be addressed is "How do I know the literature I am reading to inform my inquiry is reputable?" Cochran-Smith & Lytle (2009) note that teacher-inquirers "treat both their own practice as the site for intentional investigation and the knowledge and theory produced by others as generative material for interrogation and interpretation (p. 131). A teacher researcher does not look at the literature she collects to inform her study with an uncritical eye. It's important to analyze and critique literature as it relates to your study and to your knowledge from practice. Not all research studies are created equal. Some studies are better than others, and some pieces of literature will be more relevant to your needs than others.

As you proceed through this chapter and learn about other data collection strategies, notice the ways many teacher researchers we quote to illustrate these strategies reference literature related to their inquiry topic, just like Joan Thate did in the excerpt from her work that appears in Chapter 2. As these teacher researchers' reference to literature demonstrates, literature is an essential form of data that every teacher-inquirer should use so as to be connected to, informed by, and a contributor to the larger conversation about educational practice.

Collecting Literature as Data: The *Real* Evidence-Based Practice

By Sarah van Ingen and Susan Ariew

At one time or another, most teachers have been told to engage in some teaching practice because "research says" or because the practice is "evidence-based." Our work is designed to take back the phrase "evidence-based practice" and to give it renewed meaning. Social workers have already done this. Social work educators have equipped new social workers with the understanding that the phrase "evidence-based practice" really refers to a *process* that the practitioner engages in when using research or "evidence" to inform practice. You too can be an evidence-based practitioner. You too can use education research to inform your own teaching and inquiry.

We have found that the process of using existing research (literature) to inform a teacher's inquiry has enormous benefits but that it can be uncomfortable at first. It's a bit like beginning a new exercise routine. If you have ever tried to begin running or to start up running after a hiatus, you know how uncomfortable it is—how your lungs burn and legs ache. Looking for data from education research to inform your inquiry may feel a bit like your lungs are burning. But if you can stick with it, you can also experience a similar rush of having had a great run and being ready for more.

We've included here an outline of the first three steps of a simple five-step process we use to prepare teachers to use literature to inform teaching. Within each of the three steps, we have provided tips or "water breaks" that can help you push through the discomfort to realize the power you have to be informed by and to contribute to a global conversation on how to improve teaching and learning.

STEP 1: CONSIDER YOUR QUESTION.

After reading Chapter 2 of this book, you have already thought quite a bit about your wondering. Before embarking on a search for literature, think *even more* about your wondering.

TIP: Get specific. If your wondering is broad in nature, talk to someone else (another strategy from Chapter 2) with the purpose of getting more specific. For example, you may wonder about how to increase student motivation in math class. In talking with a peer about what is really behind this wondering, you may realize that it's not all students who are not motivated, but your concern is really for your English language learners. And, when you say "motivation" you really mean their willingness to participate in class discussions. Do you see that this question has narrowed from how to motivate students in math class to how to support mathematical discussions among ELL students? Training yourself to get very specific at this stage will help you in your literature search. The studies reported in journal articles often must answer very specific research questions. Of course, after or during your search, you might refine or revise your question (more on that in Step 2), but it will help to start with specific questions. We call these researchable questions.

STEP 2: BEGIN THE SEARCH.

With a refined, specific question, now the hunt for data from the research literature begins.

TIP 1: Come up with a list of key words. Think about all the words related to your specific question and try to identify synonyms for key words. Thinking of the example earlier, you might have this list: English language learners, mathematics, discussion, discourse, participation. There is no one "right" list, but having several key words provides you flexibility in your search.

TIP 2: Come up with a plan for where you will search. This will require a bit of creativity because, unfortunately, not all education research is "open access." This means that to read some articles, a person or institution must pay money. We do *not* recommend paying for access to journal articles. Instead, try using one of these strategies to find articles related to your inquiry question.

A. Use a resource that provides research summaries. The US government has created the What Works Clearinghouse (http://ies.ed.gov/ncee/wwc) that provides research summaries written just for teachers. Outside of the United States, the International Bureau of Education (www.ibe.unesco.org) has an Educational Practice Series that provides research summaries for teachers. These are great resources, but they may or may not include information on your particular question. In addition, whenever you read a research summary that someone else created, there is the added question of what research they left out. Why did they choose the articles they did?

B. Use a research database. ERIC is a free research database sponsored by the US government (http://eric.ed.gov). Your local public library may give you

(Continued)

(Continued)

access to other research databases. Of particular interest to educators are Google Scholar and Education Full Text.

C. Use journals published by professional organizations. Your school and/or district may have institutional memberships to professional organizations such as the National Council of Teachers of Mathematics (NCTM). As is the case with NCTM, a membership allows you online access to excellent articles from the journals that the organization publishes.

D. Use open-access journals. These journals are, as their name implies, free and available to anyone who would like to look at them. There is a growing trend for prestigious universities, such as Stanford, to require their researchers to publish in open-access journals or university digital repositories. This means that you can find some really good information here. The Directory of Open Access Journals (www.doaj.org) can help you find a journal relevant to your interests.

E. Use your partnerships. If your school is part of a university-school partnership, you could ask your university partners if they can find research articles on your specific topic. In this case, it would be best if you and the university faculty member sat down and did the search together. This way you have input over the article selection.

F. Use your public or university library. If you live near a public university, you can visit that library and search their subscription databases and journals. Most of them have work stations reserved for public access. In addition, the majority of public libraries have interlibrary loan services for you to request items not available through your local library system.

TIP 3: Think binoculars. If you've ever used a pair of binoculars to watch birds, you know that to focus them on one bird requires a process of going out too far and in too close until that bird comes into focus. The process of searching for research literature is quite similar. When you start searching, you may find that your search terms are too broad, and the articles you find are not specific enough to your question. Then you need to enter in more search terms or use more specific terms. On the other hand, you might come up with too few articles. This means you have to broaden your terms. The task of focusing your search and finding relevant articles requires patience and perseverance. Keep at it! If one strategy seems like a dead end, find another. Work with a partner. There is a treasure trove of information out there, and the search is worth the effort!

TIP 4: Think blue bird. In a tree full of crows, you may be looking specifically for blue birds. Likewise, in a list of articles that pop up during a search, we suggest you look specifically for research summaries aimed at teachers and empirical articles. Empirical articles provide results from a specific intervention or wondering. These are in contrast to theoretical articles that provide information on new ideas. We suggest selecting three to five research articles as a starting place for your literature data collection. Fewer than three articles may give you too little information on your topic, but more than five articles may be too daunting to process. Note that a meta-analysis or a meta-synthesis is an article that synthesized the findings from several studies. These meta articles will give you more information than an article on one study only and might be a good choice to include in your selection of three to five articles.

TIP 5: Ask a librarian! This may be the most important tip we can offer. If you run into problems with the suggested steps and tips listed here, a librarian has the training and resources to assist you. Most public and university libraries have "Ask a Librarian" services where you can talk to a librarian by phone or online chat to get some specific help on finding the information you need.

STEP 3: READ AND SYNTHESIZE THE LITERATURE.

Now that you have found literature that addresses your question, it's time to find out what this literature says. Think more patience, more perseverance! When reading a report from a research study (empirical article), you are likely to encounter this basic heading structure: abstract, introduction, methods, results, discussion, and references.

A. Abstract: This comes at the very beginning of the document and gives you an overview of that article. It is a great place to begin your reading.

B. Introduction: This may contain a discussion, called a literature review, about other studies done on this topic. This is a great find because it can lead you to several other articles on your topic. The author provides the full citation for those additional articles at the end of the paper in the reference section. The introduction can also inform you of the key words researchers use when talking about your topic. You may learn of new words or phrases about your topic and then can go back to Step 2 and search again for more articles on your topic.

C. Methods and Results: Here the author describes what was done in the study. This section might contain technical, statistical details. Although these are important because they speak to the strength of the research, it often requires specialized training in statistics and research methods to understand. You may want to skim these sections.

D. Discussion: Here the author discusses the meaning of the research and answers the question, "So what?" Often the author has a paragraph or more about the implications of the research for the classroom teacher. Obviously, this information is of great interest and relevance for you.

TIP: Take the time to summarize and synthesize. Write a one- to two-paragraph summary of each research article you read. When summarizing, think specifically about how the study informs your initial inquiry question. Feel free to talk back to the article a bit. How does this article help to answer your question? What additional questions does this article raise? How is the setting of this article similar to or different from your own classroom? After you complete the summarizing stage, write a one-page synthesis of what you now know about your topic after reading all of your research articles. You can use this summary to inform your own research plan.

Strategy 2: Field Notes

In the previous chapter, when we discussed the first reason for collaboration, we noted that the life of a classroom teacher is quite demanding—teaching and engaging in inquiry is hard work! One of the reasons the work of teaching is so demanding is that schools and classrooms are busy places, jam-packed with *action*. Teachers inter*act* with children, children inter*act* with each other, and teachers and children inter*act* with subject matter. All of these inter*actions* occur within a particular context mediated by values (e.g., all children can learn), norms (e.g., students must raise their hands and be called on before answering a question), and rituals (e.g., each morning the class salutes the flag).

To capture *action* in the classroom, many teacher researchers take field notes as they observe. Field notes can come in many shapes, forms, and varieties. Some of these include scripting dialogue and conversation, diagramming the classroom or a particular part of the classroom, noting what a student or group of students are doing at particular time intervals (e.g., every two minutes), and recording every question a teacher asks. Field notes are not interpretations but rather focus on capturing what is occurring without commenting as to why the action might be occurring or how one judges a particular act.

The forms your field notes take depend on your wondering. For instance, in Nancy Sunner's study of her questioning techniques, her field notes listed every question she asked during selected lessons. The connections between your wondering and the form your field notes take will become more apparent in subsequent examples of field notes shared throughout this section.

You may take field notes as you engage in the teaching act or have them taken for you by others. An example of field notes taken by teachers as they inquired comes from the work of intern Beth Schickel and mentor Darice Hampton introduced in the previous chapter. Recall that Beth and Darice were interested in the development of phonemic awareness in two of their kindergarten learners. As they worked with these children, one way they took field notes was by scripting the responses the children had to different phonemic awareness activities. One activity they developed for these learners involved finding pictures with the same initial phonemes. To illustrate scripting a student's response, an excerpt from their scripted field notes that was collected during this activity is shared in Figure 4.1.

Scripting as a form of field notes simply involves writing down verbatim (or as close to verbatim as possible) what your learners are saying. The first time you script notes for yourself, it may feel awkward or unnatural.

Figure 4.1   Scripted Field Notes by Darice and Beth

SOURCE: Used with permission of Beth Schickel and Darice Hampton.

Some of the teacher-inquirers we know have found little "tricks" to help in the process. For example, when Amy Ruth was scripting at the kindergarten writing table, she found the children were more interested in what and why she was writing than in completing their own work. Frustrated after her first attempt to collect data by scripting, as it seemed to interfere more with her teaching than help her inquire into her teaching, she found a way to fold data collection unobtrusively into her teaching in the following way. Amy constructed a red folder that looked just like the red folders all of her kindergarteners worked with at their writing center. The cover of the red folder Amy constructed for herself was marked in big black magic marker letters as follows: "Miss Ruth's Writing Folder." She shared the folder with her students, noting that over the next few weeks, "Miss Ruth is going to be writing at the writing center just like you! When you do your writing, I will be doing mine." Amy used that folder when engaged in scripting, and the children understood that Miss Ruth was working just like they were and never questioned her about it again.

Similarly, another kindergarten teacher-inquirer we know, Lynn Dobash, became frustrated when she discovered that important actions she wanted to capture never occurred in a single sitting but rather were sprinkled throughout her day. It was not practical for Lynn to run to her desk to grab her field notebook each time she wanted to make a note. To solve this problem, she began wearing a very fashionable necklace—a yellow Post-it notepad with a pen attached. When a child said or did something that she wished to capture, she simply jotted it down on a Post-it note and continued on in her teaching. At the end of the day, she stuck each Post-it in her notebook. A little ingenuity can go a long way when making data collection a part of, not apart from, your teaching.

While Post-it notes are a wonderful invention that can help teacher-inquirers with field noting and other phases of their research, many teacher-inquirers are experimenting with the integration of technology that doesn't require a paper and pencil into their collection of data. The University of Wisconsin–Madison School of Education Literacies, Cultures and Languages Institute (under the direction of Cathy Compton-Lilly), the Madison Metropolitan School District's Classroom Action Research Program (under the direction of Mary Klehr), and the University of Wisconsin Office of Educational Outreach (under the direction of Mark Dzeidzic and Lisa Hebgen) recently introduced "The iPad as a Teacher Research Tool for Literacy Educators Program" to teacher-inquirers in their local vicinity, advertising the opportunity as follows:

> Knowing your students' literacy strengths and reflecting on their literacy practices are keys to excellent literacy instruction. This summer/fall course is designed for novice and experienced teacher researchers who are interested in literacy learning and exploring the role iPads can play in data collection and analysis. iPads provide portable, flexible, and multifaceted tools that teacher researchers can use in their classrooms to explore instructional issues. iPads can record audio and video, take photographs, and store data. They can easily be used to take anecdotal notes in busy classrooms as well as store electronic copies of student work or class projects. Finally, books and articles that support research can be stored and accessed through the iPad.

The program filled quickly and has an enormous waitlist. According to Mary, the integration of iPads into the data collection process for teacher researchers in her district is "brave new world stuff for us, but people are excited about it and we hope it will be productive" (personal communication, 9/15/2013).

Sometimes, unlike Amy and Lynn or teacher-inquirers from the Madison Metropolitan Area School District who are excitedly experimenting with iPads to take field notes and support other aspects of their research, some teacher-inquirers just cannot find a comfortable way to take field notes for themselves, or they want to capture action when they are an integral part of that action (e.g., giving directions, leading a discussion, asking questions). In these cases, it is impossible to record in writing your own directions as you are giving them or your own questions as you pose them. If this is the case for you, two other options are available: (1) audio record yourself or (2) find a colleague to help script the observation for you. If you are recording, you will make the recording, listen to it later, and transcribe what has occurred by taking notes or enlisting another person to script notes from the recording for you. While listening to yourself on audio recordings can be extremely insightful, many teacher-inquirers we know find it difficult to make this a part of their teaching and opt for having others take notes for them instead. For example, intern Gail Romig and mentor-teacher Brian Peters were engaged in a shared inquiry project to investigate the ways they might use science talks to enhance student understanding of science concepts. Early in their inquiry, they recorded the science talks as they occurred but changed to taking turns scripting the talks for each other as follows:

> Throughout our inquiry process, we took turns facilitating the talks and gathering data. While one person sat with the group and helped to guide the conversation, the other person sat outside the circle and kept track of who was talking and what kind of information they were sharing. The person who collected data sat outside the circle so as to not distract or intimidate the students. If the students thought their ideas were being judged or scrutinized, perhaps they would not have been as likely to share. This seemed to be the reaction of some children when they knew they were being audio-recorded.
>
> Early on we tape-recorded a few of our Science Talks. It seemed, however, that some students were reluctant to talk when they saw the microphone. During one of our small group talks later in the marking period, one child asked why we don't tape record the talks anymore. Gail told him that it seemed like people were afraid to talk if they thought they were being recorded. The student said that he didn't like to talk when we recorded because he thought his voice "sounded dumb" on recordings.
>
> In addition to students being uncomfortable with audio recording, we found that listening to the tapes in the evening after school was insightful but too time consuming and not worth the time it was taking to rehash the entirety of the Science Talk discussion. Audio recording captured more than we needed to capture. To gain insights into our wondering, we just needed to know who was talking and what type of talk it seemed to be. Consequently, we developed a system for taking field notes that involved noting who was talking, paraphrasing what was said, and coding the comment with one of four different codes: "S" for simple, "D" for detailed, "R" for repeat, and "0" for no response. Along with this system we also made notes of what we observed happening during the talks, for example, if students were sharing with a child next to them. (Peters & Romig, 2001)

As with Amy and Lynn, it took some time for Gail and Brian to find a comfortable way to capture the classroom action in their field notes. For two sound reasons (i.e., some students feeling self-conscious and the time-consuming nature of listening to the recordings), they moved from audio recording as a form of data collection to taking field notes for each other. If you choose field notes as one of your data collection strategies, realize that it might take some time and experimentation to find a form of note taking that works for you and for your inquiry, and as with the teacher-inquirers in the Madison Metropolitan School District, you may wish to experiment with technology to find what works for you.

If you are completing your first inquiry as a prospective teacher currently in student teaching or another field-experience practicum, a logical note taker for you may be your university supervisor or cooperating teacher. Over time, traditional visits by your university supervisor can move from the supervisor taking charge of the direction of the observation and providing evaluative feedback to you, to you taking charge of the direction of the observations by sharing with your supervisor the nature of your inquiry question and asking him or her to script certain lessons for you (Silva & Dana, 2001). For example, one way Julie Russell collected data for her study of teaching writing to second graders was by asking her supervisor to make data collection around her inquiry a priority during her weekly observations (see Figure 4.2).

If you do not have another adult readily available in your classroom to take field notes for you and want to collect data in this way, you may need to get a bit more creative. For example, you might adjust your schedule to teach the lesson you would like scripted during the time a fellow teacher friend has a scheduled special or planning period and ask your teacher friend to come in and take notes for you. Fourth-grade teachers Cheryl McCarty and Priya Poehner exemplified this type of creativity and flexibility in their study of peer coaching and the ways engaging in this process could give them insights into questions they held about their teaching. The following excerpt from Cheryl and Priya's inquiry shares each of their thought processes that led them to a particular form of field noting for each other, plus an example of that field note form (McCarty & Poehner, 2002).

Priya's Narrative

My inquiry question focused on one of my lower ability reading groups and their use of the discussion strategies that I had taught them. I was often frustrated that these students were unable to carry on a conversation without me being there to keep them on task and keep the conversation flowing. I was interested in seeing whether this was really the case, and if it was, to get some ideas on how to improve the situation.

I sat down with Cheryl after school one day and talked about the layout and the focus of the observation that she was about to perform. I told her my frustrations with this literature group

Figure 4.2 Scripted Notes Taken for Julie

PENN STATE

INQUIRY NOTES:
TARGET 2 areas:
•Rubric
•Brainstorming

COLLEGE *of* EDUCATION
Office of Pre-Service Teaching

p. 1

NAME *Julie Russell*   DATE/DAY 3/27/02
SUBJECT/GRADE 2   TIME 9:15
NO. OF STUDENTS 22   OBSERVER *N Diana*
SCHOOL MV   DISTRICT SCASD

What's this check list for?
   To help us write complete stories.

What does a beginning need?
   C - reads
   D - make your story that people want to read more.
      - characters
   C - dazzling action words
What did endings need?
   E - happy ending
      solve problem
   H - you have a problem that makes sense to your
      story
Are we allowed to use happily ever after?
No - why not?
   K - They need to know more
We're going to read Cabbage Rose. Look at your rubric. How
   would you score writer?
Look at this rubric. How did the author do?
   D - can you grab the book and read the first sentence?
A - I'd give it a star
Why?
   Because the sun paints the world
K - What would you give it?
   A work hard on it because it sounds like a research
   book and I don't like research books

SOURCE: Used with permission of Julie Russell.

and mentioned that they were unable to have discussions without books. This was an area of concern as more advanced groups understood and enjoyed the books we were reading at a deeper level as a result of their group discussions. During our discussion, I described and talked about the students in this group so that Cheryl could identify them easily. We talked about where the group usually met, where each of the students sat, my placement within this group, and where I would like her to sit in relation to the group. I mentioned that I was interested in the flow of conversation and was also interested in how much I contributed to the group. My goal was to get the group started by asking a question that I had noted as I read the chapter they had been assigned, and modeling the discussion prompts; and then encouraging them to take turns asking their questions and leading the discussion. I asked Cheryl to use a circular seating chart with arrows to show the direction of the conversation or script of the lesson.

When Cheryl arrived in my classroom, I had already prepared the students so that they would not be unnecessarily distracted by her arrival. She sat in the previously arranged area and was ready to chart the conversation flow. We had decided that she would sit behind me so that she could scan the entire group with ease and observe both body language and verbal participation. [The first page of these notes appears in Figure 4.3.]

Cheryl's Narrative

I chose to inquire into two things: my math teaching and the level of on-task behavior in my classroom. . . . This year I was assigned a challenging math group that has been a constant source of reflection after my teaching day is complete. . . . My math class is a combination of students from three fourth-grade classrooms. The students are a mixture of students who are meeting fourth-grade objectives and are just below fourth-grade benchmarks. The typical student in my math class learns at a slower pace, requires reteaching, and has difficulty with problem solving. It is also important to mention that there are quite a few "strong personalities" in my class and, as a group, are difficult to manage.

Wanting to collect data on a lesson on fractions in my class, I asked Priya to observe me. Since Priya and I work very closely, she was completely aware of the makeup of my math class as well as my teaching style and philosophies for teaching this particular math group. We agreed upon a form for field notes and her location while in my classroom. Noting my concerns that my class was often "off-task" and not attending to my teaching, Priya would take two-minute sweeps of the room and watch the class as a whole for on-task behavior.

I explained that my math lesson would consist of four different parts: problem solving, fraction concept review, addition of fractions using number lines, and classwork and homework. We decided the best way for her to note on-task behavior would be to use a seating chart in which she would mark her observations of each student. [Figure 4.4 shows how she coded her observations for different parts of the lesson.]

Figure 4.3   Priya's Field Notes

Figure 4.4   Cheryl's Field Notes

By looking across each field note example shared here, we demonstrate that field notes can be as different and varied as the individuals who take them. Most important is to select or create a system that works for you in practice and informs your wondering.

Strategy 3: Documents/Artifacts/Student Work

As indicated, field notes capture actions as data on paper. However, even without field notes, schools and classrooms naturally generate a tremendous paper trail that captures much of the daily classroom activity. The paper trail includes student work, curriculum guides, textbooks, teacher manuals, children's literature, individualized education plans (IEPs), district memos, parent newsletters, progress reports, teacher plan books, written lesson plans, and correspondence to and from parents, the principal, and specialists. The amount of paperwork that crosses a teacher's desk can make any teacher bleary eyed. Often the papers teachers view do not hold significant meaning when read in isolation or when read quickly in order to be able to hand them back in the morning. Teachers need to "get through" paperwork in order to keep up with their work.

Yet, when teaching and inquiry are intertwined with one another, the papers become data and take on new meaning. When teacher-inquirers select and collect the papers related to their research wonderings, we call these papers documents or artifacts. Systematically collecting papers provides you with the opportunity to look within and across these documents to analyze them in new and different ways. For example, as a method of tracking student productivity in the classroom, many teachers save student work, stamping dates on the work to know when it was produced. Through looking at student work over time, claims can be made that could not occur when viewing a single piece of student work in isolation.

Depending on their wondering or the progress of an inquiry, other teacher researchers might collect student work, noting the context in which it was produced. An illustration of student work as data appears in the teacher inquiry completed by Beth and Darice. As one form of data collection, they saved the papers that the two children engaging in phonemic awareness activities produced over time. Two pieces of their data are shown in Figures 4.5 and 4.6.

Through comparing these two artifacts, as well as other data produced during their study, Darice and Beth were able to conclude that when Ted was in the company of friends, his illustrations were more detailed and sound spelling was more developed than when Ted didn't strongly socially connect with the children at his table.

As indicated, documents are naturally occurring forms of data that can be extremely powerful. Teacher-inquirers need only decide which naturally produced papers relate to their wonderings and plan a systematic way to collect, label, and organize them.

Strategy 4: Interviews

In Chapter 3, we stated that "teacher talk is important!" As talk is crucial to the life of a teacher, capturing talk can be an important form of data

Figure 4.5   Ted—Random Writing Samples From Children at the
              Writing Center

Figure 4.6   Ted—Writing Samples When Working With Best Friend collection. Field notes are one way to capture talk that occurs during class-room activities. Some teacher-inquirers go one step further by conducting individual interviews. Interviewing can be informal and spontaneous or more thoughtfully planned, and depending on your wondering, you might interview adults such as parents, administrators, other classroom teachers, and instructional support teachers in addition to students in your classroom.

When veteran teacher Kimber Mitchell wondered about the effective teaching of science through a unit on air and aviation, she returned to her students at the end of the school year. She used interviews to gain insights into what the students remembered about a particular unit after many months had elapsed as follows:

> During my student interviews I asked my students to tell me about the four forces of flight. Most of them were able to talk about two or three of the forces. None of my students, even the ones who normally have excellent memories, could name all four forces. Their understanding of the forces of flight was sketchier than what they remembered about air. We had only one day of investigations on each of the four forces of flight in contrast to eight lessons related to air. It seems obvious to me that the students need repeated and parallel investigations on the same topic for it to become a part of their long-term science knowledge. This means that I have to make choices as a teacher about what things are most important and what things I can leave out. It is a difficult process but one that is helped by returning to one of my original questions: Which investigations help the children to understand how air-planes fly? In an interview, one of my students summed it up this way: "If you do a lot of experiments about one thing and do the experiments over and over (many trials), it will explain things." (Emily Dong in Mitchell, 2000)

Interviewing students in the classroom can be a rich source of data, but for this to happen, it is important not to get "hung up" on the word *inter-view* and imagine that the act of interviewing as it relates to inquiry is anything different than what great teachers, like Kimber, do on a regular basis. Asking students about their thinking and their learning is a natural part of lessons and instructional activities, and when related to an inquiry question, naturally occurring conversations with students can automatically become "interviews."

In the example of interviewing that follows, the teacher was inquiring into ways to teach mathematics conceptually rather than just procedurally. To garner initial understandings of her students' conceptual knowledge, she circulated as students in her class worked on a fraction problem and asked them to explain their thinking.

Teacher:	Can you explain to me how you're finding an equivalent fraction here?
Student:	Well there's a fraction law that says you have to do the same thing on the bottom and the top so I'm multiplying by two on the top and multiplying by two on the bottom.
Teacher:	Do you know why you have to multiply by the same number on the top and the bottom?
Student:	Because that's what the fraction law tells me to do.
Teacher:	But there has to be a reason for the law. Do you know what it is?
Student:	No.

She used interviews such as these as "baseline" data to track the development of her students' conceptual understandings of fractions over time. Later, after introducing manipulative materials and working with students on concrete representations of a problem, an interview with the same student revealed his developing ability to approach a problem conceptually.

Teacher:	Using the fraction bars, can you show me the first fraction, 1/2?
Student:	(pulls out the two half pieces and points at one of them)
Teacher:	Good. You have shown me one half piece. You found earlier that 2/4 was an equivalent fraction to 1/2. Can you show me 2/4 with the fraction bars?
Student:	(pulls out fourth pieces and points at two of them)
Teacher:	So what makes those fractions equivalent?
Student:	Well, they take up the same amount of space.
Teacher:	Great! So then how did you get from 1/2 to 2/4?
Student:	Oh! I get it now! I couldn't explain it before without the fraction bars, but now I see that the one half piece turned into two fourth pieces. It multiplied by two. And the total number of pieces in 1/2 is two. The total number of pieces in 1/4 is 4. It multiplied by two. That's why the fraction law says I have to do the same thing on the bottom and on the top.
Teacher:	What would happen if you multiplied by different numbers on the top and bottom?
Student:	(after thinking for a minute) Can I use the fraction bars to figure it out?
Teacher:	Sure!

Student:	(works through the process by showing two different fractions with the fraction bars) Well if I multiplied the top number by two then I get two like I did before. If I multiply the bottom number by three instead of two, then I get six. (uses the sixth pieces to show 2/6 and puts it next to the 1/2 tiles) These fractions aren't equivalent because they don't take up the same amount of space.

"Interviewing" as a form of data collection can be as simple as circulating during instruction and asking questions to students about their learning. What makes the instructional activity of asking students questions an "interview" is that this act relates directly to the wondering you are exploring for your inquiry. In the former case, the teacher was inquiring into building conceptual understandings of fractions with her fourth-grade learners.

Strategy 5: Focus Groups

Focus groups offer teachers another vehicle for collecting the talk and thoughts of children in the classroom. In many ways, focus groups occur daily in the form of whole-class or small-group discussion. The focus-group discussion can serve as a tool for understanding students' perceptions. For example, a focus group can provide insight into how students experience a new instructional strategy. Teacher researcher Marisa Ramirez conducted an inquiry into differentiating mathematics instruction in her first-grade classroom through the design and implementation of "Challenge Baskets," a system of tiered activities built from previously introduced skills. Each of these baskets contained a variety of activities for the students to complete independently, providing them with extra practice or enrichment in previously introduced skills and an individualized schedule of which activities to complete from which basket based on their ability level and needs. Marisa writes:

I could tell from the beginning that my students were excited when it was Challenge Basket time, but I wanted to hear from them the reasons why they liked it. I also wanted to know what their dislikes and suggestions for improvement would be. We held a Class Meeting to discuss their thoughts and feelings. I charted their comments on three large pieces of paper labeled "Reasons Why We Like Challenge Baskets," "Things We Don't Like," and "Ideas or Suggestions," as they shared them in class. The students took this meeting very seriously and were glad to share their suggestions. This made the Challenge Baskets even more exciting to them since I asked for their opinions and even implemented some of their suggestions. (Ramirez, 2007, p. 104)

In essence, Marisa's use of the class meeting served as a focus-group interview. Many teacher researchers also use focus-group interviews to ascertain what prior knowledge students possess about a particular content area. Teachers who use graphic organizers such as "What We Know, What We Want to Know, What We Learned" (K-W-L) strategies are conducting a form of focus group that can serve as a source of data that can inform inquiry. Although focus groups can serve as a quick way to obtain data, they have some limitations. For example, focus groups are more likely to capture breadth of opinion because the goal is often to understand the group's perspective. In addition, sometimes due to the presence of diverging opinions, less confident focus-group members refrain from sharing their thoughts.

Strategy 6: Digital Pictures

Interviews and focus groups can capture words as data. A very old proverb you are likely familiar with is "A picture is worth a thousand words." Another wonderful way to capture action that occurs in the classroom as data is through digital photography.

For example, when taking a course entitled Integrating Technology into Instruction at the University of Florida, which included a heavy field experience component requiring engagement in teacher inquiry (Dawson & Dana, 2007), one prospective teacher studied the ways a toothpick bridge-building project stimulated student thinking in a fourth-grade math and science gifted classroom. These fourth-grade students were assigned to groups to build a bridge out of toothpicks. Simulating an actual bridge-building corporation, students in each group selected the jobs of architect, accountant, materials manager, carpenter, or project manager. With a fictional budget of five million dollars to start, the accountant managed the money, writing "checks" and keeping a balance of money expended using a Microsoft Excel spreadsheet. When the bridges were finished, the students created a video and PowerPoint presentation to document their progress from the start of the project through the final bridge construction.

For her inquiry, the prospective teacher in this classroom wished to capture and understand the ways working in a group contributed to the thinking of these young, gifted learners at each step in the process. How did the group members negotiate? How did their interactions with one another contribute to these learners' individual knowledge construction during this project? To gain insights into these wonderings, teacher observations were captured as field notes, weekly reflections were written by the students and the prospective teacher, student interviews were conducted, and digital pictures were taken. The digital pictures served two purposes—they documented group progress over time and were subsequently used during the student interviews as prompts to ask each group of students to describe the ways their group collaborated to complete each phase of this bridge-building process. Figures 4.7 and 4.8 illustrate two of these digital photos taken at an early stage in bridge construction and when the bridge was completed.

Figure 4.7   Bridge Building Project—Early Stage in Group 3's Work

SOURCE: Used with permission of Kara Dawson.

Figure 4.8   Bridge Building Project—Completed Bridge by Group 3

SOURCE: Used with permission of Kara Dawson.

Strategy 7: Video as Data

Digital pictures capture a single snippet of action in the classroom at one point in time. Video as a form of data collection takes digital pictures one step further by capturing an entire segment of action in the classroom over a set time period. Given that teachers often collect their best data by seeing and listening to the activities within their classroom, video becomes a powerful form of data collection for the teacher researcher. Teacher researchers have found that using video can help them collect descriptive information, better understand an unfolding behavior, capture the process used, study the learning situation, and make visible products or outcomes. More specifically, through observing video of one's own teaching, teachers can observe attitudes, skill and knowledge levels, nature of interactions, nonverbal behavior, instructional clarity, and the influence of physical surroundings (Cloutier, Lilley, Phillips, Weber, & Sanderson, 1987).

For example, when implementing a unit of study similar to the bridge-building project described in the previous section, one middle school teacher researcher we know used video to capture his ability to differentiate instruction and create student understanding of bridge construction. The video work captured the instruction, group work, content exploration, presentation, and product. The unique part of this teacher research was that the teacher researcher involved his students in the video work in three ways. First, his students often served as videographers as they took turns filming. Their choice of what to film also was an information source. Second, the students reviewed portions of the video with their teacher to provide their own insight and analysis of the learning process. By engaging the students in the analysis, they became metacognitively aware of the components that facilitated or inhibited their learning. Third, the teacher used the video to capture and document participant perspectives. By carefully interviewing his students on video, this teacher researcher was able to more completely understand his students' experiences.

In a similar fashion, high school chemistry teacher Stephen Burgin (2007a) used video in an interesting way to gain insights into his wondering, "How can I better utilize demonstrations in a way that empowers my students' learning of high school chemistry?" In this inquiry, Stephen developed a month-long curriculum that consisted of a discrepant event demonstration for each and every time his class met. Because his school was on a block schedule, his classes met three times a week, for a total of 13 demonstrations used in the teaching unit. During the unit, students video-recorded Stephen performing each of the 13 demonstrations. Students were then quizzed and tested on the content of the Demo-A-Day unit. During these assessments, the videos were played back for the students to help stimulate their thought processes and remind them of what they had previously observed in class. Used in this way, the videos both captured the events for Stephen as a teacher researcher and aided his students in reconstructing the discrepant event demonstrations and the chemistry behind them during a quiz.

Following these assessments, Stephen then placed his students in groups of four. Each group selected one of the 13 demonstrations they had previously observed in the Demo-A-Day unit. Groups then prepared the necessary solutions, planned a script to present their demonstration to a group of local elementary students, and practiced their demonstrations in front of their peers. Once again, Stephen enlisted video at this point in his inquiry. Groups were video-recorded as they performed their demonstration shows for the elementary students. Following the show, students were asked to write a reflective paper on both the Demo-A-Day unit and the demonstration show. Stephen again shared excerpts of the videos with his students to spawn their reflections prior to writing their papers. In this way, Stephen's use of video once again served two purposes:

1. Video captured his students' performance of the demonstrations for elementary students, so Stephen could use video excerpts to stimulate his own reflections on what occurred during this portion of the inquiry and provide documentation for his own teacher research.

2. Video was used as a precursor to students' writing of a reflective paper to help them be more articulate and thoughtful in their reflections.

Given that video can be used as both an observation tool as well as a tool to capture the experiences of students and stimulate their thought processes, video is an underused but powerful form of technology for documenting the work of teacher researchers.

Strategy 8: Reflective Journals

Thus far, we have discussed ways to make data collection a part of your teaching by capturing what naturally occurs in your teaching day—action in the classroom through field notes, digital pictures, and video; student progress in your classroom through document analysis; and talk in the classroom or school through interviews and focus groups. One of the ways that interviewing and focus groups serve as powerful data collection strategies is through the *talk* of interviewing, because a teacher-inquirer gains access into the *thinking* of the child or adult being interviewed.

Capturing "thinking" is a challenge for any researcher. One way a teacher researcher captures the thinking that occurs in the school and classroom and within his or her own mind is through journaling. Journals provide teachers a tool for reflecting on their own thought processes and can also serve as a tool for students to record their thinking related to the project at hand. An example of a journal entry from Julie Russell's inquiry appears in Figure 4.9.

Figure 4.9 Journal Entry

Julie Russell

February 22, 2002

Inquiry Lesson #3

This week's lesson was really exciting for me because I am really beginning to see that my efforts are making a difference. I always imagined creating a writing atmosphere in which my students felt comfortable and confident about presenting their work alongside that of published, established authors. In my classroom library, I am going to have a section for "Classroom Authors." When one of my students publishes a story, they will get a copy to take home and will make another copy to leave in the library. As we went around the circle and the students named their own characters, I felt so excited for these children. They are in an incredibly powerful creative space right now in which they feel capable. I can remember writing my own chapter book with no hesitation when I was eight years old. Now, I would be terrified to tackle that sort of job. I suppose that is the source of my passion for developing writing instruction for primary students. My dream is to help my children see themselves as "real" authors and feel proud of their work before they begin to doubt their abilities. I would be so proud to make a difference in that way.

I think this inquiry project has taught me a very important lesson about pacing. One of my biggest weaknesses is expecting way too much. I know what those expectations can do to me, and I never want to put that kind of pressure on my children. Honestly, I think I would have done more harm than good if I continued to push so hard. Before the writing segment of my second inquiry lesson, the children were so excited to begin writing. When I started my third lesson, C. actually asked, "Do we have to write a WHOLE story AGAIN?" I felt horrible! I was so glad that we had lightened the work load. I think the whole flow of the lesson felt better. I am a much better teacher when I do not feel rushed and overwhelmed. I have noticed how incredibly sensitive the children are to how I am feeling. Do you remember when I scolded them and they apologized during that reading group? They do that often lately. They seem to want to behave and achieve to please me, and they get upset if they think I am not pleased. It's a big responsibility to have someone care that much about your opinion. It becomes a constant process of reflection and negotiation, because their sensitivity to my expectations makes me really sensitive to whether or not my expectations are appropriate. I think that breaking the writing into more manageable chunks made a huge difference. The children did not get burned out, and I was able to relax and really enjoy the lesson. Part of my goal for this project was to share my passion for writing, and I can't do that if I am not enjoying the writing lesson.

I think that the connection to literature is very effective. Many of the children—even those for whom writing is a struggle—are starting to include beautiful literary language in their stories. I saw this emerge particularly during this lesson. I think the students have more time to write and I had more time to emphasize the literature. Their comments as we discussed both their fairy tales and the published fairy tales indicate that they are becoming more aware of the strategies that good authors use. One of the central ideas in my philosophy as a writing teacher is that even very young children can recognize what they like so they can begin to apply it in their own writing. It's exciting for me to see my role in writing instruction emerge, because that was one of the things I was questioning.

SOURCE: Used with permission of Julie Russell.

Strategy 9: Weblogs

Similar to a journal, weblogs are another excellent way teacher researchers can capture their thinking as an inquiry unfolds. Will Richardson (2006) defines a weblog, or blog, in its most general sense as "an easily created, easily updateable Web site that allows an author (or authors) to publish instantly to the Internet from any Internet connection" (p. 17). As blogs consist of a series of entries arranged in reverse chronological order, they can serve as a sort of "online diary" where teacher researchers can post commentary or news about the research they are currently engaged in. Unlike the journal as a form of data collection, the teacher researcher who blogs can combine text, images, and links to other blogs as well as post comments in an interactive format. The comment feature of blogs provides the opportunity for teacher researchers to receive feedback from anyone in the world (in an open blog community) or other teacher researchers (in a closed community).

For example, third-grade teacher Wendy Drexler used a blog to both capture her own reflection throughout the duration of an inquiry as well as to serve as the object of her inquiry when she investigated a K–12/ university blogging collaboration between preservice teachers and her third-grade students. Wendy gained insight into her wondering, "What happens to third-grade students' attitude toward writing, quality of a final writing product, and motivation to write when they participate with preservice teachers in a blogging project related to the study of Native American culture?" by collecting data in the following ways: writing survey, student blogs, interviews, student concept maps, and student five-paragraph presentations. In addition, Wendy kept a teacher's reflective blog to capture details that were taking place on a daily basis as well as her feelings as the project evolved.

Sample entries from Wendy's blog and one of her student's blogs appear in Figures 4.10 and 4.11.

As indicated in Figure 4.10, Wendy's personal blog helped her combine the benefits of field notes and journaling in one place. Through careful analysis of her own blog over time, as well as the blogs of her students (see Figure 4.11) and the other forms of data she collected, Wendy learned that collaborative blogging improved her students' writing and supported development of related skills and knowledge (Drexler, Dawson, & Ferdig, 2007).

Both journaling and blogging as a form of data collection can be very powerful tools, but sometimes it is difficult for the novice teacher researcher to view his or her own reflections as important data! Ironically, as teachers (in charge of facilitating the thinking of others), we have not been socialized into thinking that our *own* thinking matters! Yet capturing your own thinking over time can lead to critical insights into your teaching that may only occur when you revisit a thought that occurred to you while teaching at a later date or when you string a number of thoughts together that have occurred intermittently over a longer period of time. If you

Figure 4.10   Wendy's Blog Entry

October 14, 2006

Wendy

[Logged in users] Narrowing Topics and Concept Maps
Posted by Wendy | 0 comment(s) | Edit | Delete | Trackback URI

The children blogged on Monday about the three topics on which the research essay will focus. The university partners responded with good comments and some additional resources. On Friday, each child created an Inspiration concept map to help visualize where more content was needed to round out the research. This was an excellent exercise for the students. Previously, they were having difficulty organizing long lists of facts. Ultimately, the Inspiration concept map will be viewed in outline form to help the students organize the actual paper. One very valuable aspect of this type of project is allowing those students who excel and enjoy the research process to include as much detail in the paper as can be found. The students who work more slowly or those who struggle are still able to work with more simplistic topics. It was also interesting to observe one student who is notoriously slow on most assignments. He often appears distracted and requires a lot of verbal cues to pull him back in. In this case, he was engrossed in the content, specifically focused on the language of his tribe. Again, time is the greatest challenge in these types of projects. As a teacher, I am encouraged by his focus and desire to learn more. However, there is only so much time available. We decided to change one of his three topics to language. But, I still had to scoot him along to make sure he completed enough of the assignment to keep him from falling further behind. Since all of the children have Internet access at home, they can continue most aspects of the project outside of school. However, at this age (third grade), they are not accustomed to taking that kind of responsibility for out-of-school learning. Most still require very concrete, specific instructions for homework assignments. I'm going to think more about this. How wonderful it would be for each student to have as much time as needed to approach the learning process in his or her own way without always being hurried. Next week, we will finish the concept maps and post them on the website for the university partners to see.

Keywords: educational technology, hurried child, Integrating technology with social studies, Native American Projects, special projects

---

SOURCE: Used with permission of Wendy Drexler.

Figure 4.11   Student Blog Entry

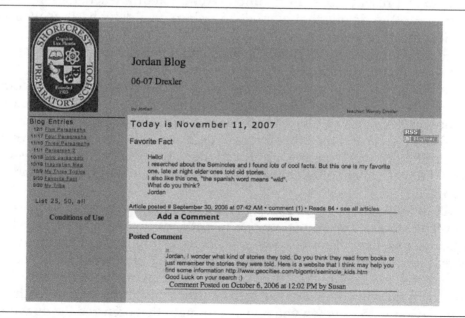

SOURCE: Used with permission of Wendy Drexler, teacher at Shorecrest Preparatory School.

(or any of your students) are a Harry Potter fan, you will recall that the wise teacher and headmaster, Albus Dumbledore, has the ability to extract thoughts and recollections of events from his head and place them in a "pensieve." At critical times in the Harry Potter stories, Albus enters the pensieve, sometimes with Harry, to explore these old memories and thoughts, and gains new insights with each visit. Journaling or blogging can serve as your personal pensieve to capture and store your thoughts and recollections safely so you can share them with teaching colleagues and return to them at various times in the evolution of your inquiry, gaining new and deeper insights with each visit.

A good way to make your personal pensieve as effective as it can be is to plan for your journal writing or blogging ahead of time. This means committing to a specific time to journal or blog throughout your inquiry as well as a structure for journaling/blogging that makes sense in relationship to what you wish to learn. For example, in Ashley Pennypacker Hill's study of how she could support the self-regulation of learners receiving Tier 3 intensive instruction within a new 21st-century architecturally designed school, Ashley used a journal in the following way:

> I answered two prompts daily: What did I learn about self-regulation in reading today? What did I learn about how my students might transfer self-regulation strategies to other contexts? The use of a teacher's journal allowed me to capture my own thinking. I established a time that I wrote in my journal daily, which was for ten minutes directly after teaching. . . . This supported me through the success, areas of growth, and provided me a structured outlet in deciding the next steps that needed to be taken in the study. (Hill, 2013, pp. 47–48)

At the end of her study, after analyzing data and writing up her results, Ashley reflected on her approach to journal writing as one form of data she collected, offering suggestions to other teacher inquirers, like yourself.

> Many texts about the process of practitioner research suggest journaling as one method of data collection. What texts about the practitioner research process often do not do, however, is suggest that teacher researchers highly structure their journaling process. In this study, I established a time that I would write in my journal daily. Establishing this time ensured that I had dedicated time to methodically reflect on my teaching. If I would not have established this time, I would have engaged in writing a journal haphazardly and I would not have collected systematic data. In addition, in my journal I responded to the same two prompts every day: "What did I learn about self-regulation in reading today?" and "What did I learn about how my students might transfer self-regulation strategies to other contexts?" These two prompts directly connected to my research

questions and provided focus to my daily reflections. Without these prompts, my journal would have been a tool for reflection, but the data within it would have likely been much broader and less helpful to me as I analyzed my data over time. Therefore, practitioner researchers, at the onset of their studies, might consider highly structuring the use of the journal by committing to a regularly scheduled time to write in it and by using consistent prompts that directly connect to their research questions. (Hill, 2013, pp. 128–129)

If you choose journaling or blogging as one form of data you will collect, consider taking Ashley's advice.

Strategy 10: Surveys

Some teacher-inquirers employ more formal mechanisms (such as sociograms and surveys) to capture the action, talk, thinking, and productivity that are a part of each and every school day. The most common formal mechanism we have observed in our work with teacher-inquirers is surveys. Surveys can give students a space to share their thoughts and opinions about a teaching technique or strategy, a unit, or their knowledge about particular subject matter.

Recall Brian Peters and Gail Romig's inquiry into science talks. In the following excerpt, note how the use of surveys gave Brian and Gail access to their students' thinking about their experiences during science talks:

Upon entering into the process of using Science Talks as a means of instructing and assessing students, we were looking for answers to many questions. Could we use Science Talks as another mode of instruction? Would Science Talks enhance what we were already doing in terms of instruction? Would the use of Science Talks enable us to better assess what the students know and yet need to learn? Would Science Talks provide a vehicle for those who struggle with written forms of assessment to express their understanding meaningfully? Dickenson and Young (1998) state that science can provide "common experiences" that children can speak and write about. Would Science Talks enhance how the children communicate about these common experiences?

In addition to articulating the perspectives about Science Talks that we developed as teachers as a result of answering these questions through inquiry, we wished to discover how the students felt about the Science Talks. If the students felt comfortable and had some ownership in the activity, there may be greater participation. We used a survey which asked for information regarding the following: "What do you like about having Science Talks?," "What don't you like about Science Talks?," and "Do you have any suggestions for improving our Science Talks?"

The children's responses to this survey gleaned some interesting information and led us to the conclusion that all members of our class enjoyed Science Talks. The following two survey responses were typical of all of the responses we received:

"I like Science Talks because you might need a question answered and the teacher doesn't know the answer. With more people, more questions can be answered. I can't think of anything I don't like because science rules. I don't want to change anything 'cause things are cool as they are."

"I like Science Talks. They are cool. It is fun because we can share what we have to say. We don't even have to raise our hands."

The entire class completed the survey and not one student stated that the use of Science Talks was disliked. There were some portions of the process that were not enjoyed, and some students offered suggestions. The main item of dissatisfaction that appeared in the survey was that more than one student talked at once or that one could not speak because of others dominating the discussion. Twenty-nine percent of the class expressed this opinion.

Many students gave suggestions to improve our Science Talks. There was a desire to have smaller groups for Science Talks. One student suggested that each person in the circle have a turn and be allowed to share or pass. One child did not like the physical arrangements of the talks because she did not like sitting on the floor. Another did not like the time of day our Science Talk was held. Two students suggested that we should extend our Science Talks to other subjects. . . . We were able to learn plenty from our surveys. (Peters & Romig, 2001)

Depending on the inquiry, some teachers survey students as the first part of their investigation and have the students complete the same survey at the end of an inquiry. This is particularly useful when surveys focus on students' understandings of content or attitude toward particular components of the school day and a teacher-inquirer wishes to capture growth or change over time. Surveys can also be used in similar ways with adults.

First-grade teacher Candy Bryan and third-grade teacher Kelly Reilly-Kaminski completed a shared inquiry project that focused on understanding effective parent communication, relying primarily on surveys to gather information. In the following excerpt, note the way their wondering(s) about parent communication logically led to using a survey as the main form of data collection. Also note the ways in which their data collection plan changed over time.

As a result of enrolling in a professional development course on teacher inquiry, we found the opportunity to discuss an area of concern in our classrooms. Both of us believed that parent involvement is directly related to student success in the classroom. Children will be more successful academically, complete more homework, achieve higher grades, have more positive attitudes, and behave better if parents are more involved. After all, who is a child's first and most important teacher? The answer to this question is obvious. By involving parents, teachers gain a unique perspective that provides valuable information into a child's education. According to the National PTA:

> Over 30 years' research has proven beyond dispute the positive connection between parent involvement and student success. Effectively engaging parents and families in the education of their children has the potential to be far more transformational than any other type of educational reform. (1997, p. 5)

We wondered about what methods of communication parents found valuable, what we could do to be more effective and what trends appear as students mature from the primary grades (beginning with Candy in first grade) to the intermediate grades (beginning with Kelly at third grade). At the conclusion of our research project, it was our intention to make changes to our current practices that parents would find valuable and insightful. These changes would provide parents with more information concerning their child's education and benefit all parties involved: students, parents, and teachers.

Figure 4.12   Parental Survey I

I will use the results of this survey to improve communication between home and school. Please fill the survey out honestly and if you have any questions, please contact me at the school.

1. What forms of communication from me do you find useful (e.g., home-school journals, newsletters, website)?

2. Do you read the newsletter with your child? What sections do you find the most valuable, if any? What sections are not of value to you, if any?

3. Do you have any suggestions on how I can improve the current newsletter? If so, please describe them.

4. Do you visit the classroom website? What components do you find the most valuable, if any? What sections are not of value to you, if any?

5. Do you have any suggestions for how I can improve the current classroom website? If so, please describe them.

6. Do you find home-school journals valuable? In what ways?

7. Are there any other forms of communication that you would find valuable? If so, please explain.

SOURCE: Bryan & Reilly-Kaminski, 2002.

To gather the data, we needed to find out more about the parents' need for communication. We relied heavily on parent surveys to gather information. We surveyed the parents once at the beginning of the project using the survey labeled Parental Survey 1 [see Figure 4.12]. We asked questions about home-school journals, newsletters, and websites and asked for suggestions about other forms of communication that they might find useful. After reviewing the surveys we realized that we needed to ask clarifying questions. Unfortunately, the first survey was done anonymously. We were hoping to receive more honest answers if we didn't require the parents to sign the survey. This was a problem because we needed to survey some of the parents again in order to clarify their responses. We were hoping to follow-up by using short parent interviews over the phone. Instead, because we didn't know who filled out which survey, we had to survey the entire population again. In the second survey, labeled Parental Survey 2 [see Figure 4.13], we asked for the parents' preferences and suggestions about communication and participation as a volunteer in the classroom. We added the piece about participation because of input from the first survey. We also added a few questions about e-mail as a communication tool. (Bryan & Reilly-Kaminski, 2002)

An important lesson learned about data collection from Candy and Kelly is that shifting gears midway through your inquiry, and adjusting your original plan as your inquiry unfolds, is not unusual. Originally, Candy and Kelly planned on doing one survey and follow-up phone interviews. Based on information that emerged on the first survey as well as the realization that they were unable to target particular parents with follow-up interviews because the first survey was completed anonymously, Candy and Kelly constructed a second survey.

Departing from your original data collection plan is a natural part of the inquiry process. If you find as your inquiry unfolds that forms of data collection you employed need to be adjusted—adjust accordingly! If you find as your inquiry unfolds that different forms of data collection you hadn't planned on using may be insightful to your wondering—use them! Just keep track of the decisions you make as an inquirer along the way, as articulating changes in course can also be an important piece of what you are learning.

In our final example of survey data, we return to high school chemistry teacher Stephen Burgin. In the school year that followed his Demo-A-Day inquiry, Stephen was dissatisfied with the ways his required afterschool help sessions were going. He had observed that a small group of his students were not paying attention in class because they could rely on the extra-help sessions to pick up anything they missed. In an effort to make his extra-help sessions more meaningful to students, and less frustrating for Stephen, he again used the process of inquiry to explore the overarching

Figure 4.13   Parental Survey 2

Dear Parents,

I am still working on my research project about parent communication. I have some questions about home-school journals and parent volunteers.

Home-school journals are journals that would be kept in your child's homework folder. They are meant to act as a two-way communication tool. If you had a question or comment to make, you could just write the note in the journal. I would read the journal and respond. I could also use it to communicate individually with parents when I have something to tell you.

Please answer Yes or No.

_____ Do you think you would use a journal like this?

_____ Do you have e-mail?

_____ Would you like to use e-mail to communicate?

If so, please provide the address. _____

_____ Would you prefer e-mail to a home-school journal?

Would you like to participate or volunteer more in the classroom?

Yes or No

If you responded by circling the Yes, please check the items below that you would like to help with.

_____ Typing students' stories

_____ Helping with trips

In addition to helping with these two options, how else do you think I could use parent volunteers?

Please write your name below and return this form to school.

_____

SOURCE: Bryan & Reilly-Kaminski, 2002.

question, "What is the most productive way to structure afterschool help?" Stephen's subquestions included the following:

- What are students' perceptions and expectations for extra help?
- What is the relationship between misbehavior during class and attendance at afterschool help?
- What skills do my students need to take charge of their extra help?
- What is the chemistry skill level of my students who seek help outside of class?

Note the ways in which Stephen's subquestions led to the development of a survey, administered to all of his chemistry students, to begin his inquiry (see Figure 4.14).

Once Stephen administered this survey, he tallied and compared responses with his record of attendance at extra-help sessions and observational notes he had taken since the beginning of the year. As a result of reflecting on his initial survey, attendance, and observation data, Stephen was able to name and sort his students into four distinct categories.

> Upon reflection it became apparent that four groups of students were emerging. The first group of students attended my help sessions regularly and benefited from them based on my observations and survey responses. The second group of students attended my help sessions but gained nothing from them according to my observations and survey data. The third group of students did not attend help sessions and their achievement in my class seemed to indicate that they did not need to. And the fourth group of students was those who did not attend help sessions, but probably should. In order to gain further insights into these four distinct groups of students, I proceeded to collect data through interviews. I selected some students that fit into each of these categories to talk with and compare their responses to similar questions. (Burgin, 2007b)

Figure 4.14   Chemistry "Help Session" Student Survey

Instructions: Please respond to these statements anonymously according to the following scale:

1	2	3	4	5
Strongly Agree	Agree	Neutral	Disagree	Strongly Disagree

1. I pay attention most of the time during chemistry class.

1	2	3	4	5

2. I have attended multiple help sessions this year.

1	2	3	4	5

3. I only attend help sessions if there is a quiz or test coming up.

1	2	3	4	5

4. I feel like my attendance at help sessions has impacted my understanding of chemistry.

1	2	3	4	5

5. I come to help sessions because I want to do well in chemistry class.

1	2	3	4	5

(Continued)

Figure 4.14   (Continued)

---

6. I come to help sessions because my parents and/or teachers make me.

    1   2   3   4   5

7. I think that help sessions should be led by my teacher.

    1   2   3   4   5

8. I think that help sessions should be led based on questions that I have.

    1   2   3   4   5

SOURCE: Used with permission of Stephen Burgin.

Stephen's research offers another important lesson about data collection. When engaging in teacher research for the first time, it is easy to conceptualize data collection and data analysis as concrete, distinct entities that teachers progress through in a lockstep manner (i.e., First I will collect my data. After all my data are collected, then I will analyze them). Rather, data collection and data analysis are often iterative processes that teacher researchers vacillate between over the course of their inquiries. According to Thorne (2000),

> Because data collection and analysis processes tend to be concurrent, with new analytic steps informing the process of additional data collection and new data informing the analytic processes, it is important to recognize that qualitative data analysis processes are not entirely distinguishable from the actual data collection. The theoretical lens from which the [teacher] researcher approaches the phenomenon, the strategies that the researcher uses to collect or construct data, and the understandings that the researcher has about what might count as relevant or important data in answering the research question are all analytic processes. (p. 3)

In Stephen's case, the collection and subsequent analysis of his survey data, observation data, and attendance data led Stephen to the collection of additional data and a specified procedure for how to collect it—student interviews sampled from four categories of students. We revisit the close relationship between data collection and data analysis in Chapter 5.

Strategy 11: Quantitative Measures of Student Achievement (Standardized Test Scores, Assessment Measures, Grades)

In this era of high-stakes testing and accountability, numerous quantitative measures of student performance abound, and these measures can be valuable sources of data for the teacher researcher. For example, high school biology teacher Mickey MacDonald was struck by the differences in the grades she and her ninth-grade teaching colleagues in English, world cultures, and Algebra I had assigned their students when they met for their routine end-of-the-quarter team meeting to share, compare, and discuss students who received grades of D and F in their courses. This led Mickey to use teacher research to better understand these grading discrepancies. In the following excerpt from Mickey's work, note how her grading dilemma leads her to select grades and achievement test data as one source to glean insights into her wondering.

> I am a high school science teacher in my third year of teaching at P. K. Yonge Developmental Research School. Like most teachers, I want my students to succeed in my class. More importantly, I want to prepare my students to be successful in other science classes. I am disturbed that my students' grades, at least at a cursory level, appear "deflated" in comparison with my team's grades and in comparison with our overall middle and high school grade distributions.
>
> Based on all of the questions running through my mind, I narrowed down my wondering to this: In what ways can examining my class grades, other instructors' grades, and standardized test scores enable me to address the apparent grade deflation that my students experience? Within this wondering, I will use these subquestions to guide me as I attempt to address my dilemma. They are as follows:
>
> - Is there a relationship between my students' first semester science grades and math grades?
> - Is there a correlation between my students' first semester science grades and their FCAT (Florida Comprehensive Assessment Test) reading and math scores?
> - Are there any differences in science grades based on gender or grade level?
>
> As I was developing what my inquiry would look like, I began to research what the literature said about grade deflation. Although a search on the term *grade deflation* did not provide any research, a search on *grade inflation* did. Two articles that I read both indicated that grade inflation exists in high schools. In a June 2004 report, Cook (2004) writes, "Even though SAT scores remain . . . unchanged, college applicants are receiving more As than ever as grade inflation reaches new heights in the nation's high schools . . . " This statistic was first noted in a *Forbes* article in which the author wrote, "Between 1991 and 2001, a period when SAT-measured aptitude was essentially flat, the proportion of test-takers receiving grade point averages of at least A- rose

from 29% to 41%" (Seligman, 2002). *U.S. News and World Report* also reported in 2000 that although students reported being "tuned out" in high school, a record number were receiving As, even though there were no indicators that levels of achievement had improved over the past 30 years (Wildavsky, 2000). Based on the literature, my students were not experiencing the grade inflation trend. If anything, it appeared that my students were experiencing the opposite.

In designing my inquiry, I knew that I had a plethora of raw data available to me. The key was choosing the data that would provide the best insight into my wondering. I decided that I would limit the data that I had available to teacher-issued data and achievement test data. For teacher-issued data, I chose to look at grades from our first semester in biology and math. For achievement test data, I chose the Florida Comprehensive Assessment Test (FCAT) Sunshine State Standard reading and math scores and achievement levels. I compiled all of these data into an Excel spreadsheet, which I could sort by grades, achievement levels, class, gender, and other indicators. (MacDonald, 2007, p. 51)

Because Mickey's dilemma and wondering were directly related to test scores and grades, this form of data collection was a natural selection for her inquiry. Because these data were already collected and available at her school, all Mickey needed to do was compile the data of her students in an Excel spreadsheet that would enable her to sort and view this data in different ways. Figure 4.15 contains a sample spreadsheet.

For an example of assessment data, we turn to the work of fourth-grade teacher Debbi Hubbell (2006), who decided to look closely at one of her teaching passions—reading—through inquiry. Debbi knew that one of the best predictors of performance on Florida's yearly standardized test, the FCAT (Florida Comprehensive Assessment Test), was reading fluency and that research has shown a direct correlation between fluency and comprehension. She wanted to help her students become more successful readers and believed that if they became more fluent they would develop their reading comprehension. In the end, this would also allow them to perform better on the FCAT.

Worried about seven students she felt were at risk and less fluent than others in her class, she decided to explore in more detail the research related to developing fluency in elementary readers. She attended numerous workshops and read a variety of research-based articles that developed her knowledge of fluency. As a result of this knowledge development, Debbi introduced the rereading of fractured fairy tale plays to these seven learners to see if this activity might increase reading fluency. The fractured fairy tales differed from the more traditional skill and drill activity these students often encountered in daily reading instruction.

Figure 4.15   Mickey's Spreadsheet

Gender	Grade Level	05–06 First Sem. Biology Grade	Math Subject	05–06 First Sem. Math Grade	SSS Reading AL	SSS Reading Scale Score	SSS Math AL	SSS Math Scale Score
F	10	A	Geometry	B	1	274	3	307
M	10	A	Geometry	A	2	287	3	324
F	10	A	Geometry	A	2	304	3	312
M	10	A	Geometry Hon.	A	2	315	4	342
F	9	A	Geometry Hon.	A	4	353	4	351
F	9	A	Alg. I Hon.	B	4	358	3	336
M	10	B	App Math II	B	1	268	2	271
F	10	B	Geometry	D	1	280	3	319
M	10	B	Geometry	C	2	285	2	290
F	10	B	Geometry Hon.	B	2	289	4	345
F	10	B	App Math II	C	2	292	2	268
M	10	B	Geometry	B	2	301	3	307
M	10	B	Geometry	B	2	307	3	326
F	9	B	Algebra I	B	3	310	3	330
M	9	B	Algebra I	A	3	313	3	334
F	9	B	Algebra I	C	3	314	3	319
F	10	B	Geometry	B	2	319	4	345
M	10	B	Geometry	C	2	321	3	312
F	9	B	Algebra I	B	3	322	3	316
F	10	B	Algebra II	C	3	328	3	325
M	10	B	Geometry Hon.	B	3	339	4	332
M	10	B	Algebra II Hon.	C	3	343	4	354
M	10	B	Geometry Hon.	B	3	345	4	354
M	9	B	Alg. I Hon.	B	3	349	4	352
M	10	B	Geometry	B	4	359	3	303
M	9	B	Alg. I Hon.	B	4	370	4	370
F	9	B	Alg. II Hon.	A	4	371	5	399
M	9	B	Algebra I	B				

(Continued)

Figure 4.15   (Continued)

Gender	Grade Level	05–06 First Sem. Biology Grade	Math Subject	05–06 First Sem. Math Grade	SSS Reading AL	SSS Reading Scale Score	SSS Math AL	SSS Math Scale Score
M	10	B	Algebra I	B				
M	10	C	Geometry Hon.	C	1	253	3	325
M	10	C	Inf. Geom	B	1	265	3	330
M	10	C	Geometry Hon.	C	1	267	4	333
F	9	C	Geometry Hon.	B	2	278	4	359
M	10	C	Geometry	B	1	281	3	305
M	10	C	Geometry Hon.	B	2	285	4	336
M	10	C	Geometry	C	2	286	3	310
F	10	C	Geometry	C	2	289	3	309
F	10	C	Geometry	D	2	290	3	301
M	10	C	Geometry	C	2	290	2	291

SOURCE: Used with permission of Mickey MacDonald.

To gain insights into her wondering, "What is the relationship between my fourth-graders' fluency development and the reading of fractured fairy tale plays?," Debbi's first form of data collection was her administration and scoring of Dynamic Indicators of Basic Early Literacy Skills (DIBELS) at different time periods throughout her research. The Dynamic Indicators of Basic Early Literacy Skills are a set of standardized, individually administered measures of early literacy development. They are designed to be short, one-minute fluency measures used to regularly monitor the development of prereading and early reading skills. This assessment measure was a practice her school already engaged in and provided Debbi with data to assess her students' fluency development over time (see Figure 4.16).

One note of caution regarding standardized test scores, grades, and assessment measures: Because these types of data take the form of numbers, they are consonant with traditional notions of research many teachers hold. In fact, one of the first images teachers conjure up when they hear the word *research* is often number crunching and statistical analyses. Because of this image, as well as the prevalence and focus on these types of data in schools today, standardized test scores, assessment measures, and grades are sometimes the first and only type of data teacher researchers think about collecting (Dana & Yendol-Hoppey, 2008b). Yet Roland

Figure 4.16 Debbi's DIBELS Data

	10/18	12/1	2/10	2/21	4/6	
			DIBELS Test Date			
J	48*	53*	55*	60*	73*	
B	81*	98-	114-	105-	164	at risk*
C	90-	98-	95-	100-	130	less fluent-
Ja	64*	70*	92-	85*	119-	
T	93-	96-	88*	97-	121	
S	94-	91-	86*	78*	113-	
M	84-	101-	99-	107-	127	

SOURCE: Used with permission of Debbi Hubbell.

Barth (2001) reminds us that "good education is more than good scores and good teaching is more than generating good scores" (p. 156). Similarly, good teacher research is about more than generating good test scores or showing the relationship between one's teaching practice and one's students' performance on state tests. If you are planning on using standardized test scores, assessment measures, or grades as a form of data collection for your inquiry, it is critical to delve deeply into this data, understanding what the test/assessment you are relying on was designed to measure and being sure to use the measure in the ways it was designed to be used. Consider the following real scenario depicting a superficial use and reliance on standardized test score data reported by Love (2004).

> When educators in one Texas high school saw African-American students' performance drop slightly below 50% on their state mathematics test, putting the school on the state's list of low-performing schools, they reacted quickly. Decision makers immediately suggested that all African-American students, whether or not they failed the test be assigned peer tutors (Olsen, 2003). Based on one piece of data and one way of looking at that data, these decision makers made assumptions and leapt to action before fully understanding the issue or verifying their assumptions with other data sources. They ignored past trends, which indicated that African-American students' scores were on an upward trajectory. They failed to consider that the decline was so small that it could better be explained by chance or measuring error than by their instructional program. They considered only the percent failing without digging deeper into the data to consider what students needed.

Finally, they proposed intervention targeted only for African-American students, while overlooking Hispanic and white students who also failed the test. (p. 22)

To guard against your own teacher research unfolding as the scenario just described, remember that standardized test scores and other assessment data can provide valuable information for the teacher researcher but need to be interpreted carefully and considered along with other data sources as well. Debbi Hubbell learned this valuable lesson in her fractured fairy tale inquiry, where she admits that when she was first planning this inquiry, she intended to rely solely on the DIBELS scores to ascertain the meaning fractured fairy tale pedagogy held for her students. After discussing her proposed inquiry with colleagues, she was questioned regarding this single form of data collection, and she added to her data collection plan two additional strategies. In addition to DIBELS data, Debbi took anecdotal notes each time she used fractured fairy tale plays with these fourth-grade students, documenting their reactions and engagement and her assessment of their fluency development with each rereading of a play. Finally, Debbi relied on student work or artifacts as a third data source. At the end of the fractured fairy tale series, Debbi asked her students to write "Dear Mrs. Hubbell" letters, telling her about their perceptions and experiences with the fractured fairy tale unit of study.

In reflecting on what she learned as a result of engaging in this research, Debbi shared the following:

What I did not expect to learn seems more important than the DIBELS data to me. I learned:

1. Students love to be engaged in meaningful reading (even those who previously did not want to EVER read—this year or before). A student, who when asked, had hated school and was failing, actually said later he enjoyed this aspect of school and improved at least by a grade or more in *each* subject.

2. Excellent prosody could be obtained, more than I expected, through the reading of fractured fairy tales. I only expected "words per minute" to be increased, but was very amazed at the expression that was produced by these very motivated students.

3. A student, who had complications with comprehension that I could not account for, seemed to overcome these difficulties and become successful on reading tests that assessed comprehension.

4. Positive social interactions occurred between students who previously had difficulty communicating in a positive way. Students enjoyed helping each other in a kinder way when someone made a mistake, and tolerance as well as admiration was practiced with more difficult relationships.

5. Students will give up a time (recess) that is valuable to them to produce a theatrical version of a play.

6. Students reported these things in a letter to me:

   - It helped me read better and made me smarter.
   - I learned to try your best and do not be embarrassed.
   - I'm a more fluent reader.
   - The fairy tales bring more happiness to the school day and more laughter to the morning.
   - We don't have to be perfect.
   - The tales improved my vocabulary.
   - The plays helped me read with more expression. (Hubbell, 2006, p. 7)

By drawing on multiple sources of data, Debbi was able to develop a much richer picture of what was occurring in relationship to her use of fractured fairy tale plays to deliver reading instruction than she would have been able to develop had she collected and relied on DIBELS data exclusively. One of the reasons we engage in teacher research is that it honors all the great complexity of teaching. In most cases, no single source of data (whether it be field notes, student work, interviews, focus groups, pictures, video, journals, blogs, surveys, or standardized test scores and assessments) can adequately capture all the great complexity inherent in teaching. Therefore, it is important for teacher researchers to use multiple forms of data as they design their inquiries in order to develop the richest possible picture they can of what is occurring in the classroom. We further discuss the importance of multiple data sources in the section of this chapter entitled "When Do I Collect Data and How Much Do I Collect?"

Strategy 12: Critical Friend Group Feedback

Like Debbi Hubbell in the previous example, versed in the importance of drawing on multiple sources of data, in her inquiry on grade deflation, Mickey MacDonald also collected data in more ways than standardized test scores and grades. One of the additional ways she collected data is through critical friend group feedback. As introduced in Chapter 1, critical friends groups (CFGs) are one version of professional learning communities developed by the National School Reform Faculty (www.nsrfharmony .org). The National School Reform Faculty (NSRF) defines a CFG as "a Professional Learning Community consisting of approximately 8–12 educators who come together voluntarily at least once a month for about two hours. Group members are committed to improving their practice through collaborative learning" (NSRF, 2007). Protocols developed by NSRF and available on their website systematize and guide the dialogue that occurs between teachers at these meetings. Mickey writes:

One data piece that I knew would be very insightful would be to get my colleagues to help me interpret my data. I enlisted their input using P. K. Yonge's three secondary Critical Friends Groups. Each group was given the Excel spreadsheet data that I had compiled [see Figure 4.15]. Using the protocol called *Making Meaning from Text*, each group described, asked questions, and speculated about the meaning/significance of my Excel spreadsheet, and discussed the implications of my spreadsheet to their work (http://www.harmonyschool.org, retrieved November 11, 2006). As teachers "read" the text (my spreadsheet), they wrote comments and highlighted things they noticed. As each group began to discuss the text, comments were recorded as minutes. (MacDonald, 2007, p. 53)

Figure 4.17 illustrates the recorded comments from this critical friends group discussion.

Figure 4.17   Mickey's Critical Friends Group Feedback

March 8, 2006, PKY Critical Friends Group Comments (Division: M. MacDonald)

What Do You See? Describing the Text

- NJD: 5 in SSS AL, yet C in math/bio. Questions the validity of these tests (standardized).
- GS: Ditto; overall, sees similar grades in both classes (math/sci correlation).
- CK: Math grades often one higher than sci grades.
- TR: Looked at high-math SSS vs. low-math class grades. But saw opposite as well; not convinced a correlation exists.
- TA: Grades seem to approximate bell curve; sci/math grades; only nine students have differential of two or more grades (e.g., A/C or B/D).
- CD: Lots of C/C/3/3 students. Interesting distribution of students who are two or more SSS AL levels apart (between reading and math AL): 2 in bio got an A, 3 got B, 12 a C, 5 a D, and none of the bio grade Fs.
- AM: 4 of 6 people who got As are below average in FCAT reading. One student (D.R.), low-level reading, expect low grade, yet math score is 3 FCAT, and D in math class. Amy thinks this is a bit swippety-swappety. Lots of high reading achievers in Cs and Ds.
- BR: Disbursements of Ds and Fs; many Fs in science but only two across the board in math. Is this because of intensive math classes?
- MM: # as same in both classes. In math, lower proportion of lower grades; science had a flip-flop, yet # of Cs about the same (between math/biology). Overall, bell curve is skewed to the right in science, and to the left in math.
- NDean: Interested in relationship between intensity level of the math class and how it might affect grade distribution.

What questions does examining this data raise?

- NDean: How do you infer grade deflation from this data?
- NJD: How can we apply this type of data to directly solve something in our courses?

- GS: Might this data reflect students who *know* the material but who lack a strong schoolwork ethic?
- CK: Difficult to draw accurate correlations; this data might not be an accurate indicator.
- TR: How do math/sci reasoning relate?
- TA: Are grades reflecting attitude and behavior more so than ability? (Assuming FCAT measures ability to begin with.) Are Mickey's grades inflated or deflated?
- CD: What if we had more data? Could we draw additional conclusions without the benefit of a computerized database?
- AM: How are grades calculated in Mickey's class? And how are they weighted? How might this information differ if it had been state-supplied (how does it affect our expectations of student performance?) Is FCAT a measure of grade inflation?
- BR: Why only one biology level, and yet multiple levels of applied math? Why are grades so much higher in intensive math? Does this reflect that a student is on the "correct" path (meeting state expectations)?
- MM: Wanted a way to compare overall grades of her classes to their other grades. Sees a similar pattern, but perhaps no direct correlation.

What questions does this text raise for you?

- CD: Could Mickey's high-performers (yet low SSS ALs) be due to particular teaching methods used?
- NJD: Worried about misuse of data in justifying our own personal agendas or matching our own expectations? Is it wrong to put more trust in data than personal methods and observations?
- TR: How will you (Mickey) let this data impact your instruction?
- MM: Adamant about late work = zero policy. Hoping that ninth-grade team meetings would result in better student work turn-in rate.
- TR: Would you use this data to affect how you weight different categories of class assignments (readings, tests, etc.)?
- MM: Possibly, but past experience shows it doesn't overall affect student work completion.
- AM: How much reading is in Mickey's bio class?
- MM: Minimal, often based on notes, quizzes, essays.
- TR: How much of biology is based on ability to read textbook vs. comprehend material and form/reason original conclusions?
- CK: Is having increased # of intervention math students in biology next year going to adversely affect overall bio grade distribution?

Implications on Our Work

- NJD: It is good to collect data; have a quantitative approach ... but not a good idea to base legislation on it ... but conversations like this are a good idea. Fears government moving forward without adequate teacher input.
- AM: Did a student's low FCAT score prevent them from taking a higher-level science? (Bio Honors, e.g.) Frustrated.
- BR: 90%+ students are within one letter grade (between sci/math); believes this an indicator of balance and the grading system in general.

SOURCE: Used with permission of Mickey MacDonald.

In this next excerpt from Mickey's work, note the ways in which CFG feedback, as a source of data, stimulated Mickey's own thinking about her research, as well as how it led to her collection of additional data through student interviews, providing another example of the ways data collection and analysis are iterative processes. Finally note the ways in which Mickey's inquiry led to action (changes she planned to make in her practice based on what she learned through this cycle of inquiry).

Using the collection of comments from each CFG discussion, I summarized each step in the *Making Meaning of Text Protocol*. In the first step, "Describing the Text," members were asked "what they saw" when looking at my Excel spreadsheet data. Members were reminded to make comments without judgments or interpretations. Some quotes from members (denoted in italics) are followed by interpretations or questions that I have about each comment (in plain print):

- *"(There are) lots of C/C/3/3 students."*

  Many of the students received semester grades of "C" in biology and their math class and also had Level 3 on their reading and math FCAT scores.

- *"In the D-range for biology, there are a larger number of Level 1s and 2s in reading and math scores."*

  I need to see how many students with a semester grade of "D" are Level 1 or Level 2 in FCAT reading and math.

In the second step of the Making Meaning of Text Protocol, CFG members posed questions that my spreadsheet raised for them. Some questions shared by my colleagues (denoted in italics and followed by my interpretations/questions in plain print) included the following:

- *"Disbursements of Ds and Fs . . . (There are) many Fs in science but only two across the board in math. Is this because of intensive math classes?"*

  All of my students are in one level of science. The same students are split into seven levels of math classes ranging from Intensive Math 1 (a remedial mathematics course) through Geometry Honors.

- *"How can we apply this type of data to directly solve something in our courses?"*

  This question concerning data-driven instruction is asked more and more frequently of teachers.

- *"Might this data reflect students who know the material but who lack a strong school work ethic?"*

I need to examine the homework grades and compare these to biology test scores to see if, in fact, these students do know the material but do not complete homework.

In the third step of the Making Meaning from Text Protocol, my critical friends were asked the questions, "What is significant about my spreadsheet?" and "What meaning can you construct from it?" Comments (denoted in italics and followed by my interpretations/questions in plain print) included the following:

- *"There shouldn't be this many Biology 1 students."*

Maybe we should offer alternate choices for the science class that students can take in ninth and tenth grade. With the new legislation that the Florida Department of Education is implementing with the incoming ninth-grade class of 2007–2008, we will need to offer a "major" in the area of science. This may allow for more choices for our students.

- *"Worried about misuse of data. . . . Is it wrong to put more trust in (this kind of) data than personal methods and observations?"*

Looking at number data may negate a critical form of assessment that teachers use all the time to ensure student learning.

- *"Would you use this data to affect how you weight different categories of class assignments (readings, tests, etc.)?"*

I am not sure that this is the real issue I need to focus on. Altering the weighting may cause the grade distribution to shift left, but it doesn't change student learning in any way.

Following the CFG discussions of the data, I used colleagues' suggestions to closely examine the data by gender and by grade level. I was astonished by the grade distributions of my male students compared to my female students. Although the female grade distribution looked much like a bell curve, the male distribution was extremely skewed to the right, with a high percentage of Ds and Fs. This data clearly shows that I am not reaching my male population.

Based on another recommendation from the CFG discussion, I sorted my data based on grade level. When I analyzed this data, the grade distributions by gender and grade level were again the same for both ninth- and tenth-grade males. They were all skewed to the right. For the ninth- and tenth-grade females, the graphs were the shape of bell curves. Regardless of the grade level of my students, I am not reaching my male students.

Following the CFG insights into my student data and my own detailed analysis of my student data, I decided to interview two subgroups of students. First, I wanted to talk to female students who were achieving at a high level in biology, even though they were below grade level in reading. Next, I wanted to interview male students who were not achieving in biology but were at or above grade level in reading and math.

My first interview was with a tenth-grade female student who received an "A" in biology, although she had scored a Level 1 in reading on the FCAT. I asked her the following question: "Biology requires extensive reading. Your FCAT reading score is low, and yet you scored an 'A' for first semester in biology. What do you feel allowed you to be so successful in biology this year?" She responded with the following:

- "Different subjects in biology holds interest better than the FCAT reading topics."
- "(We) repeat material in biology over and over and follow the textbook."
- "I learn from listening, not reading."
- "Reading strategies used in Intensive Reading are also used in biology, like highlighting and anticipation guides."
- "Teacher explanations (are helpful)."

A second tenth-grade female, an "A" student in biology who also performed at a Level 1 in reading on the FCAT, responded with the following:

- "I try really hard—good grades are important to me."
- "I always do my homework."
- "I ask questions."
- "I have more time in biology than on the FCAT—I'm not stressed in class."

Next, I interviewed a tenth-grade male student who received a "D" in biology yet scored a Level 4 in reading and math on the ninth-grade FCAT. I said to this student, "Your FCAT scores are excellent in both reading and math. Your grade in biology is a D. Why do you think you are not doing better in biology?" This is what he told me:

- "I'm unorganized and the homework policy hurts me. If I can't finish work in class, it doesn't get done or it doesn't get brought back to class. I get a lot of zeros on homework."
- "There is a lot more homework in high school than in middle school. It counts more."
- "I like hands-on stuff; we don't do enough hands-on in class."
- "I don't study much."

As a teacher, these interviews tell me that I need to continue to emphasize organizational skills to my students through modeling. I need to offer different ways of learning the curriculum. This might include more hands-on activities for the kinesthetic learners. I also need to figure out a way to avoid punishing students who can learn the material without completing the repetitive assignments that other students require to be successful.

So much data, so little time . . . yet I have managed to gain some insights into what all this data means for me and how this inquiry has changed how I view my charge as a teacher. I am beginning a new academic year now. My main goal for this year is to target those male students who have poor work habits in homework completion and poor organizational skills. The two areas that I will address to help this group of students are maintaining organized, complete notebooks and increasing the number of inquiry, hands-on type activities. I will model maintaining an organized notebook. Open notebook quizzes which reward students who stay organized will be utilized regularly. I will sit down with specific students to be certain that they complete their notebook as demonstrated.

I will also use more hands-on, inquiry type activities with my regular Earth Science classes in order to increase student engagement. Hands-on activities will require that the students work in groups for extended times. Because management of behavior during hands-on activities is a concern for me, I will be working with two middle school teachers who facilitate group work regularly, as well as two high school science teachers who have been doing inquiry science within their classes. I also plan to attend a Kagan Workshop on cooperative learning. This is offered as a professional development opportunity at our school.

This is my second inquiry project in as many years. The value of looking at my practice and choosing what I feel will help me as a teacher, as well as my students as learners, is immeasurable. The questions answered through inquiry have led me to ask more questions. These can only be answered through more cycles of inquiry. A new school year and so many new inquiry prospects . . . what an exciting process! (MacDonald, 2007, pp. 53–57)

WHEN DO I COLLECT DATA AND HOW MUCH DO I COLLECT?

Now that you have seen some examples of what data collection might look like, you are ready to think about your own wondering and which forms of data collection might work for you. Like Debbi and Mickey, most teacher-inquirers find more than one data collection strategy will connect to their wondering and, subsequently, evoke more than one form of data collection in the design of their study. Using multiple sources of data can enhance your inquiry as you gain different perspectives from different strategies. In addition, by employing multiple strategies, you are able to build a strong case for your findings by pointing out the ways different data sources led you to the same conclusions. Research methodologists refer to the use of multiple data sources as "triangulation" (Creswell, 1998; Patton, 2002). Finally, by employing multiple data sources you enhance your opportunities for learning when different data sources lead to discrepancies. It is often through posing explanations for these discrepancies that the most powerful learning of teacher inquiry occurs and that new wonderings for subsequent inquiries are generated.

As teacher-inquirers ponder the "how" of data collection and select strategies they wish to employ, they must also ponder related questions of how long they will collect data and how much they will collect. The "when" and "how long" of data collection is often answered by natural constraints of time imposed by such things as the length of a unit if you are doing a curriculum inquiry or the due date for your paper if engaging in inquiry as part of your student teaching or a graduate course. Optimally, data collection would proceed until you reach a state where you are no longer gaining insights into your wondering or question and no new information is emerging. This state is termed saturation by research methodologists (Creswell, 1998; Patton, 2002).

The complexities of teaching are so great, however, that in teacher research, you could be collecting data and waiting for saturation to occur indefinitely. Never drawing closure to an inquiry robs you of experiencing a process that is one of the most rewarding and exhilarating components of teacher inquiry—deeply immersing yourself in your data, articulating findings, and allowing new wonderings to emerge. Therefore, it is important that you bind your study in a particular time frame. You must make decisions about when and how long as you balance what is feasible to do in the real world of your classroom and what is optimal for providing insights into your topic.

At this point it is extremely valuable to develop a comprehensive plan for your inquiry. Hubbard and Power (1999) suggest that teacher-inquirers write a research brief, defined as "a detailed outline completed before the research study begins" (p. 47). A research brief may cover such aspects as the purpose of your study, your wonderings, how you will collect data, how you will analyze data (we explore this in Chapter 6), and a time line for your study. Through the process of developing a brief, teacher-inquirers commit their energies to one idea. This commitment facilitates an inquirer's readiness to begin data collection.

We end this chapter with three very different examples of research briefs. The first brief (Figure 4.18), written by teacher Robin Livingston, is focused on a very contemporary topic many teachers in a variety of contexts and grade levels may have pondered—the integration of student cell phones into instruction. The second brief (Figure 4.19), developed by Abbey Wilson, illustrates the planning process used by a preservice teacher engaging in inquiry as a part of a field experience in a special education setting. The third and final brief (Figure 4.20) was developed by Mickey MacDonald, a highly experienced inquirer whose work was used as an example in this chapter. Looking at briefs developed in different contexts and different grade levels and that represent different levels of inquiry experience can help you decide on your own approach to planning an inquiry. Following these sample briefs, you'll find three exercises you may wish to complete to help you develop your own plan—and begin!

Figure 4.18   Inquiry Brief Example 1: Robin Livingston

Using Cell Phones to Enhance Instruction

Robin Livingston

Purpose

Approximately 84% of high school students own a cell phone (Engel & Green, 2011). Most high schools around the country have some type of strict rule about cell phone and electronic device usage. Most of those rules include leaving the devices at home or turned off in backpacks (Engel & Green, 2011). Students currently in high school appreciate active learning and multi-tasking and some seem to think that using cell phones in the classroom for educational purposes would aid in the education of our students (Humble-Thaden, 2011). Many students and teachers even disregard the rules about electronic devices. According to Anita Charles (2012), there are three steps to take at the beginning of implementing cell phones into the classroom to minimize the amount that students take advantage of the process: define inappropriate times for cell phone usage, incorporate new media into pedagogy, and develop methods for discourse when using cell phones in the class.

As a teacher in a social studies classroom at the high school level I am faced with many challenges. Two of those challenges are motivating my students to take responsibility for their learning and to prepare them for a world that consists of ever-changing technology. My classroom has the least amount of technology used for teaching and learning in the whole school. I have a projector and three working computers, compared to the

(Continued)

Figure 4.18   (Continued)

other classrooms with at least six working computers and an ActivBoard (an interactive Smartboard). With only three computers, classroom research and other computer related activities are nearly impossible. Because of this dilemma, I have asked permission from my administration to do a pilot program where students are able to utilize their own personal mobile devices (cell phones, tablets, iPods) for classroom needs to determine the benefit those devices can have on the learning in my class.

Next school year, my limited technology will no longer be an issue because my building will be torn down and a new three story building will be built in its place. Technology will be available in that new classroom, and my hope is that I will still be able to supplement mobile device technology into my classroom to create a technology rich environment. Based on the results of this inquiry and the student reflections, grant requests might also allow me to further the use of mobile devices within my classroom.

Questions

What benefits can mobile devices have on student learning and class participation when utilized for educational purposes to supplement classroom technology?

Subquestions

How will using mobile devices in class affect students without their own personal mobile devices?

How can I create a climate of mobile device etiquette so students take responsibility for learning while in class?

Methods

I will work with my World History class of 30 students. They have already been introduced to the idea of using mobile devices in class but have not gone much further than that. We will create a list of rules and etiquette to use in class when mobile devices are permissible. I have already assigned each student to a group of three based on reading level, classroom personality, and preferred learning style (visual, auditory, etc.). Each of the ten groups is named using a color. I will assign a mini-project for the students to complete during class where they answer an open-ended question, which requires Internet research. The mini-project will be during a unit on the Middle Ages. The students will have the option to use their mobile devices for research during class. Each group has at least one member in the group that owns a mobile device for classroom use.

Additionally, two surveys will be distributed (pre and post) to students to determine their excitement and level of interest in using mobile devices during class. The post survey will gauge their level of satisfaction with the mobile device usage in the classroom, issues that they encountered, and their perception of its effects on student learning.

During class time that is not spent working on the mini-project, students will have opportunities to utilize mobile devices for instant polls, notes, flashcards, and other applications discovered through research and student input.

Throughout this process, research will be conducted to find relevant literature on the topic of mobile device usage in the classroom. Because of the potential problems relating to this topic, literature will be used to modify classroom procedures if needed, educate parents and other faculty members of the benefits of mobile device technology in the classroom, and for ideas on additional ideas to incorporate mobile devices into the classroom.

Data Collection

- Observation/field notes—Journal after each class, observation of student engagement during class
- Student surveys (pre and post)
- Literature on mobile device technology use in the classroom
- Student artifacts
- Student interviews

Calendar

Date	Activities
Week of October 15–19	1. Reintroduce concept of using mobile devices during specific class time. 2. Create list of rules and etiquette for mobile device learning time. 3. Create and distribute survey on student feelings of learning and technology use in the classroom.
Week of October 22–26	1. Collect field notes. 2. Research literature on mobile devices in classrooms. 3. Assign mini-project on Middle Ages for students to use mobile devices.
Week of October 29–30	1. Collect field notes. 2. Research literature on mobile devices in classrooms. 3. Classroom activities aside from mini-project to utilize mobile devices (notes, interactive apps ...).
Week of November 5–8	1. Collect field notes. 2. Distribute another survey to students on learning and use of mobile devices in classroom.

Data Analysis

To be determined

References

Charles, A. (2012). Cell phones: Rule-setting, rule-breaking, and relationships in classrooms. *American Secondary Education, 40*(3), 4–16.

Engel, G., & Green, T. (2011). Cell phones in the classroom: Are we dialing up disaster? *Techtrends: Linking Research & Practice To Improve Learning, 55*(2), 39–45.

Humble-Thaden, B. (2011). Student reflective perceptions of high school educational cell phone technology usage. *Journal of Technology Studies, 37*(1), 10–16.

SOURCE: Used with Permission of Robin Livingston.

Figure 4.19   Inquiry Brief Example 2: Abbey Wilson

Using Manipulative Materials to Enhance Math Instruction in a Special Education Classroom

Abbey Wilson

Purpose

The purpose of this action research project is to investigate the impact of using manipulative materials to teach basic math concepts in a kindergarten through second grade special education classroom.

Guiding Question(s)

What is the relationship between the use of manipulative materials and the learning of basic math concepts for students with disabilities?
   Subquestions include:

1. What effect will the use of manipulative materials have on my students' understanding of the concepts being taught?

2. What effect will the use of manipulative materials have on my students' attitudes toward basic math concepts?

3. What are some effective ways to incorporate manipulative materials into my teaching?

4. How will students use the manipulative materials in math and in other areas of learning?

Context

The students are enrolled in an elementary special education classroom that serves children in K through second grade levels. The average class size is from five to ten students and these students are pulled out of the general education classrooms for specialized instruction throughout the day.

Data Sources & Collection Schedule	Data Analysis	Questions Data Addresses

Mathematics Knowledge
 	
1. Assessment of Knowledge
   a. Pretest of students' skills with basic math concepts.
   b. Class questions given during lesson every day. Take observations and anecdotal notes.
	1. Analyze and graph individual scores. Examine individual scores as well as group averages. Use this formative data analysis to change the focus of the lessons and use of the manipulative materials.	How did students use the manipulative materials and apply them to other areas of learning?

Data Sources & Collection Schedule	Data Analysis	Questions Data Addresses
c. Conferences. Students respond to teacher's questions about certain problems and how using manipulative materials helps them and why.	Analyze conference notes for different themes and patterns.	What effect did the use of manipulative materials have on students' attitudes toward basic math concepts?
2. Class work consists of problems done in class, on handouts, and on the chalkboard, white board, and individual dry erase boards.	2. By having students complete problems during class it allows me to observe if and in what ways students were using the manipulative materials to solve the problems. I am able to discuss with the students the steps they are taking as they work on solving the problems. I observe and record anecdotal notes of their work and discussion. Observation notes will be reviewed and analyzed for patterns and themes.	What effect did the use of manipulative materials have on students' understanding of the concepts being taught? How did students use the manipulative materials and apply them to other areas of learning?
Effective Teaching 3. Researcher journal. Write in daily to discuss how students respond to the use of the different manipulative materials for each lesson. I also will write about the comments they made. I will assess my instruction and changes I want to make.	3. Allows me to think about how things are going in the classroom and with the students. This allows me to look at the lessons and how the students are responding to them, and compare it to the graphs of the grades from their homework and quizzes.	What are some effective ways to incorporate manipulative materials into my teaching?

SOURCE: Used with Permission of Abbey Wilson.

Figure 4.20   Inquiry Brief Example 3: Mickey MacDonald

Taking Action With Assessment for Learning

Mickey MacDonald

Purpose

Over the past two years at my school, a strand of our professional development has involved Assessment for Learning (AfL), or formative assessment practices. Based on the work of the Assessment Training Institute headed by Rick Stiggins, we have begun to transform our instructional practice to include formative assessment. Most of my current knowledge about AfL has come from Knowledge for Practice, through participation in trainings on Assessment for Learning. As a classroom teacher, the more that I begin to use AfL, the more questions I have about the theory of AfL and the implications for my instructional practice and student learning.

An important component of formative assessment generally and AfL specifically is student self-assessment. The skill of self-assessment requires that students become metacognitive about their learning (Black et al., 2012; Hattie & Timperley, 2007; Ibabe & Jauregizar, 2010; Kostons et al., 2012; Pintrich, 2002). Students who internalize self-assessment skills and use them effectively tend to become self-regulated learners. Such students are self-aware of their strengths and weaknesses and know how to adjust the ways in which they interact with new material to increase their understanding (Pintrich, 2002).

As with teaching content, teachers must explicitly teach students to use metacognition in their learning (Black et al., 2012; Pintrich, 2002). Andrade and Valtcheva (2012) found that students who actively use rubrics that include clear criteria to self-assess their work produce higher quality work and improve their learning. This finding further supports the need to provide clear criteria for each learning goal and to share such criteria with students.

At my school, the 9th grade team is transitioning to a blended learning instructional format. Blended learning can take many forms within K–12 education. The model of blended learning that we use is the "Station-Rotation Model."

> Within a given course or subject (e.g., math), students rotate . . . at the teacher's discretion among classroom-based learning modalities. The rotation includes at least one station for online learning. Other stations might include activities such as small-group or full-class instruction, group projects, individual tutoring, and pencil-and-paper assignments. Some implementations involve the entire class alternating among activities together, whereas others divide the class into small-group or one-by-one rotations. (Innosight Institute, 2012, para. 2)

Part of student instruction within biology will be face to face instruction and part of instruction will be online. My intention is to utilize online learning for three important instructional purposes. First, students will complete formative assessment activities that allow me to determine where they are in relation to specific learning targets. Second, I will use this formative assessment data to lead students to instructional activities that will allow them to fill any gaps they may have with particular learning goals. Finally, as students independently interact with online content, I will pull students into small group instruction who need additional teacher support with learning. Although pulling small groups of students for additional support is commonly achieved in elementary classrooms, such instructional practice in high school settings is nearly nonexistent.

Questions

I have already begun my inquiry work at my school this year, which is an extension of my inquiry work over the past two years. My main wondering is:

In what ways will moving to a more blended learning environment allow for ongoing assessment for learning, implementation of differentiated instruction in a secondary biology classroom, and preparation for the biology end of course exam?

Within my main wondering, I have two subwonderings:

1. In what ways can a blended learning instructional model leverage student learning opportunities that promote autonomous or self-regulated learning among 9th grade biology students?

2. What classroom structures need to be in place to allow small group instruction within a high school biology classroom?

Kristin Weller, who teaches geometry using an AfL framework, and I will be completing a shared inquiry that will be a component of subwondering 1.

How can we scaffold the use of self-assessment of learning targets and formative assessment data to teach struggling students how to

- reflect on what they know;
- reflect on what they do not know; and
- develop action steps to fill in the gap before they take a summative assessment?

Methods

I will be working directly with four students during the ecology unit beginning the week of October 15th. I have chosen these particular students based on past performance in biology. Each student has scored poorly on short content quizzes and on unit tests. Although three of the four students generally complete all classroom assignments, they do not connect what they are learning in the activity with the corresponding learning target nor do they understand that the purpose for completing the activity is to learn, not simply to get the assignment done. As a result, the quality of the assignment suffers because the students' goal is completion not learning.

Prior to beginning the ecology unit, students will complete a baseline self-assessment of the ecology learning targets using a Google form. I will contact each of the parents of the four students to get their cooperation in having their student attend two afterschool group study sessions each week during the ecology unit. During each study session, students will complete a formative assessment on each learning target that was covered in class prior to the help session and they will self-assess each of the targets based upon their formative assessment scores. I will use their formative assessment scores to model how to use such data to make an action plan to fill any gaps in understanding during the

(Continued)

Figure 4.20   (Continued)

first week of study sessions. Within the subsequent study session, students will develop their own action plan and either work independently on an online activity to fill the gap or receive Tier III support from Dr. Kort, our secondary support specialist, or from me. At the end of each study session, students will complete an exit slip on the learning targets and a reflection on how the learning activity(ies) they completed connected to the learning target(s). I will complete a journal entry via a 10-minute quick write following each session to capture my thoughts about the study session, ideas I want to implement or change, and observations I make about each of the students.

Within class, I will have students track (graph) their scores on the short content quizzes and on the ecology unit test and compare these scores to their quiz and test scores from the previous two units. At the final study session, I will interview the students via a focus group to capture what they learned about the relationship among the instructional activities that they do in class and for homework, the learning targets, and the assessments.

Following the unit assessment, I will contact each student's parent(s) and discuss the results of the study sessions, their student's progress, and ways to continue to support their student's academic success.

Data Pieces

- Pre, during, and post unit self-assessment data
- Formative assessment data
- Student artifacts

  o study session exit slips on progress toward meeting learning targets
  o reflections on connections between learning activities and learning targets
  o action plans
  o tracking graphs/comparison of scores

- Student interviews via focus group
- Quiz and unit test scores
- Attendance records
- 10-minute quick write reflection journal

Calendar

Date	Activities
Week of October 8–12	**Create cohesive unit plan** 1. Decide on specific instructional activities for each learning target 2. Find alternative activities for each learning target for additional support 3. Create formative assessments for each learning target 4. Create short content quizzes 5. Create summative assessment 6. Contact each of the parents and set up study session schedule

Week of October 15–19	**Begin study sessions (2)**
	1. Collect exit slips on learning targets and copies of student reflections and action plans
	2. Pre-unit self-assessment of learning targets via Google form
	3. Students set up assessment tracking graph
	4. Complete formative assessment on learning targets covered in class followed by self-assessment of learning targets following instruction
	5. 10-minute quick writes
Week of October 22–26	**Continue study sessions (2)**
	1. Collect student artifacts (exit slips on learning targets and copies of student reflections and action plans)
	2. Complete formative assessment on learning targets covered in class followed by self-assessment of learning targets following instruction
	3. Students graph quiz scores from ecology unit
	4. 10-minute quick writes
Week of October 29–30	**Continue study sessions (1)**
	1. Collect student artifacts (exit slips on learning targets and copies of student reflections and action plans)
	2. Complete formative assessment on learning targets covered in class followed by self-assessment of learning targets following instruction
	3. Students graph quiz scores from ecology unit
	4. 10-minute quick writes
Week of November 5–8	**Final study sessions (2)**
	1. Collect student artifacts (exit slips on learning targets and copies of student reflections and action plans)
	2. Students complete post-unit self-assessment of all learning targets via Google form
	3. Students graph quiz scores and unit test scores from ecology unit
	4. Run focus group/interviews
	5. 10-minute quick writes
	6. Follow-up contact with parents

References

Andrade, H., & Valtcheva, A. (2012). Promoting learning and achievement through self-assessment. *Theory into Practice, 48*(1), 12–19. doi:10.1080/00405840802577544

(Continued)

Figure 4.20 (Continued)

Black, P., McCormick, R., James, M., & Pedder, D. (2012). Learning how to learn and assessment for learning: A theoretical inquiry. *Research Papers in Education, 21*(2), 119–132. doi:10.1080/02671520600615612

Hattie, J., & Timperley, H. (2007). The power of feedback. *Review of Educational Research, 77*(1), 81–112. doi:10.3102/003465430298487

Ibabe, I., & Jauregizar, J. (2010). Online assessment with feedback and metacognitive knowledge. *Higher Education, 59*(6), 243–258. doi:10.1007/s10734–009–9245–6

Innosight Institute (2012). Innosight institute—Blended-learning model definitions. Retrieved from www.innosightinstitute.org/media-room/publications/blended-learning/blended-learning-model-definitions.

Kostons, D., van Gog, T., & Paas, F. (2012). Training self-assessment and task selection skills: A cognitive approach to improving self-regulated learning. *Learning and Instruction, 22*(2), 121–132. doi:10.1016/j.learninstruc.2011.08.004

Pintrich, P. (2002). The role of metacognitive knowledge in learning, teaching, and assessing. *Theory into Practice, 41*(4), 219–225. Retrieved from www.jstor.org/stable/1477406.

CHAPTER 4 EXERCISES

1. Begin your own data collection process with the strategy every teacher researcher should use—the collection of some literature related to your inquiry topic. Using the search strategies we described in this chapter, find three to five reputable pieces of literature related to your inquiry topic. What insights do these pieces of literature provide for you related to your inquiry topic? How does the study you are developing connect or relate to this literature? In what ways, if any, might you refine the wondering you developed in Chapter 2 based on your reading of this literature?

2. Brainstorm what types of data collection strategies you might employ by creating a data collection chart. Title your chart with your main inquiry question and generate two columns: (1) information that would help me answer my question and (2) data collection strategies that would generate this information. An example based on Brian and Gail's work appears in Table 4.1.

Table 4.1 In What Ways Do Science Talks Enhance Student Understandings of Science Concepts?

Information That Would Help Me Answer My Question	Data Collection Strategies That Would Generate This Information
Knowing how students' conceptual knowledge develops during our astronomy unit	Collect the students' science journals
Knowing what students are saying during Science Talks	Audio taping Science Talks, taking field notes

Information That Would Help Me Answer My Question	Data Collection Strategies That Would Generate This Information
My thinking about what happened during the Science Talks after they occur	Teacher journal
Students' opinions about Science Talks	Surveys
Literature on Science Talks; I'm already familiar with Karen Gallas's book *Talking Their Way Into Science*	Searching for other books or articles connected to Science Talks, building conceptual knowledge in science, teaching elementary science, and so on

3. Create your own inquiry brief that includes all of the aspects of conducting a teacher inquiry we have explored so far (e.g., wonderings and questions, collaborative support, and data collection strategies). Begin your brief with a statement that summarizes the purpose of your inquiry. End your brief with a detailed time line for completing your study. Once you have developed a draft of your brief, you may wish to consult Chapter 3 of the text *Digging Deeper Into Action Research* (Dana, 2013) to refine and fine-tune your plan.

Considering the Ethical Dimensions of Your Work as an Inquirer

At this point in the book, you've developed a wondering as well as a plan to gain insights into that wondering through the collection of multiple forms of data and are likely ready to move forward full steam ahead with the data collection process. Before moving forward however, it is important to pause for a brief moment to engage in a careful and close examination of any ethical issues that might be related to your study. With an inquiry brief developed and a plan for your research taking shape, this is the perfect time to consider the ethical dimensions of your work as an inquirer and make any changes or adjustments to your inquiry plans based on what you learn from your consideration of this topic.

WHAT SHOULD I CONSIDER WHEN THINKING ABOUT ETHICS IN RELATIONSHIP TO PRACTITIONER RESEARCH?

Most professions have a code of ethics that delineates the guidelines and responsibilities for those who work within it. Teaching is no different, with several organizations and individual states publishing a code of ethics to guide educators. For example, the National Education Association's (NEA) Code of Ethics states the following:

> The educator, believing in the worth and dignity of each human being, recognizes the supreme importance of the pursuit of truth, devotion to excellence, and the nurture of the democratic principles. Essential to these goals is the protection of freedom to learn and to teach and the guarantee of equal educational opportunity for all. The educator accepts the responsibility to adhere to the highest ethical standards. (NEA, 2013)

Similar to many other professional standards for teaching, these NEA standards are based on two principles—a commitment to the student and a commitment to the profession. Each of these principles states an overarching obligation, followed by the ways educators fulfill that obligation. For example, the student principle states the following:

> The educator strives to help each student realize his or her potential as a worthy and effective member of society. The educator therefore works to stimulate the spirit of inquiry, the acquisition of knowledge and understanding, and the thoughtful formulation of worthy goals." (NEA, 2013)

A glance at these ethical standards for teaching helps to illuminate that when teachers engage in the process of inquiry, they are engaging in a process that is a natural and normal part of what good, ethical teaching is all about.

- Good and ethical teaching involves looking carefully and closely at student work that is generated in teachers' classrooms to better understand students' progress and what adjustments can be made to instruction to help *all* students learn.
- Good and ethical teaching involves assessing all students on a regular basis and analyzing scores on various assessment measures to help students master goals and objectives and achieve to their highest potential.
- Good and ethical teaching involves asking students questions about their learning to ascertain their understanding of content to inform instructional decisions that will ensure successful learning opportunities for *all*.
- Good and ethical teaching involves closely observing students as they work—watching for any behavior that provides insights into students' acquisition of knowledge and understanding and adjusting teaching according to these insights.

When the process of teacher inquiry is used as a professional development mechanism to help teachers learn and improve their own practice locally as well as to contribute to school improvement efforts, teachers are not doing anything differently than they would normally do as a good, ethical teacher. Engagement in teacher inquiry as a form of professional development simply makes the normal, everyday work of teaching less happenstance and more visible, heightening the opportunity for teachers to improve learning conditions in their classrooms on a regular basis. When inquiry is approached in this way, choosing *not* to engage in the process can almost be viewed as *un*ethical. Working in the best interest of the students you teach means carefully and systematically investigating your teaching and the relationship it has to your own students' learning. As such, it is important for all teacher-inquirers to keep general codes of ethical teaching conduct in mind as they teach and investigate their own teaching practice.

Yet a murkiness occurs when the ethics for the teaching profession in general meet the ethics for conducting research that govern academics working in a university setting. While engagement in teacher inquiry is different from engagement in the types of research done in higher education by academic researchers (as discussed in Chapter 1), both types of study share some common language and processes, although the language and processes mean different things. For example, Pritchard (2002) notes that even the word *research* itself is defined differently by practitioner inquirers and Institutional Review Boards (committees at universities that review, approve, and monitor research conducted at the institution to ensure ethical treatment and rights of humans in all research studies). According to Pritchard (2002), practitioner researchers "understand research as an integral part of what they do in the ordinary course of events as a way of improving their regular practice; practitioner research is a way for practitioners to learn on the job" (p. 4). In contrast, Pritchard notes that "IRB members rely on the regulatory definition of research":

> *Research* means a systematic investigation, including research development, testing, and evaluation, designed to develop or contribute to generalizable knowledge (34 Code of Federal Regulations 9CFR) 97.102[d]). (Pritchard, 2002, p. 4)

With differing understandings of and use of the word *research*, ethical considerations for the profession of teaching itself and ethical considerations for the conduct of research become muddled when engagement in teacher inquiry is part of university activities such as coursework or serves as a culminating project for a graduate degree program in the form of a master's thesis or dissertation. These complexities can lead to a lack of clarity for teacher inquirers regarding such university procedures as obtaining Institutional Review Board approval, as all involved in the practitioner inquiry movement ponder the question, "At what point does teaching become research?" (Nolen & Putten, 2007).

The answer to this question needs to be continually revisited, discussed, and debated in relationship to every inquiry you undertake. Pritchard (2002) notes,

A considerable portion of practitioner research falls outside the IRB's purview. Practitioner researchers may seek to improve their understanding of their own practice without pursuing generalizable findings (e.g., a teacher whose purpose is examining the development of a collective identity by a particular class or students). Or their research may not collect information from research subjects or design activities in ways that subordinate the participants' interests to the interest of knowledge (e.g., teachers whose research consists entirely of reviewing and developing curricula, or who observe and analyze peer interactions on the school playground). Research ethicists generally agree with the regulations that research is always shaped by the aim of generating knowledge; practitioners whose actions are designed exclusively to generate some benefit, while being aware that knowledge may accrue as a result, are not doing research. (Pritchard, 2002, p. 4)

As Pritchard continues his discussion of the relationship between practitioner research and IRBs, however, he illuminates why the answer to the question, "At what point does teaching become research?" is not crystal clear:

Practitioner research that meets the criterion of aiming to generate knowledge is complex because its dual purposes of generating knowledge and achieving a practical end are entangled, bringing into play both the research ethics perspective and the ethical demands of the practical activity. (Pritchard, 2002, p. 4)

In general, whether you are "teaching," "researching," or seamlessly intertwining the two, the role of ethics in any teaching endeavor ought be considered "in terms of how each of us treats the individuals with whom we interact at our school setting: students, parents, volunteers, administrators, and teaching colleagues" (Mills, 2014, p. 31). As Smith (1990) so eloquently states, "At a commonsense level, caring, fairness, openness, and truth seem to be the important values undergirding the relationships and the activity of inquiring" (p. 260). Keeping caring, fairness, openness, and truth at the forefront of your work as a teacher-inquirer is critical to ethical work.

WHAT ROLE DO SCHOOL DISTRICT RESEARCH POLICIES PLAY IN THE INQUIRY PROCESS?

If you are engaging in inquiry as a part of your school or district's professional development plan for teachers, be aware that individual school districts approach engagement in inquiry differently, and it's important to be attentive to and follow any school or district guidelines for this form of professional learning. While most school districts have policy and procedure in place to review and approve any research activity that occurs in schools and classrooms, teacher inquiry is often exempt from a formal review process by a district research office as it is considered a natural and normal part of the work teachers do to continually improve their own instructional practice.

For example, Fairfax County Public Schools, a district with a long, rich history in supporting teacher research, has the following statement in their district policy regarding research:

> Internal research studies . . . may be conducted without approval of the research screening process on behalf of Fairfax County Public Schools by staff members carrying out their assigned responsibilities to maintain and improve instructional programs and administrative practices. Parents and staff members shall have the right to inspect such studies, and materials used in connection with such studies, on request. Any data collection, reporting, and/ or related research activity undertaken within, or by, Fairfax County Public Schools shall protect the privacy of students, parents, and employees.

The Fairfax County Public School Policy brings up an important point to keep in mind as you engage in inquiry—the protection of the privacy of your students, parents, and colleagues. Hence, when sharing your inquiry work with others, it's important to consider removing any student, parent, or colleague identifying information from the discussion of your inquiry and even consider the use of pseudonyms when discussing individual students. For example, in the previous chapter, note the ways Mickey MacDonald and Debbi Hubbell did not include any student-identifying information in their presentation of data in Figures 4.15 and 4.16.

Related to the protection of privacy, when partnering with universities on inquiry work, districts are often most concerned with the Family Educational Rights and Privacy Act (FERPA), a federal law that protects the privacy of student education records. FERPA (www2.ed.gov/policy/ gen/guid/fpco/ferpa/index.html) has rules related to the types of student information that can be shared and with whom. FERPA does not have to be an insurmountable hurdle to districts and universities partnering to inform practice and improve learning conditions for children in classrooms through the process of inquiry.

For example, in order to cover course assignments that include inquiry work at their institution, the University of South Florida partnered with Hillsborough County Schools to develop a course task approval process so that every USF education student would not need to submit an individual request to use student data in inquiry-related activities. The approval process requires the college to collect from the university course instructors a list of inquiry task descriptions that are collectively presented to the district for review and approval. Next, the district reviews the assignments, asking for clarification when needed, and sends a single letter of approval to the college indicating which assignments have been approved. Finally, course instructors include the following information in course syllabi with each approved assignment/task:

> This project has been approved through the Hillsborough County Public School Research Review process. Note that individual student information is protected under the Family Educational Rights and Privacy Act (FERPA). The University of South Florida and Hillsborough County Public Schools both want to ensure that student records are protected and that teachers and potential teachers have the most appropriate training opportunities. Student Information (K–12) collected for this task will *not* include information that identified the individual student and any student identifiable information/data collected will *not* be retained (e.g., videos with students in them, copies of student work, audio recordings of student interviews, etc.) past the completion of the course and the assignment of a grade by the instructor/professor.

If you are engaging in inquiry as a part of university activity, be aware of FERPA and any district regulations related to it. You should also be aware of IRB processes and procedures.

WHAT ROLE DO UNIVERSITY INSTITUTIONAL REVIEW BOARDS PLAY IN THE INQUIRY PROCESS?

Just like school districts, institutions of higher education vary, and while IRBs often do not require approval for inquiry conducted as part of a university course, "the determining factor in the decision (usually) relates to whether or not the outcomes of the proposed study will be published or presented at a professional conference" (Mills, 2014, p. 30). A general rule of thumb at most universities is that if the inquiry will be published as a thesis or dissertation, or shared through publication in a national journal or presentation at a national meeting, the aim of the inquiry is to generate knowledge, and IRB approval should be obtained.

If IRB approval will be a part of your work as a teacher-inquirer, an important aspect of your application will be obtaining informed consent from the people you will be studying. In most cases for the teacher-inquirer, this refers to students, and if your students are under 18 years of age (which will be the case for almost all K–12 teacher inquirers), informed consent must be obtained from parents. The following letter, used by Ashley Pennypacker Hill in her inquiry into her teaching of self-regulation to learners receiving Tier 3 instruction in reading, serves as an example that may be useful in crafting your own informed consent form for an IRB application.

Dear Parent/Guardian,

I am a doctoral student in the School of Teaching and Learning at the University of Florida, conducting research on self-regulated learning under the supervision of Dr. Nancy Dana. The purpose of this study is to understand how to teach self-regulation to 5th-grade students receiving intensive Tier 3 reading supports and to help these learners transfer their self-regulation strategies to other contexts. The results of the study may help teachers better understand how to teach self-regulation. With your permission, I would like to ask your child to volunteer for this research.

Participation in this study does not change the instruction your student is currently receiving in reading. With your permission, I will collect artifacts of your child's work and perform a review of their academic data. Your child's identity will be kept confidential to the extent provided by law. Students' names will be replaced with a pseudonym. When the study is completed and the data have been analyzed, all will be destroyed. No names will be used in any reports. Participation or nonparticipation in this study will not affect grades or placement in any programs.

You and your child have the right to withdraw consent for your child's participation at any time without consequence. There are no known risks or immediate benefits to the participants. No compensation is offered for participation. If you have any questions about this research protocol, please contact me at XXX-XXXX or my faculty supervisor, Dr. Dana, at XXX-XXXX. Questions or concerns about your child's rights as research participant may be directed to the IRB02 office, University of Florida, Box 112250, Gainesville, FL 32611, (352) 392–0433.

Ashley Pennypacker Hill

Doctoral Candidate

School of Teaching and Learning

College of Education

University of Florida

_____

I have read the procedure described above. I voluntarily give my consent for my child, _____, to participate in Mrs. Pennypacker Hill's self-regulation study. I have received a copy of this description.

_____   _____

Parent/Guardian   Date

Notably, at some institutions, obtaining IRB approval can bog down a project, as those who sit on review boards are not always familiar with practitioner inquiry and may not understand the legitimacy of the movement as a way for teachers to learn about teaching while in the act of teaching and make more informed instructional decisions as a result of the process. Furthermore, IRBs are often made up of mainly quantitative researchers who approach research from a positivist paradigm. Without knowledge of the teacher inquiry movement and the purpose behind engaging in practitioner research, IRB members may reject a proposal outright under the assumption that studying one's own students is inherently unacceptable as it would be impossible for a teacher to avoid coercion of students into participation in the research (Brown, 2010). On another note, IRB members may view teacher research as "not quite meeting the definition of 'real' research, so that as long as proposed teacher research will not be conducted in unusual educational settings, it is automatically exempt" (Brown, 2010, p. 279).

Even if your work might be slowed down by ethical questions that emerge from others out of lack of knowledge about the practitioner inquiry movement, the ethics of your work is not something to shy away from but embrace. You can use ethical discussions to teach and inform others about the nature of a teacher's work and the ways engagement in the process of inquiry informs it. For example, when undergoing an internship period as a new IRB member, Oklahoma State University professor Pamela Brown questioned her IRB mentor on a teacher research proposal they had reviewed together:

> My mentor wanted to reject the proposal as written, claiming it would be impossible for a researcher soliciting participation from his own students to avoid coercion. I countered, ultimately successfully, that the field of teacher research was well respected and that rejecting the proposal for that reason would logically extend to all teacher research proposals, since by definition they involve teachers engaging in research in their own teaching settings. This stance by the IRB would stifle important voices and would be unacceptable. (Brown, 2010, p. 278)

Students, as well as their professors, can help educate reviewers about the practitioner inquiry movement by defining practitioner inquiry within their IRB proposals. For example, note the way Ashley Pennypacker Hill both included a definition of practitioner inquiry and pointed out the ways her study was a natural part of her teaching practice in the completion of the "Scientific Purpose of the Study" portion on her IRB application.

Scientific Purpose of the Study

Practitioner inquiry is defined as "systematic, intentional study by teachers of their own practice" (Cochran-Smith & Lytle, 1993). Engagement in practitioner inquiry has been an integral part of my growth as a professional educator, and I wish to use this method of systematic reflection to complete the capstone experience for the attainment of the Ed.D. degree.

Specifically, the purpose of my study is to understand how to teach self-regulation to 5th-grade students who struggle with reading and to help these learners transfer their self-regulation strategies to other contexts during the school day. Self-regulation is defined as the cycle of self-generated feelings, thoughts, and behaviors to strategically achieve personal goals (Paris & Paris, 2001; Perry, 1998; Zimmerman, 2000). Specifically, students are taught to reflect on their own learning before, during, and after assignments and to use their reflections to set personal goals for future achievement.

As a reading support specialist, I work daily with small groups of students to build their reading skills. Research indicates that self-regulation is an important skill for students to attain and has many benefits. Hence, I wish to incorporate the teaching of self-regulation strategies into my normal everyday practice as a teacher, and to document the teaching of these strategies to better understand the ways these strategies are working for my students. The incorporation of self-regulation teaching strategies into my daily practice as a classroom teacher will be utilized as the capstone experience for the attainment of my Ed.D. degree, and my work teaching self-regulation will be written about in form of a dissertation.

Regardless of whether you are engaging in inquiry as a mechanism for your own professional development within your school or district or engaging in inquiry as a part of your pathway to the attainment of a degree at a university (or a combination of both), you can embrace working through the ethical dimensions of your work by engaging in a "self-interrogation" of sorts, posing ongoing questions that need to be continually revisited as you teach and inquire into your teaching practice. Among others, for example, Brown (2010) suggests the following questions for the self-interrogation of teacher inquirers:

- What is the purpose of this proposed research?
- What data do I plan to collect—audiotapes, videotapes, student work samples, journal entries, observations?
- Might a layered consent/assent form be useful, in which participants check levels of participation to which they agree, such as use of work samples, use of journal entries, use of audiotapes, use of digital video?
- How can I make sure my research does not interfere with the academic mission of my role as a teacher?
- What is my place in terms of power? My students' place?
- Who might be negatively affected by my research? How do I guard against negative impact? (pp. 280–281)

In sum, the ultimate responsibility for ethical conduct as a teacher and a teacher-inquirer resides with you, with the ultimate goal of doing no harm to the students you teach or any other people involved in your inquiry. Whether you go through any mandatory research approval processes or not, "it is important you develop your own criteria for what you consider to be ethical behavior" (Mills, 2014, p. 32). We hope this discussion of inquiry and ethics provides a solid start for your consideration. For further reading on the subject, we suggest the following articles:

- Brown, P. (2010). Teacher research and university institutional review boards. *Journal of Early Childhood Teacher Education, 31,* 276–283.
- Pritchard, I. A. (2002). Travelers and trolls: Practitioner research and institutional review boards. *Educational Research, 31*(3), 3–13.

CHAPTER 5 EXERCISES

1. Engage in a discussion about the ethics of teaching and the ethics of doing research with one or more colleagues. Discuss and debate the question posed in this chapter, "At what point does teaching become research?"

2. Review the inquiry brief you created at the end of Chapter 4 in light of your discussion with colleagues of the question, "At what point does teaching become research?" Discuss your research briefs with one another to consider the ethical dimensions of the work you plan to undertake. Use the questions Brown (2010) suggests as you review each brief to inform your discussion. Make adjustments to your brief as needed as you take into account the ethical dimensions of your work as an inquirer.

6

Finding Your Findings

Data Analysis

Congratulations! As you begin this chapter, you are well on your way to completing your first inquiry. The good news is, with a wondering developed, a collaborative structure to support you, and data collected, you are ready to begin analyzing your data and writing up your work. This is also one of the most rewarding, exciting, thought-provoking, and growth-oriented components of inquiry!

You will learn in this chapter that there are two types of data analysis. The first type of data analysis we describe is ongoing throughout your entire inquiry and occurs *as* you are collecting your data. The second type of data analysis we describe takes place toward the end of your inquiry and occurs *after* you have finished data collection. Both types of analysis play an important role in the inquiry process.

WHAT IS FORMATIVE DATA ANALYSIS?

Recall Stephen Burgin's work studying extra-help sessions and the ways he could make these sessions more effective presented in Chapter 4. At about the midpoint of his inquiry, Stephen paused in his data collection process to carefully consider the data he had collected to date and what that data might tell him about where to go next in his study. At this point,

Stephen was able to name and sort his students into four categories of participation in help sessions based on looking at their completion of a survey at the start of his inquiry, considering attendance patterns at the extra-help sessions he had offered since then, and simply observing his students at extra help. The four categories of students that emerged for Stephen were students who attended and benefited from extra-help sessions, students who attended help sessions but did not benefit, students who did not attend help sessions and performed well in class, and students who did not attend help sessions but were struggling academically. He decided to proceed with his inquiry by strategically interviewing some students from each of these categories to gain insights into his wondering, "What is the most productive way to structure afterschool help?" The process of carefully considering data *as* you collect it, and using your consideration of it to help inform instructional decisions and next steps in your inquiry, is called *formative* data analysis.

WHAT MIGHT FORMATIVE DATA ANALYSIS LOOK LIKE?

In this section, we provide two examples of formative data analysis. The first example is taken from the work of May Steward, a middle school teacher supported in the inquiry process by her coach, Darby Delane. This example demonstrates the formative data analysis process in relationship to qualitative data collected (specifically focus group interview data) and foreshadows our discussion of the steps associated with the summative data analysis process that comes later in this chapter. The second example is taken from the work of Megan Hefner, a preservice teacher supported in the inquiry process by David Hoppey from the University of South Florida. This example demonstrates the formative data analysis process in relationship to quantitative data collected (specifically progress monitoring tools) and how such tracking over time can help a teacher make instructional decisions as an inquiry unfolds.

Example 1: A Seventh-Grade Science Teacher Analyzes Data at the Start of Her Inquiry

In line with the National Science Standards, May Steward was dedicated to investigation-based science teaching, where her students would actually experience the scientific process as much as possible, like real scientists. May liked to design her lessons to be action oriented, having students spend a majority of their time engaged in activities such as "asking questions, mixing chemicals, dissecting flowers, observing ants, and forming hypotheses before trying them out" (Wolk, 2008, p. 118). Yet, after a two-week break in the teaching routine because of testing and spring break, students were not behaving in ways conducive to May's implementation of an investigation-based curriculum and a positive classroom-learning environment. May found herself retreating from her investigation-based teaching methods and turned to direct, lecture-based instruction in an effort to "control" her students. Through discussions with her seventh-grade team, May realized she missed her investigation-based teaching methods and lamented that she was no longer able to teach science in ways consonant with her philosophy and best teaching practices advocated by the National Science Teachers Association. May realized that in order to return to investigation-based work at the end of the school year with her students, she needed to take a step back in order to take a step forward, looking closely at her classroom management. And so May turned to teacher research and embarked on her first cycle of the inquiry process by wondering, "How can I create the classroom management conditions needed so my students can be successful science learners?" (Delane, Dana, & Steward, 2010).

The inquiry plan she constructed called for the initial collection of data through leading a whole-class focus group interview with her fourth-period students to involve them in envisioning what a classroom environment conducive to learning science would look like. She began class by sharing with the students her observations of their behavior since coming back from two weeks of state testing and spring break, noting that because of their behavior, she had retreated from teaching science in the ways they all enjoy. She posed this whole-class focus group interview question to the class: "How can we work together to create the classroom conditions needed so we can all learn science in interesting ways?"

Students offered their ideas, while May recorded them on a large piece of chart paper at the front of the room. As May was recording responses, she noticed that only a handful of her entire class of students was participating. She remembered reading in Chapter 4 of this book that one of the limitations of focus group interviews was that "less confident focus-group members refrain from sharing their thoughts." With this in mind, May told her students they were going to end their discussion with each class member writing down one wish for their class so that at the end of the year, they would all feel that they were successful science learners. May thought by collecting written responses, every student's "voice" would be heard.

In order to analyze these responses, that evening, May typed up the 21 wishes that were turned in on her computer. After reading through all responses a few times, May experimented with grouping these responses in various ways. For example, she sorted the responses by gender. She took careful note of the responses made by her most struggling students. Finally, she settled on grouping the responses into three different categories and highlighted each category separately:

Category 1 (7 responses): Wishes for more fun and less pressure from school

Category 2 (5 responses): Wishes for a more calm and respectful environment

Category 3 (9 responses): Wishes for more consistency in class routine

Student Wish List Responses

1. Give respect to Ms. Steward and other classmates. Let's be kind and no arguing at one another.

2. I wish everyone would get an A and that we had more field trips.

3. Have our agenda done when Ms. Steward comes into the classroom. We can have out our paper and pencil and be ready to learn and have our homework out.

4. Come in and get ready and start on time. Maybe the deputy could come to class from lunch. That might help us.

5. Listen and be quiet.

6. I wish I could get us less homework.

7. I wish we could come to class, sit down, and get started on our work!

8. My wish for the whole class is to respect Mrs. Steward.

9. I wish people would stop being loud in Ms. Steward's class. It is loud sometimes.

10. We need to have more fun and more parties. And all A's.

11. Get ready for class all together would be good. Some do and some don't.

12. People need to come to class to learn! They need to focus. I wish they would focus.

13. To give me an A for no reason and to just be kind to people. Having a little bit of fun and not having all this homework. To be Friday every day!

14. My wish is to get more field trips out of town, and to give us less homework. Homework Mon.-Thurs. and Friday no homework.

15. Class would be good if it started on time every time.

16. I want to show Ms. Steward my respect. I want to have an S (Satisfactory) for conduct.

17. My wish is to have us all on the same page from the bell.

18. I wish L and T wouldn't bring in so much of their drama into class so we could get going on time.

19. I wish I was the richest person in the world.

20. Saying there is no homework! Saying we don't have to do nothing to pass!

21. I wish things would go in order the same way. So I know what to do.

May could certainly understand her students' craving for less pressure, especially because the school year was coming to a close and due to the fact that many of her students qualified for free and reduced lunch and faced uncertainty during the summer months. What was most significant to May, however, was that a good two-thirds of the class was looking for less drama and more stability in the classroom. May used this knowledge to fine-tune and reorder the interventions she had designed to implement as a part of her inquiry and focused the next phase of her research on developing a consistent class routine.

Example 2: An ESE Teacher Uses a Progress Monitoring Tool to Gain Insights Into Student Progress as Her Inquiry Unfolds

Megan Hefner, a special education preservice teacher, used inquiry informed by universal screening and progress-monitoring formative data to improve five kindergarten students' letter and sound recognition. Guided by her instructor and her mentor teacher, she followed four specific progress-monitoring steps: (1) student selection and problem description, (2) action planning, (3) intervention, and (4) outcome assessment.

Step 1: Student Selection and Problem Description

In line with the first step of the RtI process, Megan began her inquiry by identifying the student learning problem. In illustrating this first step, Megan reviewed data that indicated her students' inability to name letters and determine initial letter sounds as indicated by classroom performance and the district kindergarten universal screening inventory that included the Dynamic Indicators of Basic Early Literacy Skills (DIBELS) assessments. As a result, she asked, "How can I help this group of kindergarten students labeled as high risk for failure improve their letter and sound recognition?" In this example, Megan used data to identify a question related to a specific student learning need.

Step 2: Action Planning

To begin the second step in the process, Megan provided data that indicated her students' needs in early literacy skill development. She developed a goal for the academic intervention related to the action research question. For example, Megan's goal for one of the five students in her small group was that "by December 6 James will increase his letter identification rate from 11% accuracy to 85% accuracy during weekly trials." Next, Megan and her mentor collaboratively reviewed the early literacy literature to identify evidence-based practices that matched the small groups' needs and collaboratively designed when and what intervention(s) were necessary to change student performance for the targeted skills. These included phonemic awareness activities, manipulative letter work, Elkonin boxes, music-based activities, and multisensory strategies. Last, she designed a specific time line for action plan implementation. This process included ongoing data collection and analysis. Her plan included the frequency, time, and schedule for the intervention sessions as well as developed ongoing data collection and data analysis using a systemic progress monitoring plan. Once the RtI design worksheet was completed (see Figure 6.1), Megan started to implement the intervention.

Step 3: Intervention

Once the action plan was developed and approved, Megan began the intervention. Throughout the semester, she maintained a regular schedule of progress monitoring. By regularly scoring weekly monitoring probes and recording results, Megan developed data collection and analysis skills. She used graphing templates to assist in identifying learning trends during the progress monitoring period.

The collection of data, as displayed in Megan's graphs (Figures 6.2 and 6.3), allowed her to easily track progress, determine how a student was responding to the intervention, and adjust the intervention accordingly. The graphs of student data present Megan's representation of her students' learning gains across intervention sessions. As evident in the figures, Megan carefully included enough progress monitoring points to accurately create a trend line (e.g., typically 6–8) as well as a goal line (indicated by the dark black line in Figures 6.2 and 6.3). She also indicated that her targeted goals were consistent with the intervention plan by having the graph monitor the same need prioritized and addressed in the intervention plan. She also assured that there was adequate data for each student.

Figure 6.1 RtI Design Worksheet

Tier 2 - Small Group Intervention Form

Student(s): _____   DOB: _____

School: _____   Teacher(s): _____

Meeting Date: _____   Target Skill: _____

DIRECTIONS: This form is to be completed and approved before starting your strategy implementation project

Additional Data Indicating Need for Intervention (Benchmark and progress monitoring data must be attached.):	Instructional Procedures:	Times per week: 3 (Tues.-Thurs.)
Benchmark assessments	Orton Gillingham strategies including:	**Length of sessions:** 30 minutes
☐ *DIBELS indicated that this group of students are considered high risk for failure. They also scored low to high risk on the Initial Sound Fluency (ISF) measure. Student could identify 4 of 26 uppercase letters and 0 of 26 lowercase letters (10th percentile) and identifying from 0-11 initial sounds (ranged from the 6th and 44th percentile).*	☐ Hands on activities (sand writing Manipulative Letter Work/ Elkonin Boxes) ☐ Phonemic Awareness (oral Sound) work included using multi sensory strategies, (choral responding) and music based activities (*Alphabet Boogie, Who Let the Letters Out*).	**Tier 2 Initiation Date:** October 4 **Progress Monitoring Plan:** *Weekly using flash cards and a coding sheet for initial letter sounds as well as letter identification. Assessment will be determined based on the number of letters and sounds correctly identified.* *DIBELS ISF subtests assessment every two weeks.*
☐ *As indicated on the kindergarten inventory students weaknesses include naming the days of the week, recognizing basic shapes, and recognizing letters.*		*Daily observation notes on what is proving to work or not work during each session will be taken. Intervention will be adjusted accordingly.*

Goal Statement (This is one Example as each student had multiple goals for letter recognition and initial sound fluency.)

By December 6, James will increase his letter identification rate from 11% accuracy (3 of 26) to 85% accuracy (22 of 26) during weekly trials.

163

Step 4: Outcome Assessment

In sum, the data collected instructed Megan on whether to continue the current intervention, tweak or revise the intervention, discontinue the intervention and begin another, or refer her students for further evaluation based on the outcomes of this project. In the final report, Megan reflected on their work to decide whether the intervention was implemented with fidelity, the progress monitoring plan was appropriate, and the data were valid. She also gauged the relative success of the intervention and provided future recommendations. Megan's outcome assessment indicated that she was pleased with the progress of her students. Her visual representation of her data and writing summary suggests that students overall have improved their letter and sound recognition, though two students in particular struggled more than the others.

As illustrated, the integration of universal screening required Megan's attention to ongoing, tightly coupled assessment with instruction. This process included the integration of benchmark screening and diagnostic assessments as data sources for her inquiry. Using these tools

Figure 6.2 Letter Recognition

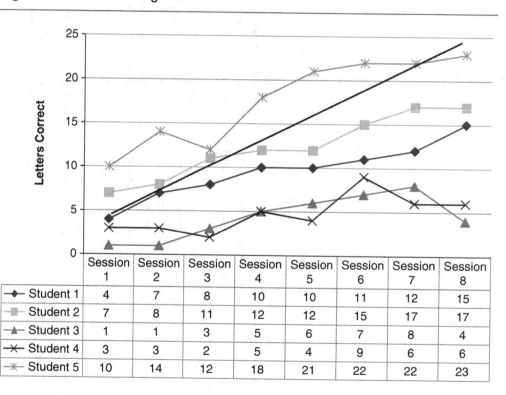

	Session 1	Session 2	Session 3	Session 4	Session 5	Session 6	Session 7	Session 8
Student 1	4	7	8	10	10	11	12	15
Student 2	7	8	11	12	12	15	17	17
Student 3	1	1	3	5	6	7	8	4
Student 4	3	3	2	5	4	9	6	6
Student 5	10	14	12	18	21	22	22	23

Figure 6.3   Sound Recognition

Sound Recognition

	Session 1	Session 2	Session 3	Session 4	Session 5	Session 6	Session 7	Session 8
Student 1	3	4	5	7	8	12	13	19
Student 2	4	6	6	7	10	12	21	19
Student 3	2	3	4	4	5	4	12	11
Student 4	1	2	3	3	4	3	11	6
Student 5	4	4	7	10	14	15	18	21

Megan formally assessed student progress using curriculum-based measurements. This strategy helped Megan to determine the effectiveness of her instructional interventions. By using these assessments, Megan was able to determine her students' progress using data-based decision making derived from observable and measureable outcomes. In combination, Megan used inquiry, progress monitoring, and universal screening assessments to help determine the effectiveness of her instruction.

We learn from the examples of May and Megan that analyzing data as you are in the midst of collecting it can provide great insights into your teaching and your inquiry as it unfolds. When you have completed the collection of all of your data however, there are more insights to be gained by considering your entire data set as a whole, rather than pieces or subsets of it over time throughout the course of your inquiry. After you have finished collecting all data, it's time to analyze and summarize what you've learned about yourself, your students, and your teaching as a whole. This process is called *summative* data analysis.

WHAT IS SUMMATIVE DATA ANAYSIS AND HOW DO I GET STARTED?

When teacher-inquirers get to this point in their inquiries, they often ponder, "OK, I've collected all of this 'stuff' (I have a whole crate full of data)—*now* what do I do with it?" Figuring out what to do with the mounds of data that have been collected over the course of an inquiry may be quite similar to the feeling you had when you began your inquiry. Overwhelmed by the complexities inherent in teaching and the subsequent numerous possibilities for inquiry, you may have found it difficult to decide on and develop a wondering. You asked yourself, "Where do I begin?" Recall in Chapter 2 that when we discussed the question of "Where do I begin?" we noted that wonderings do not materialize out of thin air.

The same is true of the conclusions you draw from summative analysis of your data as you near the end of a particular inquiry. Findings and conclusions do not materialize out of thin air—they come from careful scrutiny of your data as you proceed through a systematic process of making sense of what you learned.

Research methodologists have developed, described, and named a long list of systematic processes that facilitate summative data analysis. Two of the processes most frequently discussed in the social sciences are coding and memoing. We turn to Schwandt's (1997) *Qualitative Inquiry: A Dictionary of Terms* to provide brief, technical definitions of these concepts.

> *Coding*—To begin the process of analyzing the large volume of data generated in the form of transcripts, field notes, photographs, and the like, the qualitative inquirer engages in the activity of coding. Coding is a procedure that disaggregates that data, breaks it down into manageable segments and identifies or names those segments. . . . Coding requires constantly comparing and contrasting various successive segments of the data and subsequently categorizing them. (p. 16)

> *Memoing*—A procedure suggested by Barney Glaser (1978) for explaining or elaborating on the coded categories that the field-worker develops in analyzing data. Memos are conceptual in intent, vary in length, and are primarily written to oneself. The content of memos can include commentary on the meaning of a coded category, explanation of a sense of pattern developing among categories, a *description* of some specific aspect of a setting or phenomenon, and so forth. Typically, the final analysis and interpretation is based on integration and analysis of memos. (pp. 89–90)

While the summative data analysis work of a teacher-inquirer does draw from the field of social science and borrows the processes described by these scholars, getting bogged down in the jargon or technical language is easy. Phrases such as "disaggregating data," "coded categories," "phenomenon," and "final analysis and interpretation" may feel foreign to your teaching practice and set up a roadblock to data analysis. To help you around this roadblock, throughout this chapter, we describe the processes of summative data analysis using language, phrases, and metaphors that are consonant with your life and work as a teacher.

In addition to the technical jargon used by researchers, baggage that we carry with us about our own prior conceptions of what research is can make summative data analysis difficult. Many people conceptualize research and summative analysis as quantitative "number crunching" rather than qualitative "storytelling." Frankly, good research can be either. The research method and summative analysis procedures needed depend on your research question. Quantitative methods may be a part of your work if you've used Likert-scaled surveys, standardized test scores, grades, and/or assessment measures as part of your study. However, our experience suggests that teacher questions and the resulting summative analysis techniques tend to be more qualitative in nature since teacher questions often seek to understand a process or the nature of a classroom phenomenon. Thus, the summative data analysis process we discuss in this chapter is much more inductive in nature. Even though this process may be antithetical to the ways you've thought about research (what data are and how you've analyzed data in the past), letting go of these conceptions is an essential part of beginning the summative data analysis process.

A final reason summative data analysis can appear difficult is that the inductive process you are about to enter into is uncertain. Many qualitative researchers we have worked with have described analysis as "murky," "messy," and "creative." To help you understand the process and scale the three hurdles to data analysis (technical jargon, prior conceptions of research, and uncertainty), we end this section by defining and describing the summative analysis process as a metaphorical jigsaw puzzle.

If you are a jigsaw puzzle enthusiast, a useful way to understand the process of summative data analysis is to imagine yourself putting together what is touted in every hobby store across the nation as the "world's most challenging puzzle." One of the reasons for this description is that the puzzle comes in a bag, not the traditional box with a cover that pictures the completed puzzle. Hence, as you work, you know that the different pieces you are putting together will result in a picture, but you are uncertain of what it is going to look like in the end. To top it off, the directions to completing this puzzle indicate that there are more pieces in your bag than you will need, and other pieces may still be at the store!

Anxious to begin the puzzle, you start the process by just spreading all of the jigsaw pieces out on your table, with no other objective than to just look at what you have. Next, you begin to assess the puzzle pieces that lie before you by pondering, "What do I notice about these pieces that might give me insights into what this puzzle is going to be?" Based on what you notice, you begin a process of grouping or sorting. Perhaps you group all the pieces by similar color (e.g., blue), thinking that all of these blue pieces might fit together to create a sky, or you group by straight edges, knowing that these will form the perimeter of the completed piece. As you actually begin fitting pieces together and the picture begins to take shape, you may realize that some of the ways you grouped the remaining puzzle pieces are not correct (e.g., "Some of these blue pieces I thought might be sky really are part of a blue boat that is taking shape in the bottom right-hand corner of the puzzle"). You regroup as you continue your work on the puzzle, creating new, additional groupings or condensing two groupings into one.

At times the summative data analysis process feels overwhelming, as you may search for hours to find where one certain piece fits, only to conclude later that it is not even a part of the puzzle. Later, you realize you are missing two important pieces and subsequently must go back to the hobby store to find them. Although there are frustrations along the way, when you finally complete the puzzle, you take pride in your accomplishment.

When doing teacher inquiry and searching for what you have learned, the puzzle pieces are your data, and you are piecing your data together in different ways to create a picture of what you have learned for yourself and for others. The process is "messy," "murky," and "creative," because, just as the puzzle enthusiast must proceed without a box cover, at the start of the summative analysis process, you are not quite sure what this picture of your learning will look like—you must be patient as you allow your data to "speak" for itself and to lead you to your findings. Ashley Pennypacker Hill reflects on the importance of patience and trusting the process.

> When it became clear that summative data analysis was the next step in my inquiry, I felt like I had hit a brick wall. I was standing at the top of a mountain of data, and I knew I needed to dig my way through to get to the bottom of what I had learned through this inquiry, but didn't have an efficient digging strategy. I read about a four-step process in *The Reflective Educator's Guide to Classroom Research,* but wasn't there a quicker way to do this? I feared that the data analysis process was going to be so inefficient that I would pick my head up in 6 months and still not have anything figured out.
>
> I had to keep moving forward and I had to tackle this. I had to start the process and just take the leap—jump right on in to all the data that I had collected, while continuing to focus on my driving questions. Within a few hours of beginning the four-step process I had read about, I started making connections and seeing patterns in the data. I began to trust the process and released myself from

the need to be efficient. It was OK that things were messy and that there were twists and turns and lots of repetition. It was not only OK, but I realized later that this was an integral part of the data analysis process. (Hill, personal communication, 9/21/13)

Like Ashley's reflection alluded to, many teacher-inquirers move through a four-step process to tackle summative data analysis: description, sense making, interpretation, and implication drawing.

To begin, you read and reread your entire data set, with no other objective than to get a descriptive sense of what you have collected. The goal of this first step of analysis is to describe your inquiry data using the following questions: "What did you see as you inquired?," "What was happening?," and "What are your initial insights into the data?" You might complete the description step by talking it through with another member of your inquiry community, writing it out, or choosing a combined approach and taking detailed notes as you talk.

Next, you begin the sense-making step by reading your entire data set and asking questions such as, "What sorts of things are happening in my data?," "What do I notice?," "How might different pieces of my data fit together?," and "What pieces of my data stand out from the rest?" To answer these questions, you may take notes in the margins of your data. You may physically cut your data apart and place the evidence in discrete piles or categories. You may decide to write down your answers to these and other questions on a separate sheet of paper, noting the location of the evidence. Like May did to analyze a small portion of data she had collected at the start of her inquiry, you may group data by using a different color marker for each theme or pattern you identify. You may highlight all excerpts from your data that fit this theme or pattern. Organizing your data is one of the most creative parts of the sense-making process.

Sometimes inquirers get stuck at this stage and need some prompts to help begin this sense-making process. Table 6.1 offers some organizing units that can serve as prompts for helping us begin our analysis. For example,

Table 6.1   Examples of Organizing Units

Examples of Organizing Units		
Chronology	Key events	Various settings
People	Processes	Behaviors
Issues	Relationships	Groups
Styles	Changes	Meanings
Practices	Strategies	Episodes
Encounters	Roles	Feelings

you might look at your data to see if a story emerges that takes a chronological form. Or you may notice that your data seem to organize around key events. Or you may see some combination of organizing units that is helpful. Be sure to understand that this table is by no means exhaustive and is offered just to provide some examples. As you make sense of your data, you should let the organizing units emerge from the data rather than force an external set of units. If you do decide to cut the data apart, you might want to consider keeping a complete set of data as a backup. Your answers to the description-level questions and your emerging sense-making units begin the process of grouping or sorting your data by theme or category.

Just as the jigsaw puzzle enthusiast realizes that some of the puzzle pieces are not necessary, and some are still at the store, as you analyze your data you will notice that not all of the data you collected will be highlighted/coded or will fit with your developing patterns or themes. These diverging data excerpts should be acknowledged and explained if possible. Likewise, you may find that you need to collect additional data to explore an emerging pattern. For example, recall from Chapter 4 that Mickey MacDonald interviewed students after receiving feedback from her CFG on data she had collected and analyzed in her study. In addition to collecting additional data as a result of summative data analysis, as your findings emerge, you may even regroup, rename, expand, or condense the original ways you grouped your data.

The process of sense making may take many iterations. For example, this may mean that you made data categories, named the categories, combined the named categories, renamed the categories, and eventually combined some of the combined renamed categories. As you move through this process be sure to keep track of how you arrive at the final sense making of your data. You may do this in a narrative form or you may draw a concept map for each iteration of your analysis. No matter which method you choose to map out your sense-making process—do it! The documentation will really help you as you begin the interpretive step of analysis, write up your inquiry, and discuss your findings with others.

As the puzzle nears completion and you begin the interpretive step of inquiry analysis, you need to construct statements that express what you learned and what the learning means. Teacher-inquirers often construct these statements by looking at the patterns that were coded and asking and answering questions such as, "What was my initial wondering, and how do these patterns inform it?," "What is happening in each pattern and across patterns?," and "How are these happenings connected to . . . my teaching? . . . my students? . . . the subject matter and my curriculum? . . . my classroom/school context?"

The findings from this step can be illustrated by the teacher-inquirer in a number of ways including but not limited to the following: themes, patterns, categories, metaphors, similes, claims/assertions, typologies, and vignettes. For example, instead of describing each individual unit that

Jennifer Thulin identified as she inquired into how to use music to facilitate the growth of a struggling reader, she captured the findings using the three following musical similes: "Music as a motivator," "Music as a confidence builder," and "Music as a context for making meaningful connections." Table 6.2 outlines possible illustrative techniques and provides examples.

Table 6.2   Strategies for Illustrating Your Findings

Themes/Patterns/Categories/Labels/Naming—A composite of traits or features; a topic for discourse or discussion; a specifically defined division; a descriptive term set apart from others.

Examples: collaboration, ownership, care, growth

Metaphors—A term that is transferred from the object it ordinarily represents to an object it represents only by implicit comparison or analogy.

Examples: "The Illustrator," "The Translator," "The Reporter," "The Guide," and "Casting the Play"

Simile—Two unlike things are compared, often in a phrase introduced by "like" or "as."

Examples: "music as a motivator," "music as a confidence builder," "music as a context for making meaningful connections," and "writing as conversation"

Claims/Assertions—A statement of fact or assertion of truth.

Example: "Inappropriate expectations discouraged many of the learners in my classroom and hindered my effectiveness as a writing teacher."

Typologies—A systematic classification of types.

Examples: Different uses for puppets—instructional, entertainment, therapeutic

Vignettes—A brief descriptive literary sketch.

Example: "The Struggle for Power: Who Is in Control"

The children were engaged in conversation at the meetings, jobs were continuing to get done, but there was still a struggle centering around who was in control. With the way the class decided to make a list of jobs, break the jobs up into groups, choose the people they wanted to work with, there were breaks in communication. Conflicts were arising with the groups. Everyone was mostly aiming to get "their own" way.

These strategies help illustrate, organize, and communicate inquiry findings to your audience. Once you have outlined your organizing strategy, you will need to identify the data that support each finding presented in your outline. Excerpts from these data sources can be used as evidence for your claims.

Finally, upon completing each of these steps teacher-inquirers ask and answer one last set of implication questions as follows:

1. "What have I learned about myself as a teacher?"

2. "What have I learned about children?"

3. "What have I learned about the larger context of schools and schooling?"

4. "What are the implications of what I have learned on my teaching?"

5. "What changes might I make in my practice?"

6. "What new wonderings do I have?"

These questions call for teacher researchers to interpret what they have learned, to take action for change based on their study, and to generate new questions. For, unlike the puzzle enthusiast, who can marvel at the completed piece, the puzzle for a teacher-inquirer is never quite finished, even after intensive analysis. Hubbard and Power (1999) note that "good research analyses raise more questions than they answer" (p. 117). While you may never be able to marvel at a perfected, polished, definitive set of findings based on summative data analysis from one particular inquiry, you can marvel at the enormity of what you have learned through engaging in the process and the power it holds for transforming both your identity as a teacher and your teaching practice. Cochran-Smith and Lytle (2001) propose that

> a legitimate and essential purpose of professional development is the development of an inquiry stance on teaching that is critical and transformative, a stance linked not only to high standards for the learning of all students but also to social change and social justice and to the individual and collective growth of teachers. (p. 46)

After completing summative data analysis, marvel at your growth and the impact you can have as an individual teacher who has joined a larger community of teacher researchers. Through engagement in inquiry as a member of this community, you are contributing to the transformation of the teaching profession!

WHAT MIGHT SUMMATIVE DATA ANALYSIS LOOK LIKE?

To exemplify the process of summative data analysis we just described, we turn to the first piece of teacher inquiry completed by veteran teacher researcher Amy Ruth (Ruth, 1999, 2001, 2002). Recall that Amy completed her first teacher inquiry as an intern in a professional development school by looking closely at an individual English as a second language learner she called Adam. Amy was particularly interested in learning about the ways peer interaction facilitated Adam's written language development.

To gain insights into her wondering, Amy collected data in three ways over a two-month time period. Amy's first mode of data collection was her own taking of field notes. She developed a data collection sheet to complete each time she worked with Adam at the writing center. On the data sheet, Amy diagrammed the seating arrangement to keep track of where group members chose to sit each time they came to the writing center. Next on the data collection sheet, Amy had a space for observations. In this space, Amy noted anything that stood out to her during the time Adam's group was at the center. There was also a place on the data collection sheet labeled Notable Dialogue where she scripted comments that occurred between peers during their interactions. Finally, Amy had a place labeled Additional Comments where she noted anything else occurring during time at the writing center that was interesting or intriguing.

Amy's second mode of data collection was to keep a personal journal on each day that she met Adam's group at the writing center. Amy notes, "These entries helped me to gather my thoughts, ideas, and further questions concerning my initial wonderings" (Ruth, 1999, p. 7). Finally, one of us, as Amy's supervisor, scripted notes of interactions at the writing center while Amy taught.

After two months of collecting data in these three forms, Amy approached the almost-full box in which she was keeping all of this data, plus articles and books she had found on the writing process and ESL students. She set aside a few hours on a Saturday morning to begin the process of creating a picture of what she had learned. To begin, she took each piece of data out of the box and organized them chronologically, beginning with the first piece collected and ending with the last, and read through every piece. By reading through her entire data set, Amy was reminded of incidents that occurred throughout the duration of her inquiry (through her own field notes and those scripted by her supervisor), as well as her thoughts about Adam, peer interaction, and the writing process as her inquiry unfolded (through her journal entries). In addition, reviewing readings that had appeared in such journals as *Journal of Second Language Writing* and *TESOL Journal* contributed to Amy's developing understanding of her work with Adam. The process of reading the data set in its entirety "freshened up" and provided a description of all that Amy had been thinking about and doing for the past two months.

With all she had collected fresh in her mind, Amy read through the entire data set a second time. On this second time through, Amy began sense making. As she read she asked herself, "What am I noticing about my data?" She constructed a list as she read titled "Inquiry—What I'm Noticing" (see Figure 6.4).

From looking at this list, Amy decided that her next step was to read the data again but, this time through, to focus solely on Adam and her initial wondering, stated as, "How does peer interaction facilitate Adam's writing at the kindergarten writing center?" She wrote this question on an index card and laid it in front of her to remind her of what she was looking for in

Figure 6.4   Amy's List of "What I'm Noticing"

Themes? 4/99

Inquiry → What I'm Noticing

Adam - asks B. to draw pictures. Directs B. w/ descriptive words. B. draws for him, asking questions (clarifying questions

Small group - K. A. & S. do a lot of small talk w/ K - I'm noticing how much more she has to say about her story than what's on page

a m class - more independent writers

K. - eager to share w/ me, but not peers

S. - so artistically centered w/ drawings (little written) ? my question: How is crafting (cutting + gluing) tied to writing?

B. - did not want to write words till peer suggestion made

Adam & B. - still requesting B. to draw particular animals for him → Adam draws w/ him simultaneously → upon urging, Adam & B. will write out words on paper.

this third read of her entire data set. This time, she decided to mark her data by highlighting any pieces of it that pertained to this question in pink.

Once this process was completed, Amy took a break for lunch and then returned to her data for a fourth reading. During this fourth sweep, however, Amy read only what had been highlighted in pink. Through reading only the pink data excerpts, she generated a list of seven patterns that seemed to describe and capture the essence of what was occurring over and over in her data. She named each of these patterns as follows: (1) requesting drawings from peers, (2) Adam's verbalization as drawing object, (3) labeling objects around the room, (4) outgoing personality, (5) role taking in group, (6) burdens others, and (7) asking for clarification.

Next, Amy created a coding mechanism for each of her named patterns, creating a symbol that corresponded to each pattern (e.g., a "tree" corresponded to pattern 1, a "bubble" corresponded to pattern 2, the word *dog* corresponded to pattern 3, a "smiley face" corresponded to pattern 4, a "hat" corresponded to pattern 5, a "sad face" corresponded to pattern 6, and a "check" corresponded to pattern 7. Just as Amy had done previously when she wrote her question on an index card and laid it in front of her to remind her of what she was looking for as she read, Amy noted each pattern and symbol on an index card and kept this card in front of her as she read through the entire data set a fifth time. This time through, she underlined and used her symbols to code the data. Amy's index card denoting the pattern symbols, as well as one piece of coded data from each of the three ways it was collected, appear in Figures 6.5 to 6.8.

A few days later, Amy sorted her data by pattern, reading through only the excerpts that pertained to each pattern that was coded. As she read through each pattern, she began the interpretive step of analysis. She asked herself, "What is happening in each pattern?," "How are the patterns connected to each other?," and "What do these patterns mean in relation to my initial wondering?" This time through, Amy noted the ways some patterns were connected to each other. For example, Amy saw connections between the four categories: (1) Adam's outgoing personality, (2) requests for drawings from peers, (3) different roles at the writing center, and (4) burdening others. She regrouped her data accordingly.

That week, Amy talked with her own peers at a seminar about what she was seeing. As she talked about the patterns, Amy noted that aspects of who Adam was as a person and learner that were strong attributes (i.e., Adam had an outgoing personality and Adam was acquiring more and more spoken English words) were positive forces in the development of his writing. Adam was able to use his personality and the blossoming of his spoken English language as critical aids to his progress as a writer by asking peers for help, especially the child who had taken on the role of artist in the group. Amy noted that requests for drawings from the group's artist were frequent in her data and were appropriate and productive for Adam. As Adam's request for drawings from the child who took on the role of artist at the writing center became more frequent, the artist became reluctant to respond to Adam's requests. Amy shared with her colleagues incidences that appeared in her data such as the following:

> Adam said, "Books! Draw books." The artist replied, "Books? I can draw one book." Adam held up three fingers and replied,

Figure 6.5   Amy's Index Card Denoting Symbols Used for Coding

SOURCE: Used with permission of Amy Ruth.

"No, three books." The artist shook his head no. Adam said again, "Four? Four books." The artist drew just one book, and eventually, Adam drew the rest.

In talking about her data, Amy also shared that what she had coded as a burden for the child who took on the role of the artist also seemed to lead that same child to become more immersed in his own writing. Amy shared that as the inquiry proceeded, the artist seemed more interested in doing his own writing and drawing. His own stories were growing more elaborate, and it appeared that he was trying to spend more time and effort on his own stories.

Through engaging in dialogue, Amy's colleagues helped her capture what she was learning in a single statement or assertion: "A productive tension exists between Adam, his personality, his oral language development, and the ways he uses these attributes in interactions with peers at the writing center."

Fitting together these four different patterns revealed to Amy the complex nature and delicate balance of the interactions that were occurring at the writing center. Through her inquiry and summative analysis of data, Amy gained new understandings of what was occurring—understandings

Figure 6.6   Example of Coded Data—Journal

Amy Ruth

Inquiry Journal

Tuesday, March 2, 1999

After finally deciding to concentrate my inquiry focus on "Adam", a ESL student, I have really started concentrating on his interactions and writing at the Writing Table during Lang Arts centers. I am curious about how his interactions with peers will *Initial Question* influence, encourage, and help the progress and growth of his writing. Lately, Adam has been asking peers (B., in particular) to draw objects on his paper for him. Mostly everyone in the classroom knows that B. is particularly skilled and practiced at drawing dinosaurs and whales. They were the first two animals that I witnessed Adam requesting. Adam also goes as far as to tell B. what colors he would like things to be. After B. draws the request, Adam then adds details to the picture, usually talking as he does so. For example: a dinosaur drawn by B. and then Adam added a tree that the dinosaur was eating. Adam verbalized "tree" and eating sounds as he drew.

It is particularly interesting to see Adam requesting drawings by his peers, due to the use of the English language that we have seen really emerging recently. Within the past month we have seen tremendous growth in Adam's use of vocabulary. He is formulating longer sentences and is very eager to share his ideas through words now. I have noticed that he is more interested in full group activities in which he may have the chance to share his ideas. He raises his hand frequently, and volunteers many answers.

I am interested in seeing how this begins to play out in his writing. I am beginning to think of strategies that will encourage him to add words to his drawings.

SOURCE: Used with permission of Amy Ruth.

that would never have emerged in the absence of systematic study. Amy used the new knowledge she had constructed to make adjustments in her teaching and navigate the productive tension between Adam and the artist in the room by increasing her own interactions with Adam but still allowing for peer interactions to continue.

Figure 6.7   Example of Coded Data—Field Notes Taken by Amy

Date: ___2/22/99___

Inquiry Data Collection Sheet

6p 9

Seating Arrangement:

K.

A.   b.   Adam

me   S.

Observations:

B. & Adam working together on picture of whale, then a dinosaur
    B. drew whale & dinosaur, Adam adds detail.

Adam sounds out parts of rocket picture B. already did, to describe
    what it is B. is to draw next. oo

-S. appears to be translator

Notable Dialogue:

Adam asks B. to draw him a fish.   A "A green fish! "
                                     "Fish, Big! "

A- "B., Look what I have, do you remember my picture? The one I drew
        with blue hair?"

A- "I don't want any words, just my shame because I am
        giving it to B."

B- "Don't ever do that again! " (To A. after dropping marker)   translator.
Additional Comments: " He doesn't understand ' (-S.)

+ K. wrote independently and quietly shared with me only after
    I asked

- Me - "Do you think books you read at home help you put ideas
    into your writing?
            S. - Maybe, they help me think.

SOURCE: Used with permission of Amy Ruth.

I did not want Adam's requests and demands to hold back his
peer's writing, although I still believe that those interactions
were important for the progress of both children's writing. I
tried to hold more of my own conversations with Adam, posing
questions to him about his drawings, and assisting him whenever possible with words he would use to label his drawings.
(Ruth, 1999, p. 10)

Figure 6.8   Example of Coded Data—Field Notes Scripted by Supervisor

③

Gives children reminders at the project table. "It is almost time for me to knock."

Transition
- Amy knocks - Children line up to switch centers. She waits for all children, gives some individual reminders and knocks.

Center Rotation #2
- "How do you stay healthy?"
- Mentor arrives at project table.

Amy at Writing Table (INQUIRY)
"DOG"
- A. talking to children about O circles - globe
- Children say that "It is one of A.'s words."
- A. gets up and spins the globe.
- "Miss Ruth" - A. gets Amy's attention. He points again to globe
- Amy asks A to draw some of those countries. He hands paper to little girl across from him.
- "K. needs to work on her story too."
- A. not working - looking around room, back to globe,
- "A. be careful! Come and add some more on here.
- Amy moves over to direct A.'s writing. A. knows some but not all sounds. He has difficulty find the "T" even when Amy tells him. Someone helps him with "R" Two other children are huddled over the alphabet list. They are trying to help.

SOURCE: Used with permission of Amy Ruth.

The completed picture of Amy's learning and what that learning meant for her practice was taking shape through summative data analysis.

At this time in the data analysis process, Amy abandoned her initial wondering and generated a new wondering: "What does writing mean to Adam?" Amy continued to analyze her data and collect more data over the next few weeks with this question in mind. At the close of her summative data analysis process, Amy reflected as follows:

It is very exciting to look over the themes I found, and to realize that there was something very important going on with Adam and his peers at the writing center! Had I not posed the original question, I may never have really noticed what it was that was actually occurring. I now know how important the process of collecting data is. My data and themes did not necessarily definitively answer my initial question. But more importantly, they allowed me to see what was really growing and developing at our kindergarten writing center. Plus, I answered an entirely new question!

I have found out, through this inquiry project, that there really are not any concrete answers to the initial question. It is where the initial question leads that is important. The initial question allowed me to open up to seeing, hearing, and experiencing all that was going on at the writing table. I let the data collection and analysis lead me to my findings, instead of me leading the data collection and analysis to what I was hoping to find. (Ruth, 1999, pp. 12–13)

As you reflect on Amy's example of data analysis, remember the three words we used to describe the data analysis process: "messy," "murky," and "creative." With this in mind, realize that summative analysis of your data might not proceed exactly as Amy's. Every teacher is unique, every inquiry is unique, and, hence, every piecing together of the inquiry data to create a picture of the learning that has occurred is unique. Yet, as you finish this chapter, you now have knowledge of a common set of general procedures used to analyze data and a sense of how those general procedures may play out in a particular teacher-inquirer's work.

You may wish to complete additional studies of the data analysis process before you begin or as you engage in the process yourself. We conclude this chapter with suggested exercises for summative data analysis, as well as a list of references you may find useful as you engage in this most difficult, but most rewarding, component of inquiry.

CHAPTER 6 EXERCISES

1. The first step of analysis is *to describe* your inquiry. Read through your data carefully. Take notes as your read. After reading your data, respond to the following questions:

   - What did you see as you inquired?
   - What was happening?
   - What are your initial insights into the data?

2. The second step of analysis is to begin *making sense of* your data. The organizing units presented in Table 6.1 can serve as prompts for helping you begin your analysis.

- Use the chart to help you identify or construct possible organizing units for your data. Be sure to consider organizing units that emerge from within your inquiry.
- Now take a stab at organizing your data and identifying the units of analysis that emerge in your inquiry data. For example, maybe the important story in your data involves "changes" and you identify categories such as "changes for kids," "changes in content," and "changes in instruction."

3. Once you have a general idea of the important units of data and an idea of the emerging story, you need to decide how you will present the data. Read through the list of strategies presented in Table 6.2; they are designed to help you illustrate your *interpretive* findings. Remember, this is by no means an exhaustive list.

  - Now, you will need to choose a strategy or strategies for illustrating and organizing your own findings for your audience. Once again, use your creativity to organize your thoughts.
  - Outline the elements of your organizing strategy and identify the data you will use to support each component of your outline.

4. You probably thought the most difficult step of the analysis process was completed. However, the final *implications* step remains. Your remaining responsibility is to move from interpretation of the findings that you present in Exercise 3 to articulating the implications or "So what?" of your study. Some helpful questions follow that may prompt your thinking in this area:

  - What have I learned about myself as a teacher?
  - What have I learned about children?
  - What are the implications of my findings for the content I teach?
  - What have I learned about the larger context of schools and schooling?
  - What are the implications of what I have learned for my teaching?
  - What changes might I make in my own practice?
  - What new wonderings do I have?

Data Analysis References

Bernhardt, V. (2004). *Data analysis for continuous school improvement.* Larchmont, NY: Eye on Education.

Boudett, K. P., City, W. A., Murnane, R. J. (2005). *Data wise: A step-by-step guide to using assessment results to improve teaching and learning.* Cambridge, MA: Harvard Education Press.

Creswell, J. W. (2008). *Research design: Qualitative, quantitative, and mixed methods approaches* (2nd ed.). Thousand Oaks, CA: Sage.

Creswell, J. W. (2012). *Qualitative inquiry and research design.* Thousand Oaks, CA: Sage.

Mills, G. E. (2014). *Action research: A guide for the teacher researcher* (5th ed.). Saddle River, NJ: Pearson Education.

Patton, M. Q. (2002). *Qualitative research & evaluation methods* (3rd ed.). Thousand Oaks, CA: Sage.

Wolcott, H. F. (1994). *Transforming qualitative data: Description, analysis, and interpretation.* Thousand Oaks, CA: Sage.

Wolcott, H. F. (2008). *Writing up qualitative research* (3rd ed.). Thousand Oaks, CA: Sage.

7

Extending Your Learning

The Inquiry Write-Up

Y ou have just completed the process of data analysis, during which time you sorted, re-sorted, and made sense of all you had collected throughout the duration of your inquiry project. You thought about your inquiry as a whole. You thought about what was happening in the data. You thought about what you learned. You thought about the implications of what you learned for your own teaching practice. In short, you did a lot of thinking!

A wonderful way to think about your inquiry is to write. Noted educational ethnographer Harry Wolcott (1990) goes so far as to state that writing and thinking are synonymous: "The conventional wisdom is that writing reflects thinking. I am drawn to a different position: Writing is thinking" (p. 21). Referring specifically to the process of teacher inquiry, Mills (2014) further states that there is great value in writing up research because

> the process of writing requires the writer to clarify meaning—choose words carefully, thoughtfully describe that which is experienced or seen, reflect on experiences, and refine phrasing when putting words on a page. You may learn something important about your students and their learning—something you may have

missed had you not considered your words on the page—as you formally write about your research. (p. 179)

For this reason, we recommend writing as an extension of data analysis and as a wonderful way to extend your learning.

WHY SHOULD I WRITE?

Unfortunately, while writing is a terrific mechanism for clarifying thinking as you summarize what you have learned and for giving your learning a form that can be shared with others, writing is not a part of a teacher's daily work, and it takes a great deal of time. Mills (2014) suggests challenging the time constraint by making writing a part of your professional life and responsibility. Mills suggests capturing the minutes and hours—before school; after school; during preparation periods; or in lieu of canceled faculty meetings, failed parent conferences, and "sit-and-get" professional development days. When all else fails, use personal time to get writing done.

If you can get past the time constraint and the resistance to engaging in an activity that Wolcott (1990) describes at its best as "always challenging and sometimes satisfying" (p. 12), we believe that the times it is satisfying will outweigh all the difficulty and frustration inherent in writing and that through the writing process, you will take your own individual inquiry to a new level. Mills (2014) suggests sound reasons for writing. We end this section with his five most compelling reasons to write.

Clarification—Writing your research requires clarity and accuracy of expression. Writing about your research activities encourages thought and reflection, and perhaps creates new questions that are resolved, which shape and complete your research.

Validation—Publishing your research and the feedback you will receive from your reviewers and readers will validate who you are as a professional educator and what you do.

Empowerment—Reflecting on your practices through writing will empower you to continue to challenge the status quo and be an advocate for your children.

Generative—Writing is a generative activity that culminates in a product, something tangible that you can share with colleagues, supervisors, and parents.

Accomplishment—Writing up your research will provide you with a sense of accomplishment. It is both humbling and exciting when colleagues read your work and compliment you on your accomplishments! (p. 180)

WHAT MIGHT MY WRITING LOOK LIKE?

If you recall, Julie Russell was passionate about writing, and this passion led to her inquiry into second-graders' writing. Julie's passion for writing makes her a logical teacher-inquirer to feature in this chapter as an example of what your work may look like in written form. Julie's work provides only one example of "the look" of an inquiry write-up. We encourage you to view other write-ups as models, such as journals that publish teacher inquiries, published collections of teacher research and action-research websites (see, for example, Masingila, 2006; Meyers & Rust, 2003; Caro-Bruce, Flessner, Klehr, & Zeichner, 2007).

Note that the example of Julie's work we share in this chapter, as well as many of the examples you will find in journals and action research collections, are quite detailed and subsequently, lengthy. If the detail and length of Julie's or any other teacher researcher's published work overwhelms you, find a write-up form that is a better fit with who you are as a teacher and writer. For example, when we noticed some teacher researchers becoming overly stressed at the thought of writing up their work, we introduced the concept of an "executive summary write-up" into our work at the Center for School Improvement and later the Lastinger Center for Learning at the University of Florida (Dana & Baker, 2006; Dana & Delane, 2007; Dana & Yendol-Hoppey, 2008b). Executive summaries provide brief (three- to five-page) overviews of a teacher's inquiry, as well as contact information for the teacher so more detail about a teacher's work can be shared through personal contact with the author. You can view examples of executive summaries completed by teachers in districts partnering with the University of Florida in the past by visiting the following website: https://inq.education.ufl.edu/teacher-inquiry-database. Similarly, the Madison Metropolitan School District's Classroom Action Research Program offers another website that shares teachers' summary of their inquiry work: http://oldweb.madison.k12.wi.us/sod/car/carabstractintro.html. Another fine model for inquiry write-ups that may appear less daunting for the teacher researcher who doesn't enjoy writing is the inquiry brochure. This technique is used extensively in the Fairfax County Public School District as one option for teachers to share their research in a written form. Two examples of inquiry brochures from the Fairfax County Public School District appear at the end of this chapter as Figures 7.1 and 7.2. Yet another model for an inquiry write-up that we have used with preservice teachers at the University of Florida and University of South Florida is the inquiry template. During field experiences that occur four mornings a week prior to their full internship, our students select one student in consultation with their mentor teacher to study through the inquiry process. As a part of their work with this child, they design and implement an intervention targeted at helping that student address an area ripe for his or her growth and development as a learner. The template consists of one box each that contains the preservice teacher's wondering, data collection strategies, intervention description, findings, and conclusions. Writing up an inquiry becomes as simple as filling in each box. An example of the inquiry template as a form of write-up also appears at the end of this chapter as Figure 7.3.

We feel strongly that writing is an important part of the teacher-inquiry process but realize that not every teacher researcher is meant to be, nor desires to be, a published author. For this reason, we have provided examples of other models (such as the executive summary, the inquiry brochure, and the inquiry template) that provide the benefits of writing discussed previously but may be more inviting forums for some teachers to capture and share their work in written form. If we can't sell you on writing up your work in this chapter, we discuss other fine mechanisms for sharing your research in Chapter 9. Whether you intend to write a detailed accounting of your research, an executive summary, an inquiry brochure, or an inquiry template or intend to share your work using a mechanism other than writing, we feel you will find value in reading the example of Julie's writing we chose to share in this chapter.

While Julie's work is but one example, we select it for the poignant way she developed four critical features of any write-up or sharing: (1) providing background information, (2) sharing the design of the inquiry (procedures, data collection, and data analysis), (3) stating the learning and supporting the statements with data, and (4) providing concluding thoughts. In whatever way you choose to write up or share your work, we believe these four critical features can inform and help you shape this process.

Step 1: Providing Background Information

A strong way to begin your writing is to provide background information. Sharing your context, what led you to this particular study, how it is connected to others' thinking about the topic of your inquiry, and what processes you used to gain insights into a particular wondering provide a foundation for your audience to understand your work and to make judgments as to its transferability to their own teaching situation. Here, we reprint Julie's introduction to her work that was previously shared as an example of finding your wondering at the intersection of your personal and professional identities in Chapter 2. This time, as you read this excerpt, notice how Julie helped the reader understand who she was as a teacher and person ("My goal as a teacher is to help children become lifelong learners who can think critically about the world around them and create and articulate their own ideas"), what was occurring in her own classroom ("Some children wrote independently and produced several pages of text during each workshop. Others wrote one sentence at a time and frequently approached me to ask, 'Am I done yet?'"), what was occurring in the field

("As I studied children's writing development, I realized that the range of writing behaviors in my classroom were common"), what was occurring in her district ("My mentor spoke to many of the children about meeting the district's benchmark for writing by the end of the school year"), and what was occurring in her own teaching ("I began to doubt my ability to provide my students with writing instruction that would help them meet the district's writing goals and that would inspire them to enjoy writing"). Through her writing, Julie shows how all of these components coalesced to lead to this particular inquiry.

I can still remember every detail of the moment when I became a writer. The warm August air sticks to my skin, powdery chalk dust tickles my nose, and the comforting sounds of my mother making dinner fill my ears whenever I begin to put words on a page. I found my voice as a writer the summer before second grade. I was six years old, and my older sister had suddenly decided that she was too mature to play with me. She would disappear with her friends, and I was left to fill the long summer days without her. One afternoon, I wandered into the basement and started to draw on an old chalkboard that my sister and I used when we were "playing school." After a while, I stopped drawing and began writing poetry. When my mother called me for dinner, she saw my poems and became my first audience. She encouraged my efforts and gave me a small, yellow notebook so I could continue to write. My passion for writing grew as I continued to read quality literature and experienced the powerful ways in which expert authors manipulate language and develop engaging stories. Throughout my life, I have turned to written words to express my thoughts and ideas.

As I developed a teaching philosophy, I realized that my passion for teaching is intertwined with my passion for writing. My goal as a teacher is to help children become lifelong learners who can think critically about the world around them and create and articulate their own ideas. I hope that, by sharing my love for writing with my students, I can help them express the thoughts and opinions that are important and meaningful to them. Therefore, when I pictured my future classroom, I always seemed to arrive during writer's workshop. I assumed that I would be an effective, engaging writing teacher simply because I enjoyed writing. I imagined a classroom filled with eager students who loved writing and could not wait to commit their ideas to paper. I was thrilled to be an intern in a second-grade classroom, because I could remember the wonderful writing experiences I had during my own second-grade year.

As I began my internship experience, I helped provide writing instruction for a group of second graders with differing strengths, needs, and interests. I quickly realized that teaching writing is extremely complicated. Some children wrote independently and produced several pages of text during each workshop.

(Continued)

(Continued)

Others wrote one sentence at a time and frequently approached me to ask, "Am I done yet?" I often sat with a small group of students who struggled to get their thoughts down on paper. As I tried to keep these children on task and encourage them to continue writing, I asked questions and made story maps. At the end of many writing sessions, I felt uncomfortable with the amount of support I was giving to some young writers. Several children who were quite capable of writing independently often came to me and asked, "Can I write with you?" I worried that I was allowing some children to become too dependent on my help and my influence was hindering the flow of their ideas.

As I studied children's writing development, I realized that the range of writing behaviors in my classroom was common for second graders. I felt relief when I read the experts' descriptions of second-grade writers and they mirrored my feelings about the young writers in my classroom. Some children write "fluently" and approach writing with "carefree confidence" (Calkins, 1986, p. 67). These children write long, detailed narratives with ease. Other children seem to erase more than they write. Second graders are beginning to become "aware of an audience" for their writing, and the "easy confidence" they felt as first graders often turns into their first cases of "writer's block" (Calkins, 1986, p. 68). They are concerned about approaching tasks in the "right way," and that vulnerability makes writing a difficult and painstaking process for many children (Calkins, 1986, p. 69). Therefore, writing instruction in second grade must address this wide range of writing behaviors.

During the students' goal-setting conferences in the beginning of the school year, my mentor, Linda Witmer, spoke to many of the children about working toward meeting the district's benchmark for writing by the end of the year. According to this benchmark, the students must be able to write stories with beginnings, middles, and endings. These stories should be understandable and must include characters, settings, and major events. The students are also expected to include some descriptive language, use some punctuation and capitalization, and spell the district benchmark words correctly. The students must complete the writing assessment independently. After winter break, Linda and I were both concerned about our students' writing. As I looked through the students' work, I noticed that extremely capable children were often scoring below the benchmark. Many of the children were still writing incomplete stories, and endings were particularly difficult for many students. Although our students had wonderful, creative ideas, we worried that several of them would not meet the district's benchmark for writing because they did not take the reader on a complete journey from beginning to middle to end.

My initial experiences as a writing teacher were frustrating. After years of imagining myself as an effective writing teacher, I was dismayed when I realized that my efforts were not helping my students meet their writing goals. In some cases, I worried that I was doing more harm than good because my attempts to help often became persistent prompting that drowned out the students' voices in their own writing. I was heartbroken when students resisted writing, because I was so eager to share my passion for stories and language. When I conducted a survey to collect data about the students' attitudes toward writing, I was concerned when I realized that many children thought that they were good writers because of "neat handwriting," "good spelling," or "using time wisely." Although those skills are important, I noticed that most children did not mention that they were proud of their ability to create stories. Gradually, I began to doubt my ability to provide my students with writing instruction that would help them meet the district's writing goals and that would inspire them to enjoy writing. My passion for writing, which I believed would be an asset in the classroom, actually hindered my progress as a writing teacher because I struggled to relate to and communicate with students who resisted writing. As I studied writing instruction, I learned that a teacher's personal experiences with the subject matter influence the way he/she teaches his/her students (Frank, 1979). I realized that, because I had positive writing experiences as a child, I naively assumed that all of my second graders would react to writing with similar enthusiasm.

My passion for writing and teaching, as well as my frustrations about the realities of teaching writing, led me to my wonderings. I wanted to do a project that would focus on my students' development as writers and would also help me develop as a writing teacher. Therefore, I began my project with the following wonderings:

- Will my second graders write more complete stories if the elements of a story are broken down into a series of minilessons?
- Will my second graders become more independent writers and gain confidence in their writing abilities if my expectations for their writing are more explicit?
- Will collaborating with other learners help my students grow as writers?
- Will my students grow as writers if the lessons include opportunities to make connections between children's literature and their own stories?
- Will these changes in writing instruction improve the way my students feel about themselves as writers and the way I feel about myself as a writing teacher? (Russell, 2002)

This lengthy excerpt from Julie's inquiry provides contextualization for the audience, and this contextualization prepares the audience to understand Julie's particular approach to her work.

Step 2: Sharing the Design of the Inquiry (Procedures, Data Collection, and Data Analysis)

A key feature that sets inquiry apart from the daily reflection teachers engage in is that it is conducted in a systematic, intentional way. Hence, sharing your system (what you did), as well as your intentions (how you did what you did—data collection and analysis), is important. In the next excerpt, notice how Julie discusses her instructional plan for this inquiry and the ways she collected data. Also notice how she articulates the ways that data collection and analysis interacted with each other as her plan of action for instruction changed over time.

Once I developed my wonderings, I began studying both primary students' writing development and methods for writing instruction. I read resource books written by primary teachers that included actual lesson plans and anecdotes about students and their writing. I also read books by researchers who focused more on theories about writing development. I looked through my students' portfolios to learn about the problems they faced when they were writing stories. My students completed a survey that focused on their attitudes toward writing and about themselves as writers.

As I began my project, the primary division at my school was beginning the Land of Make-Believe unit. The unit fit well with my wonderings because it is language arts–intensive and it includes many examples of quality children's literature. I used some fairy tales from the unit as well as stories that were recommended in my other resources to develop a series of five literature-based minilessons. As I developed my lessons, I often referred to Susan Lunsford's (1998) *Literature-Based Mini-Lessons to Teach Writing*. Lunsford advocates using children's literature to teach writing because the literature gives students examples of how expert authors deal with the problems that all writers face. I wanted my students to feel that they were capable, valuable members of a community of writers that includes published authors. I hoped that, by using quality children's literature in my lessons, I would be able to have discussions with my students about effective writing. Once the strategies in the literature were articulated, I hoped that the children would begin to apply them in their own stories.

Initially, I planned to teach lessons about character, setting, problem, solution, and complete stories. Each lesson followed the same basic format. As a large group, the students and I read and discussed sections of children's literature that exemplified the story element we were studying. We brainstormed ideas that the students could use in their own writing. Then, the students were expected to apply the story element we studied by writing their own stories. I prepared rubrics for each story element. The rubrics were designed so that the writer, a peer, and a teacher could evaluate the way the writer used a particular story element in his/her story. I also scored the stories using the District's rubric so that the students and I could monitor our progress toward the benchmark for second grade.

As I interacted with the children and looked at my data, I changed some aspects of my lessons based on my developing understandings of effective writing instruction and second-graders' needs and abilities. After my first two workshops, I was extremely dissatisfied with my project. When I began the setting workshop, one child asked, "Do we have to write a whole story AGAIN?" The students' reluctance to write disturbed me, because I was so anxious to help them enjoy and look forward to writing. The class discussion at the beginning of the setting workshop was also quite discouraging for me because the children did not remember the concepts we studied during the character workshop the week before. When I planned the workshops, I intended to help the students build a concept of a complete story by studying one element at a time. For this plan to work, the students had to transfer the concepts from one workshop to the next. After discussing my concerns with my mentor and my supervisor, I decided to back up and change the structure of the workshops. I planned three workshops on beginnings, middles, and endings, and then a final workshop on complete stories. During the beginning, middle, and ending workshops, the students only needed to write the story element we discussed on that particular day. This change shortened the students' writing time to about twenty minutes and made the workshops more focused and less stressful. During the final workshop, the students were expected to put all of the elements together and write complete stories without assistance.

Step 3: Stating the Learning and Supporting the Statements With Data

With detailed knowledge of the "how" of the inquiry, the audience is now ready to understand Julie's findings, which she presents as "claims." As Julie engaged in the process of writing this report of her inquiry, she clarified her thinking by choosing words and phrases that carefully reflect and represent her learnings in this form. As Julie began writing and developing each claim, she also realized that her claims could be organized into four conceptual categories. She did a lot of cutting and pasting as she organized and reorganized for the reader. In the absence of the process of writing it up, Julie would not have taken her work to this organizational level and not realized the extent of her own learning. The four categories and claims associated with each category she generated as she wrote about her work were the following:

Category 1: Student Growth

Claim 1: The series of six writers' workshops that focused on the parts of stories helped several of my second graders write stories that reached the district benchmark for writing.

Category 2: Setting Expectations

Claim 2: Inappropriate expectations discouraged many of the learners in my classroom and hindered my effectiveness as a writing teacher.

(Continued)

(Continued)

Claim 3: My students were my most valuable resource as I created developmentally appropriate expectations.

Claim 4: Rubrics were helpful for some students, but they were not effective for other students.

Category 3: Collaboration

Claim 5: Collaborating with others helped some students develop ideas and grow as writers.

Claim 6: Other students found that collaborating was ineffective for them as writers.

Category 4: Connections to Literature

Claim 7: Students who make connections between writing and literature can use literature to help them solve problems when they are writing.

Claim 8: Students who are immersed in literature incorporate more literary language in their writing.

Claim 9: Students who read from a writer's perspective are comfortable thinking critically about literature.

Claim 10: The students in Room 20 are members of a writing community that includes published authors.

In the next passage from Julie's inquiry write-up, notice how Julie states each of these claims and builds an argument to support her claim by providing evidence with excerpts and vignettes from her data. When you write, in essence, you are building an argument that is not unlike a district attorney building a case to prosecute a defendant. A case built on only one piece of evidence would never go to trial. The attorney must piece together a string of evidence to create a strong case. The same is true for a teacher-inquirer. In presenting and sharing findings, the teacher-inquirer pieces together a string of evidence to support statements of his or her learning. The case is stronger when evidence is provided from multiple sources (what we learned in Chapter 4 is referred to by research methodologists as triangulation). As you read, notice how Julie weaves data excerpts from multiple sources (scripted field notes by her supervisor, her own journal entries, student work, student surveys, interviews, and literature about children's writing) throughout the discussion of each claim.

Student Growth

The series of six writer's workshops that focused on the parts of stories helped several of my second graders write stories that reached the district benchmark for writing.

As I looked through the students' portfolios at the beginning of my project, I noticed that the students who were scoring below the benchmark were not writing complete stories. They often had creative ideas and wonderful language, but they did not include crucial parts of the story. Endings were, by far, the most difficult story element for my students. Many children seemed to grow tired by the time they reached the end of their stories. They would write a few quick sentences that did not explain how the problem was solved just so they could be done. Other children had difficulty organizing their thoughts. They would write down their ideas without planning their stories, so their plots were scattered and their endings were not related to the rest of their stories.

As I planned the writing activity for the first workshop, I used my mentor's guidance to make the task similar to the district's writing assessment. After our read-aloud and our discussion about characters, I gave the students two titles. Each child had to choose one of the titles and write a story based on the title they chose. This writing activity was independent. The children had to work quietly and write their entire stories in one session.

When I scored these stories using the district's rubric, my data were consistent with my observations of the students' portfolios. Seventeen of my 18 second graders were present and wrote stories during our first writer's workshop. Of those 17 children, 11 scored below the district's benchmark because their stories were incomplete. As I looked through my comments on the stories, I noticed that 10 of the 11 stories that did not reach the benchmark lacked endings. Several stories also needed more detail in the middle to make the problems or adventures interesting and understandable.

During our sixth and final writer's workshop, the students were expected to put all of the elements of a story together. Their complete stories were eventually stapled inside of paper castles the children made and decorated. As a class, we discussed the essential elements of a complete story. Then, we brainstormed various beginnings, middles, and endings that made sense with our castle theme. The students were allowed to collaborate with their partners as they were planning their stories. My mentor, my supervisor, and I helped students organize their ideas and kept them on task. However, most of the children wrote their stories independently.

When I compared the stories from the last workshop to the stories from the first workshop, I was pleased to see that 15 of the 17 students that were present for the last workshop were able to meet the district benchmark for writing. When I checked the final scores of the 11 children who did not meet the benchmark during the first workshop, I noticed that 8 of them

(Continued)

(Continued)

were able to meet the benchmark. Two children did not meet the benchmark because their stories lacked effective endings. One child did not participate in the final writing activity because he was absent on that day. The students who were meeting the district's benchmark when I began my project continued to experience success. In fact, as the workshops progressed, 2 children raised their scores above the benchmark by incorporating dazzling language and engaging plots in their work.

After examining the students' work throughout my workshops, I can claim that the minilessons and writing activities that I developed were effective for many struggling writers. Several students linger at the borderline. They are not yet consistent in their abilities to create complete stories independently. However, many children did experience remarkable growth in only six lessons, and they made important progress toward meeting their writing goals for second grade.

Setting Expectations

Inappropriate expectations discouraged many of the learners in my classroom and hindered my effectiveness as a writing teacher.

During my initial planning for my project, I was overflowing with ideas. After several years of imagining my own approach to writing instruction, I had an opportunity to actually implement some of my own lessons. I collected children's literature, planned discussion questions, made charts for brainstorming, and developed rubrics. I pushed the students to write entire stories during one session. I was incredibly enthusiastic and I got carried away.

By my second workshop, I was feeling quite discouraged. I was trying to generate excitement and creativity, and even my most capable writers were starting to grumble and complain. The children became fidgety and distracted during the lengthy discussions. They resisted the writing activities. The rubrics that I provided were either ignored or filled in hastily and without much reflection. The stories were not improving and none of us seemed to be having fun.

The setting workshop was discouraging from the beginning. When I asked the students what they had learned in the previous workshop, they remembered that they "drew pictures of what [they] imagined in [their] minds" and discussed "picture painting words" (scripted notes, 2/21). However, I had to question them for several minutes before anyone mentioned characters, which had been the focus of the lesson. After this review, I did a read-aloud, we drew pictures, I led a discussion, we brainstormed some ideas, I read another story, and we brainstormed again. The lesson was lengthy and, to be honest, quite boring. At one point, a student asked, "Can we go back and write?" I continued with my failing lesson even though the children were clearly telling me that my efforts were not helping them.

My frustration was evident in my journal entry. As I reflected on the setting workshop, I wrote, "I think I tried to pile too much into the morning.

Their attention just could not last through all of the activities I had planned. I think my problems teaching really showed up in the children's writing, because only a few of them really described their settings in their stories." When my lessons were not developmentally appropriate, my students could sense my frustration and they got the message that writing was boring and confusing. For the first time, I began to realize that my personal experiences with writing as a young child were challenges rather than assets for me as a writing teacher. I always enjoyed writing and, in elementary school, I sought out extra opportunities to put my thoughts on paper. This passion for writing has certainly enriched my life, but it creates difficulties when I am attempting to relate to a student who does not share my enthusiasm. At the beginning of my project, I truly struggled to approach writing with a second-graders' needs and abilities in mind, and my students responded to my first few lessons with boredom and confusion.

My students were my most valuable resource as I created developmentally appropriate expectations.

As I discussed my plans and my concerns with Linda (my mentor) and Nancy (my supervisor), I began to realize that I was not truly giving the students a fair chance to practice each story part because they had to write an entire story after each lesson.

Therefore, we decided to break apart our next story and write it one piece at a time. This change would lighten the workload, shorten the work time, and give us more time to practice and reflect on each story element. As I planned, I kept thinking about the student who groaned, "Do we have to write a whole story *again*?" Above all, I wanted my students to enjoy writing and feel successful as writers. Therefore, I needed to pay attention when they gave me warnings that they were feeling frustrated and overwhelmed.

When I shortened the minilessons and made my writing expectations more appropriate for second graders, I felt much more effective as a writing teacher because I was giving my students (and myself) a chance to feel successful. I noticed that the students were more attentive during the lessons and they were more willing to write. I did not hear any grumbling or complaining about writing one section of a story, and several students actually wanted more time than I gave them to write.

I understand writing as a writer, but I do not understand it as well from a writing teacher's perspective. As I continue to meet and work with new students, I must develop strategies for deciding what types of expectations are developmentally appropriate for them as writers. During my project, I quickly learned that "children can provide important data about their own learning" (Avery, 1993, p. 420). The students were sending me urgent messages with their grumbling, their body language, their writing, and their responses to me.

When I compared the students' presurveys to their postsurveys, I noticed a few patterns. During the presurvey, when the students were asked about

(Continued)

(Continued)

their favorite kind of writing, many children mentioned writing activities such as Child of the Week, math journals, and science papers. As I read these responses, I was confronted with one of my biases. When I think of writing, I automatically think of stories. The students' responses reminded me that various genres of writing are integrated into every part of our day and these different kinds of writing experiences allow students with different strengths and needs to shine. As a teacher, I need to open my mind to the various styles of and purposes for writing so that I can engage all of my students in writing activities that give them opportunities to express their ideas and opinions.

When I read about the students' favorite and least favorite parts of writing on the postsurveys, I noticed that several students enjoyed "coming up with ideas," but "writing the words" was considered tedious and difficult. As I worked on this project, I began to realize that asking a young child to write a complete story is a daunting request. First, they must think of an idea and develop that idea until it has a beginning, a middle, and an end. Then, they must organize their thoughts and hold them in their minds long enough to get them on paper in sequence. These steps are quite difficult alone, but the task is more difficult for students who struggle with spelling, grammar, and letter formation. I am not surprised that children become frustrated when they have wonderful ideas and they have to endure the painstaking process of committing those ideas to paper. I was encouraged, however, when several children stated that they enjoyed developing ideas for their own original stories.

I found other evidence in the surveys that indicated that the writer's workshops helped some students become more confident about their writing ability. On his presurvey, one child wrote, "My least favorite part of writing is the ending because I do not like to solve the problem." When I interviewed this child, he told me that he struggled with endings and he thought that studying endings in our reading group was helpful. When I read his postsurvey, I was pleased to see that he wrote, "I like all of them the same because they are fun to do." On the postsurveys, some children were able to articulate their favorite parts of writing by using the language we used during our discussions. For example, one student wrote, "My favorite part of writing is the middles of stories because I like to make up adventures in my stories."

As a writer, I tend to be quite emotional about my work and I judge my writing based on the way I feel about it. I was fascinated when I realized that some children look at writing in a very quantitative way. When I asked them whether they were good writers, some children consistently relied on tangible evidence to support their answers. On his presurvey, a student wrote, "I think I am a good writer because I already have a published book." After the workshops were over, this student used a similar tool to measure his progress. He wrote, "I think I am a good writer because I am already working on my hardback," on his postsurvey. Other children used the scores on their stories to prove that they were good writers.

When I read one postsurvey, I became quite concerned. The student wrote that she was not a good writer because she "can't think of ideas." This response came from a child who often says that she "hates school." She resists assignments and, although she is extremely capable, she works slowly and her writing and coloring are sloppy. When I helped this student write the story that would be published in her hardback book, she would not put words down on paper unless I repeatedly prompted her. She told me her entire story, and then when I asked her what she wanted to write next, she said, "I don't know." This student is an excellent reader, and she can put wonderful language in her stories. However, her writing is often disorganized and difficult to understand. When I reviewed my comments from her portfolio and from the four stories she wrote during my writer's workshops, I consistently wrote that the parts of her stories did not relate and, therefore, her stories were not understandable and her endings did not solve the problem. I was not surprised that this student reacted negatively to writing because she has a similar reaction to most activities at school. However, I am concerned because she transferred her criticisms from the activity to herself. After she turned in her survey, I pulled her aside and told her about some aspects of her writing that I really enjoy. She just shrugged her shoulders and repeated, "I don't like it." The other students seem to either enjoy or accept writing. They are beginning to see themselves as part of a community of writers. I worry that this one student will be isolated from that community if I cannot find a way to motivate her as a writer.

Rubrics were helpful for some students, but they were not effective for other students.

When I created the rubrics for each of my lessons, I hoped that they would help the students organize their thoughts and remember the important ideas from my lessons. As I reflected on the writer's workshops in my journal, I wrote the following:

> Although the children seem to understand the parts of stories during our discussions and they seem to try to apply them in their own writing, the rubrics do not seem to be very meaningful. The children do not refer to the rubrics during their writing unless I continually prompt them, and they often just race through it at the end of their writing as an afterthought. However, I still think they should be able to see the goals clearly before, during, and after writing if they are expected to meet those goals in their stories.

Nancy helped me take a more critical look at the rubrics I had created. I divided each story element into three parts. In each of the three sections, I included the main concept and then a few notes or questions that I considered prompts. I thought that these details would encourage the students' thinking, but they actually seemed to overwhelm the children and make them unsure of whether

(Continued)

(Continued)

they had met each goal. I could tell that the rubrics were not helpful because I often found them left carelessly on the floor. During the third workshop, a student approached me with his rubric and asked, "What's this for?" My rubrics were not a useful resource for the children because the way that I thought about stories and the ways that they thought about stories were different. I needed to find a way to present the expectations for the story elements in a way that was meaningful for my second graders.

Then, while I was visiting my mother's first-grade classroom, she showed me a rubric that another first-grade class had created. The teacher listed scores from zero to six, and the children determined the characteristics of a story that would receive each score. The children had expressed their expectations in clear, simple terms. For example, a child who received a zero "did not write." These young writers knew that they were making decisions as they wrote and that those decisions had consequences for their writing. By asking students to articulate the decisions they make as they write, teachers are encouraging awareness. "Self-awareness leads to self-evaluation and, in turn, thoughtful decision making" (Avery, 1993, p. 417). I decided that my learners should be invited to be a part of setting the expectations that I was using to evaluate their stories. I hoped that, by being a part of creating the expectations, the students would feel more ownership and would begin to use the rubrics more thoughtfully.

During the fifth writer's workshop, my students and I focused on endings. After we discussed endings and the students wrote endings for their stories, I told the students that we were going to put together what we had learned about the different parts of stories. I said that the list they created during our discussion would be the checklist for their castle stories the next week. I took notes as the students suggested ideas, and I was amazed by how much information they had gathered about stories. As I recorded their ideas, I tried to use their words so that I would not add my influence to their expectations. When I created the checklist for the complete story workshop, I used the students' ideas. The expectations were expressed in clear, concise phrases. Hearing the students articulate their ideas helped me begin to understand the way an appropriate expectation for a second-grade writer should sound and look.

During the complete story workshop, I did not notice that the students used the checklists more or less than before. When I interviewed a small group of students, I invited them to compare a rubric that I wrote and the rubric that they wrote. I asked, "Did one of these checklists help you more, or were they both about the same?" One child replied, "The complete story checklist helped more because it helped you do a whole story in one day really quick." The students did not seem to care that they had written one rubric and I had written the other. I think that the students would have felt more ownership if they had been involved in creating the rubrics throughout the series of workshops. When I asked them to share their expectations for the last workshop, they basically reiterated the ideas I had emphasized during instruction. I am not surprised that they did not think of the checklist as their ideas.

During my interview, I also asked, "Do checklists help you write?" I could not tell simply by observing whether my rubrics had been effective for the students. One child replied, "Yes, because I could check down everything I did. Step by step." Another child agreed by saying, "I think it's good because the first thing I do is look at it and it says 'dazzling first sentence,' so I just think of one." Another student responded emphatically. She said, "No, because it makes you think, 'Oh, my story isn't very good, so I have to do better.'" She elaborated, "I like my stories how I like them. I don't like other people judging them just because they think they don't have any detail. I like it the way it is."

Once again, I was reminded of the wide range that characterizes second-grade writers. While one student found comfort in the opportunity to organize his thoughts, another student saw it as a threat to her as a writer. I began to realize that second-grade teachers need to develop ranges of strategies for teaching writing that are as varied as the unique writers in their rooms.

Collaboration

Collaborating with others helped some
students develop ideas and grow as writers.

I was not sure what to expect when I assigned partners and allowed the students to brainstorm with their partners before writing. However, I was anxious to add this type of prewriting to my workshops. According to Calkins (1986), talking is a better form of prewriting for second graders than drawing because their ideas are becoming more detailed and complicated. As the students chat casually about their stories, they focus on content rather than the mechanics of putting their ideas down on paper. This takes the students' attention away from the "right way" to approach their writing and helps them realize that "they have something to say and a voice with which to say it" (p. 70).

I was amazed by the way that my role in the classroom changed when I allowed the students to support each other during writer's workshop. I usually found myself talking with one writer after another. As I traveled around the room, students who were struggling would begin to trail after me with their papers clutched in their hands. I was putting all of my effort into keeping the students' pencils moving, so I didn't have time to have a meaningful discussion with a student who was struggling with writer's block or a complicated idea. When the students brainstormed with their partners, I found that my role was less frantic. I could talk quietly with a student who was concerned about his or her writing. I could eavesdrop on conversations to gain insight into the students' thinking. The students were becoming a community of writers, and they were beginning to realize that the teachers were not the only people in the room who could help them when they encountered problems in their writing.

(Continued)

(Continued)

These partnerships seemed to be the most helpful for students with average writing ability. I enjoyed participating in their conversations and I saw wonderfully creative ideas emerge as the children worked together. When a group of two boys met, they realized that one partner wrote a beginning about a dragon and the other partner wrote a beginning about a knight. They began discussing potential problems for their stories. When I visited their conference, they proudly told me that they were going to use the same problem for their stories. One writer described the problem from the dragon's perspective and the other writer described the problem from the knight's perspective. Another writer was struggling to start his castle story and his partner suggested some ideas that helped him begin. He acknowledged her help by naming the heroine of his story after her.

Other students found that collaborating with others was ineffective for them as writers.

I found that the student partnerships were not very effective for the special needs students in our room and for the most independent, fluent writers in our room. The students who were struggling as writers needed a great deal of support from teachers as they were developing their ideas and as they were putting their ideas on paper. They rarely had time to give each other feedback because they were putting all of their energy into creating their own stories.

The most fluent, independent writers in the classroom were partners during the workshops. During the interview, when I asked about working with partners, Kate replied, "It's fun, but we just have our own ideas. Charlie says something and it kind of gives me an idea, but it doesn't go well with my story. So, then I do another idea. Then, I ask Charlie if he wants to do this idea, but he changes it around, so it gets confusing." When I reviewed my supervisor's notes from watching this team's peer conference, I noticed that they did not really interact. They stated their ideas out loud, but they seemed to ignore each other. These students had their ideas in place, and they did not seem open to considering other ideas.

Finally, during the interview, another student told me that he did not enjoy working with his partner. When I asked him to elaborate, he said, "He always had to go away from me." During several workshops, we had behavior problems with this student's partner. The boys were often separated, so the partnership was not helpful for them.

Connections to Literature

Students who make connections between writing and reading can use literature to help them solve problems when they are writing.

Routman (2002) states that, as teachers, "we must immerse our students in outstanding literature every day" to "help them notice how the author has dealt with the topic, genre, organization, setting, mood, word choice, sentence construction, and more" (p. 221). Throughout this project, I was amazed by the ways that the students used the literature around them to solve problems in their own writing. When they had difficulty finding ideas, several students turned to literature for inspiration.

Dana wrote a story called "The Knights and the Dragon" shortly after we read *The Paperbag Princess* by Robert Munsch. In her story, Dana's knights defeated a dragon with clever tricks that resembled the tricks Elizabeth used in *The Paperbag Princess*:

> Then the knights came out and said is it trew [*sic*] that you can drink 30 gallons of water in only 5 seconds? The dragon said yes so he did. Then the knight said can you fly and stay up for three whole days? The dragon said yes so he did. All those three days he was still up. The dragon was egsasted [*sic*] on the third day.

In her previous story, Dana had difficulty writing an ending that solved her problem. By using Munsch as a model, she tackled this problem and was able to bring her story to a satisfying end.

When I read Jack's story, I noticed that he was making connections between writing at school and reading at home. His story, "It All Started Out from an Egg," echoes J. K. Rowling's *Harry Potter and the Sorcerer's Stone*:

> Ocne [*sic*] there was a wizared [*sic*] named Hegred. Hegred found an egg it was relly [*sic*] big so he figrd [*sic*] that it was a dragon's egg. So he took it back to his cottage in the woods and put it over his fire to keep it warm. In 15 days it hatched it was a boy dragon in five day [*sic*] he was bigger than hegred [*sic*] and sarted [*sic*] to nock [*sic*] out the walls and started to blow fire and burning [*sic*] Hegred's house down.

Jack also wrote a retelling of *Cinderella* during another writer's workshop. He has wonderful ideas and excellent language, but he seems to be more comfortable writing when he begins in a familiar place. He raises hermit crabs with his brother and sister, and he often uses the hermit crabs as characters in his stories. By starting with familiar ideas, Jack has gained the confidence to take risks by using more descriptive language and reading his stories to his classmates.

During my inquiry project, my reading group was reading a version of *The Ugly Duckling*. Charlie, a student in my reading group, mentioned his dissatisfaction with the story's message during several group discussions. In *The Ugly Dragon*, Charlie used his voice as a writer to approach issues that made him uncomfortable as a reader:

> Once upon a time in an enchanted forest with surprizes [*sic*] anywhere you went there lurked a kind and friendly dragon. It was raining cats and dogs. She laied [*sic*] 30 eggs. Every egg was silver except one. It was gold. One day when the sun was boiling like an oven the eggs

(Continued)

(Continued)

hatched. One after another. All of them looked like the mommy dragon except one. The one had gold scaly skin and cotton white teeth and the eyes were root beer brown. It was very good looking when the sun was shining on its back. All of the other dragons teased him. The one dragon was sweet and kind while the others were mean and furious and greedy.

During reading group discussions, Charlie used the illustrations in *The Ugly Duckling* to argue that the main character was different, not ugly. When I read *The Ugly Dragon*, I noticed that Charlie immediately established that his main character "was very good looking when the sun was shining on its back." Charlie also revised the end of the well-known tale. His ugly dragon met and befriended a giant without having to change his appearance at all. I was surprised and pleased when I noticed that Charlie was connecting reading experiences that happened outside of our workshops with his writing. He was truly reading as a writer, and his writing incorporated the insights that he gained as a reader.

Students who are immersed in quality literature incorporate more literary language in their writing.

For me, writing is exciting and empowering because it gives me a chance to put my voice on paper. "Voice is hard to define, but when it's in—or missing from— a piece of writing, you sense it. Writing with voice has richness and sparkle, a distinct human spirit that makes you feel you know the writer" (Routman, 2002, p. 222). Throughout the series of writer's workshops, I approached the issue of voice with my students by focusing on "dazzling" language. We searched for dazzling words as we read children's literature, we brainstormed dazzling words as we prepared to write, and we celebrated dazzling words in our peers' stories. I used literature and the checklists to encourage the children to use "dazzling first sentences" in their beginnings, "dazzling action words" in their middles, and "dazzling feeling words" in their endings. I also incorporated the search for dazzling words into my reading group instruction. As they read, the children recorded descriptive language. Then, they chose an interesting word or phrase and studied it more carefully by completing a word web.

The students responded eagerly to this aspect of the writer's workshops. Anna Quindlen's description of her heroine in *Happily Ever After* (1997) included the phrase "her eyes were the color of root beer." After I read this description to my students, I found similar phrases in at least five stories. I also noticed that the "dazzling language" appeared in stories written by students with a variety of writing abilities. This aspect of writing seemed to appeal to many of the children, and they wanted their readers to be impressed with their word choices:

"Ok said Mini in her tinest vos [*sic*]"; "One snowy cold day when the snow was falling like little cotten [*sic*] balls deep down in the forist [*sic*] there was a princess named Sofy. Her hair was the color of the sun and her eyes were the color of the sky, and her skin was the most peachiest peach you ever did see"; " . . . that nasty fox came prowling along . . . "; and "Then the room groo [*sic*] silent."

As I compared the students' stories throughout the workshops, I also noticed that their language was becoming more literary. During the first workshop, Henry tried to include the descriptive language that was discussed during the minilesson. He has many details, but his sentences sound more like a list than a story:

His name was Charlie. Charlie was a boy [*sic*] he was 26 years old and had a little brother named Cameron. Charlie has brown hair and his brother has blond hair.

During the last writer's workshop, Henry wrote a story in which the descriptive language flows more naturally:

One cold winter day in January there was a feirs [*sic*] dragon named Jack who had an advencher [*sic*] with a knight named Sam. Jack never let a sigal [*sic*] soul past him. Jack liked to practice roring [*sic*] and he liked to go into the casal [*sic*] and burn things like bowlse [*sic*] and pots.

As my students' voices began to emerge in their stories, I noticed a growing enthusiasm for sharing stories with others. When volunteers read their work aloud to the class, the students always made comments about the dazzling language.

Students who read from a writer's perspective are comfortable thinking critically about literature.

Writing can be an extremely intimidating task. Many children approach published literature as "polite guests" because they get the implicit message that printed words cannot be challenged (Calkins, 1986, p. 223). As a writing teacher, I wanted to be very careful about the message that I sent to my students as I shared literature. I hoped that my students would learn to think critically about every text they read, rather than viewing published books as "final and unquestionable" (Calkins, p. 224). Therefore, during the minilessons, I encouraged the students to respond to the literature with both praise and criticism.

Throughout the series of minilessons, I noticed that the students' comments were becoming more and more sophisticated. They were thinking about the choices that the authors made, and they were becoming more comfortable sharing their opinions about the effectiveness of the authors' writing. Their comments became more thoughtful during literature discussions, student sharings, and reading groups:

(Continued)

(Continued)

When people start to read it, they don't want to stop.

I would recommend this book to others because it teaches you a lesson. Don't be mean to others just because they are different.

He didn't name the characters. He just called them prince and princess. I think it would be good if they had names.

I'd say he needs to work more on the descriptive action words.

I would not recommend this story to another reader because the author didn't put a lot of detail at the end.

I think it's good because it's like a mystery. You want to see what happens next. (Scripted notes, 3/14)

During the final writer's workshop, I realized that my students had become quite comfortable thinking critically about published literature. I wanted to practice using the "Complete Story Checklist" with the whole group, so I read *Cabbage Rose* by M. C. Helldorfer and we completed the checklist as a class. I assumed that, because *Cabbage Rose* was a published book, the students would think it was well written. As our discussion progressed, I noticed that the children were suggesting that the author needed to keep working on many aspects of the book. They also disagreed with each other's opinions about the story:

Sarah: I think we should give it a check because there was no adventure in it.

David: I think it's a star because she went on an adventure to the castle. (Scripted notes, 3/21)

The thoughtfulness of their comments and the confidence with which those comments were delivered showed me that my students were becoming more critical thinkers.

The students in Room 20 are members of a writing community that includes published authors.

Calkins (1986) describes reading as a chance for young writers to "learn from their more skillful colleagues" (p. 221). As my project progressed, I was encouraged by evidence that suggested that my students were thinking of themselves as writers. During one morning greeting, I asked the students to share a favorite fairy tale character. I was amazed and pleased when several of them asked if they could name characters from their own writing. They were placing their writing in the same category as the books they were reading, and published authors were their equals rather than their superiors. For me as a writer and a writing teacher, this is the most satisfying outcome. If my students leave second grade knowing that they are writers, I will feel that I have succeeded as a writing teacher. (Russell, 2002)

In addition to noting the ways Julie built a case for each of her 10 claims through stringing together pieces of evidence from multiple data sources to support her learning, there are two additional noteworthy points to highlight from the main text of Julie's inquiry write-up that appears on the previous pages.

First, notice under Claim 3 that when Julie discusses patterns from her survey, she ends by discussing one child that did not fit into any of the patterns she previously mentions:

> When I read one postsurvey, I became quite concerned. The student wrote that she was not a good writer because she "can't think of ideas." This response came from a child who often says that she "hates school." She resists assignments and, although she is extremely capable, she works slowly. . . . I am not surprised that this student reacted negatively to writing because she has a similar reaction to most activities at school. . . . However, I am concerned because she transferred her criticisms from the activity to herself. . . . The other students seem to either enjoy or accept writing. They are beginning to see themselves as part of a community of writers. I worry that this one student will be isolated from that community if I cannot find a way to motivate her as a writer.

While teacher-inquirers are often quite excited about finding patterns in their data and are most apt to report those patterns when writing, it is also insightful to look at data that do not fit and also include explanations in the write-up of an inquiry of why those data do not fit. Research methodologists commonly refer to this as "negative cases." It is often through looking critically at data that do not fit and reporting this in your writing that you learn more about the patterns themselves. In addition, reporting about data that do not fit enhances the credibility of your inquiry. In the absence of sharing negative data, you risk painting an unrealistic portrait of your classroom that can be met with skepticism by your audience who know well that nothing that occurs within the vast complexities of teaching is simple. Reporting your negative data contributes to creating a picture of your learning that rings true to life.

Second, note that each of Julie's 10 claims was supported by multiple sources of data, but not nearly all the data Julie had collected over the two months of her inquiry or that she had sorted into categories during data analysis. Through her writing, Julie selected the most powerful pieces of data to represent the patterns she found and the statements of her learning. Realize that as you construct your case to support statements of your learning through inquiry, you may experience difficulty selecting which data excerpts to use. As Wolcott (1990) notes,

> The major problem we face . . . is not to get data, but to get rid of it! With writing comes the always painful task (at least from the

standpoint of the person who gathered it) of winnowing material to a manageable length, communicating only the essence rather than exhibiting the bulky catalogues that testify to one's painstaking thoroughness. (p. 18)

Once the winnowing down is completed and your arguments clearly articulated, the last step in writing up your inquiry is providing conclusions.

Step 4: Providing Concluding Thoughts

When you read a good mystery, you expect that the conclusion of the book will provide answers to solve the mystery. Similarly, as you near the end of writing up your work to share it, you may conceive of concluding thoughts as being answers to the initial questions posed by the inquiry study. Sometimes, this might be the case. However, just as often, concluding thoughts do not answer the initial research question but generate additional questions and further areas for inquiry. Recall in Chapter 5, where we discussed data analysis, we shared that the work of a teacher-researcher is never quite finished as good data analyses generate more questions than answers. It is difficult to conceive of how to finish a piece of writing when the work of a teacher researcher is never done. Many teacher-inquirers finish their work by reflecting in general on the specific inquiry just completed, generating directions for the future, and stating further wonderings. We end this chapter with the concluding passage from Julie's paper. As you read, note how she used these three techniques to bring closure to her written work.

The Next Step

During my last writer's workshop, as Linda was walking around the room, she paused at Michael's desk. Michael faces many obstacles in the classroom, and writing is particularly challenging. At the beginning of the year, we struggled to get him to pick up his pencil at all. Linda began to read over Michael's shoulder, and then she asked the whole class to stop working and listen to the beginning of Michael's new story:

One morning when the sun was makeing [sic] it's [sic] way over the montons [sic] to shine so the erth [sic] has some lite [sic]. A batel [sic] was going to begin. On a lowd speeker [sic] a king said knights begin the batel [sic]. The knights started smacking sords [sic] to gether [sic] and it sonded [sic] like thunder.

The other students complimented him enthusiastically, and he began to beam. Linda encouraged him to work hard and finish the story, and he was able to score above the benchmark for second grade.

When I heard Linda read those words, and I saw the way the other children supported Michael's efforts, I got tears in my eyes. For me, this project was filled with these magical, dazzling moments. I found that teaching writing is filled with challenges. I also found that confronting those challenges and pushing myself as a teacher make writing instruction even more engaging and exciting than I had hoped it would be. I learned that every student in my room has something dazzling to say, and my job is to help him or her find his or her voice.

Finally, I learned that my journey as a writing teacher is just beginning. I was not able to help my second graders grow as writers until I began thinking about writing from their perspective and tailoring my instruction toward them and their needs. Therefore, my workshops will change with each group of young writers that enters my classroom. After doing this project, I am able to see that challenge as a wonderful chance to grow as a teacher.

As I completed my project, many wonderings remained. One huge challenge for the future is finding a way to give young writers "the luxury of time" (Calkins, 1986, p. 23). During the interview, I asked the children to tell me how I could help them grow as writers. I was surprised when one student said, " . . . maybe you could let us be." She wanted uninterrupted time to put her thoughts on paper. I agree that students need time to just write if they are going to develop a love for writing. However, after this year, I realize that finding this time will be an enormous task. Managing time is difficult for me, but I cannot ignore this crucial part of writing instruction. As I develop a schedule next year, I will need to continue to listen to my students as I establish priorities and make decisions.

Routman encourages teachers to "take the risk of writing in front of [their] students" (2002, p. 211). I wanted to incorporate this element into my workshops, but I was not brave enough to show my writing to my students. I felt enormous tension because I was asking my students to do something that I was not willing to do myself. Next year, my first challenge as a writing teacher will be sharing my own writing with my students. I am nervous, but I am also curious about the effect my writing might have upon the workshop environment. I was incredibly impressed by the writing community that my students created this year, and I would be honored to be an active part of that community. (Russell, 2002)

CHAPTER 7 EXERCISES

1. Outline an inquiry write-up for your study using the four components of a write-up shared in this chapter: (1) providing background information, (2) sharing the design of the inquiry (procedures, data collection, and data analysis), (3) stating the learning and supporting the statements with data, and (4) providing concluding thoughts.

2. Write one component at a time, sharing drafts of completed components with a colleague, your mentor, your intern, a university supervisor, or a family member to serve as a critical friend to offer feedback on your writing.

Figure 7.1 Inquiry Brochure Example

Where the Wild Things Are:
Helping First Grade Students
Develop Self-
Regulation and
Friendships

Research Question:

What happens when adults engage first grade students in social experiences and specific lessons focused on expected school behaviors?

Contact information:
gail.ritchie@fcps.edu

Further research questions:

☼ How can I involve parents in my efforts to help students develop social competence?

☼ What happens when I emphasize intrinsic motivation instead of behavior modification?

Where the Wild Things Are:
Helping First Grade Students
Develop Self-Regulation and
Friendships

Gail V. Ritchie, MEd., NBCT
Kings Park Elementary School
2004–2005 School Year

Implications for Practice:

What Works!

☼ Patience and humor
☼ Checklists
☼ Time outs
☼ Logical consequences
☼ Strategic listening lessons
☼ Modeling manners
☼ Literature
☼ Positive reinforcement
☼ Music
☼ Talking stick
☼ Visuals
☼ Hands-on experiences

Common Threads (of effective strategies)

♪ Entertaining—read-alouds, videos, singing, hands-on experiences
♪ Positive reinforcement
♪ Negative consequences

Figure 7.2 Inquiry Brochure Example

One-Stop Shopping for Resources and Communication

The use of Blackboard (FCPS 24-7 Learning) with teachers and parents

Fairfax County Public Schools

To what extent does Blackboard (FCPS 24-7 Learning) create effective communication between staff and administrators and provide a one-stop shopping location for teacher resources?

What did we do?

- Established a Blackboard (FCPS 24-7 Learning) Plan for the school

- Established procedures for how FCPS 24-7 Learning is used

- Reviewed Blackboard plan with staff; encouraged feedback

- Trained teachers and staff on the use of FCPS 24-7 Learning

- Required all teachers to maintain a class site with specific areas that would be consistent from year to year

- Created and maintained a staff site to model the use of Blackboard and provide a teacher resource and on-line community for teacher collaboration

- Used the Discussion Board for all staff communication, including Staff News, Committee Minutes, and Office Communications

- Required staff to read Marzano's *Classroom Instruction that Works* and participate in an *On-line Discussion*

- Administered surveys and held a focus group discussion with teachers

- Reviewed course statistics to analyze use and trends

What did we find out?

- Establishing a "must use" policy encouraged teachers to go to Blackboard to access information

- Establishing an on-line discussion provided opportunities for teachers who would not normally collaborate with each other (vertical articulation)

- Accessing the staff site daily encourages teachers to begin using, maintaining, and promoting their own sites

- Making Blackboard useful to the teachers encourages them to access this resource. The design has to be clearly laid out and intuitive. If there is difficulty finding information teachers will discontinue use of the site

- Having the KP administrators model the use of Blackboard, increased teachers' use of Blackboard for parent communication

- Administrators were instrumental in the transition from Outlook public folders to FCPS 24-7 Learning

- Not all students were able to access 24-7 Learning from home

- Next year, we will continue with our Staff Site and work toward having students access their class site from school

FCPS 24-7 LEARNING

Kings Park Elementary School
Michelle Crabill, SBTS
michelle.crabill@fcps.edu
Kathleen Walts, principal
kathleen.walts@fcps.edu
Sheila Walker, assistant principal
sheila.walker@fcps.edu
703-426-7000

(Continued)

209

Figure 7.2 (Continued)

The First Steps

- Create a school Blackboard Plan
- Create an online staff site
- Enroll all teachers and staff
- Have administrators move ALL communications to Blackboard (FCPS 24-7 Learning), posting important messages in the Announcements section of the site, etc
- Organize the site to meet the needs of the school staff. Highlights of our site include:
  - *Instructional Resources—with on-line resources and lesson ideas*
  - *KP Documents*
  - *KP Forms*
  - *KP ROAR (our weekly newsletter)*
  - *Staff Directory*
  - *Links to the Instructional Gateways*

A Parent/Teacher Communication Tool

- Teachers attended trainings as needed to create Blackboard site (FCPS 24-7 Learning)
- Teacher created and maintained a classroom site for communication with parents and students
- Required areas on teacher sites:
  - *Teacher Contact information*
  - *Weekly Announcements*
  - *Assignments including Word Study, Homework, or projects*
  - *Class Information including Newsletter, Schedule, Calendars, etc.*
  - *Links to Websites including school site and curriculum resources*
- Teachers updated items on the class sites weekly, monthly, quarterly, and yearly according to the school plan
- At Back-to-School Night, teachers informed there parents of how Blackboard will be used and how to login
- Teachers monitored the use of their class sites through course statistics
- Teachers promoted the use of Blackboard throughout the year in newsletters or other communications
- Blackboard training was held for parents at a PTA meeting

An On-line Community for Teachers

Quick access to:

- Administrator's announcements
- Office Communications
- Staff News
- Memos
- Crisis Plan
- Committee Minutes
- Staff Directory
- Staff Weekly Newsletter
- Links to Instructional Resources
- The Instructional Gateways
- Subject Area postings by committees or curriculum leads
- Discussion Board chat of Marzano Instructional Strategies

Teachers like:

- 24 - 7 access to information
- Collaboration with staff
- Password protected staff information anytime, from anywhere
- "One-stop shopping" for centrally located school and staff resources
- Modeling provided by the administrators

SOURCE: Used with permission of Kings Park Elementary School.

Figure 7.3 Inquiry Template Example

Using Lunch Dates to Break One Student's Silence

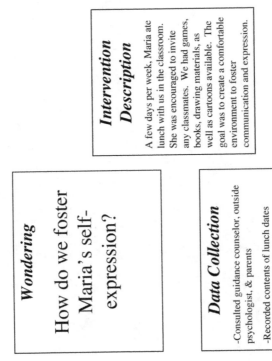

Wondering

How do we foster Maria's self-expression?

Data Collection

-Consulted guidance counselor, outside psychologist, & parents

-Recorded contents of lunch dates

-Recorded observation notes throughout school day

-Collected writing samples

Intervention Description

A few days per week, Maria ate lunch with us in the classroom. She was encouraged to invite any classmates. We had games, books, drawing materials, as well as cartoons available. The goal was to create a comfortable environment to foster communication and expression.

Findings

-Maria is strong academically despite her fear and avoidance of communication.

* *progress reports, Honor Roll, Aim High, high reading group*

-Yes or No questions are received by Maria with a greater response rate than open-ended questions.

* *She asked Maria if she had any brothers or sisters. Maria shook her head no. Teresa said, "Aw, man you're lucky!" Teresa asked Maria what she did over Spring Break. Maria did not answer and just stared. Mary asked if she played outside. Maria shook her head no. Mary said, "Don't tell me you stayed inside the whole week?!" Maria nodded yes.*

-Maria appears less apprehensive around the few students in the class who don't expect her to remain silent.

* *Jeanet asked each student in her group to name something they noticed in the picture. When it was Maria's turn, she looked at the picture and her lips quivered as if to speak. Barbara said, "She's shy." Maria looked away from the picture.*

Teresa turned to Maria and asked, "Was your name called?" Maria shook her head yes. Teresa said "Yay!" and put her hand up for Maria to give her a high-five. Maria hesitated greatly and then gave Teresa a high-five.

8

Becoming the Best Teacher and Researcher You Can Be

Assessing the Quality of Your Own and Others' Inquiry

I n Chapter 7, we strove to create a compelling argument for teacher researchers to write up their work and shared some powerful examples of inquiry write-ups as models. While we painted the writing up of your teacher research as an important part of the inquiry portrait, we begin this chapter by pointing out one danger inherent in writing up your work.

The one danger of completing a write-up of your inquiry is that when you are through, it feels final, like the end of a long journey. Therefore, you may begin to view practitioner inquiry as a linear process and focus on the outcome, the ending of one project, one exploration, one wondering . . . and then go back to the act of teaching and "business as usual." As a linear project, teacher inquiry is not a part of teaching, it is apart from it. When you complete your write-up, it's important to remember that teacher inquiry is not about doing an action research project that is completed at one point in time and is over. Rather, teacher inquiry is a continual cycle or circle that all educators spiral through throughout their professional life-times—a professional positioning or stance, owned by the teacher, where questioning, systematically studying, and subsequently improving one's own practice becomes a necessary and natural part of a teacher's work because of all the inherent complexity the act of teaching holds. Doing action research and writing up your work is one powerful way to actualize this stance. Although one's particular action research project might appear to culminate with the write-up, one's inquiry stance continues to be a pow-erful force and source of knowledge for self and others throughout the professional lifetime—just like a circle, it has no end.

As a teacher who adopts an inquiry stance toward teaching, you pro-vide a living example and inspiration for others in the teaching profession that inquiry is less about what one does (one action research project that has been written up) and more about who one is (a teacher who positions himself or herself professionally not as an implementer of a rigid, unchang-ing teaching routine year after year but as a constant and continuous ques-tioner, wonderer, and explorer throughout the professional lifetime). You understand that engaging in inquiry is not about solving every educa-tional problem; it's about finding new and better problems to study and in so doing, leading a continuous cycle of self and school improve-ment . . . truly, becoming the best that you can be.

Engaging in teacher research helps you become the best you can be in your teaching practice, but what about becoming the best you can be as a researcher? If, through inquiry, you can find a way to enhance and build your research skills in addition to the ways you enhance and build your teaching practice, the power of your inquiry magnifies exponentially with each cycle you complete. The purpose of this chapter is to help you find that way to enhance your research skills.

WHY IS IT IMPORTANT TO ASSESS THE QUALITY OF MY WORK?

When teachers complete their first inquiry project, it is often the comple-tion or end product of that work that gets all the attention. Certainly the completion of one cycle through the inquiry process should be noted, cel-ebrated, and shared with others, and we will discuss more about the importance of sharing in Chapter 9. Yet the spotlight on one particular inquiry project can potentially overshadow the importance of the inquiry stance. Remember, it is the ability of teacher research to actualize an inquiry stance toward teaching that is the reason for engaging in teacher research in the first place.

That being said, it is still natural, necessary, and important to focus on each single cycle through inquiry, as we have done in this text. It is through focusing intently on each individual cycle that teachers are enabled to take charge of their own professional development and continually improve their teaching. With each individual cycle of inquiry, the quality of the related teaching occurring in the classroom is enhanced. We believe that the degree of enhancement of classroom teaching brought about through inquiry is directly related to the quality of the inquiry. For this reason, it is important for teacher-inquirers to commit both to quality teaching *and* to quality teacher research.

One gets better as a teacher and researcher not only through engagement in their own teacher research but through the teacher research of colleagues. Cochran-Smith and Lytle (1991) remind us that

> teacher research should be valued not simply as a heuristic for the individual teacher. Rather, if it is to play a role in the formation of the knowledge base for teaching, teacher research must also be cumulative and accessible to different people over time for a variety of purposes. (p. 25)

As Cochran-Smith and Lytle note, teacher research differs from a heuristic, which usually leads rapidly to a solution of an informal problem as teacher research relies on systematic and intentional study. Teacher researchers do more than create heuristics as the work of inquiry moves beyond educated guesses or intuitive judgments considered reasonably close to the best possible answer based on loosely applicable information. Additionally, teacher researchers capture their systematic, intentional study in ways that can be shared with other teachers through writing (as discussed in the previous chapter) and/or oral presentation. As you hear and read the research of teaching colleagues, it is also important for you to understand the details of their work, not for the purpose of finding fault or becoming judgmental but for the purpose of seeking to understand and assess the ways a colleague's action research might inform your own teaching practice, a term researchers refer to as "transferability."

WHAT IS THE DIFFERENCE BETWEEN GENERALIZABILITY AND TRANSFERABILITY?

We have previously discussed that the reason we prefer the generic term *inquiry* to *action research* or *teacher research* is that the word *research* often conjures up images antithetical to the teacher research process (extensive number crunching and statistical analyses, white lab coats, experimental designs with a control and treatment group, and long hours in the library). Another image associated with the word *research* is generalizability, or the extent to which the findings of a research study will hold true and should be applied to other populations. Just as teacher research is not consonant with extensive number crunching and statistical analyses, white lab coats, experimental designs, and long hours in the library, teacher research is not meant to be generalizable to *all* teachers *everywhere*.

For example, recall Debbi Hubbell's inquiry in Chapter 4, on the relationship between the reading of fractured fairy tale plays and fluency development in seven of her struggling fourth-grade learners. If you revisit Debbi's DIBELS data (see Figure 4.16), you will note that each of the seven learners she was tracking improved his or her DIBELS performance over time. This does not mean that *every* teacher in Debbi's school ought to start using fractured fairy tale plays during reading instruction, as one might believe to be the case if the purpose of teacher research was to be generalizable. Remember, teacher action research is typically about capturing the natural actions that occur in the busy, real world of the classroom. Debbi selected DIBELS as one form of data to capture action in *her* classroom, not as a proven valid and reliable measure of fluency development so that her work can be generalized to all fourth-grade teachers everywhere! Additionally, Debbi's sample size (seven learners) was small. Debbi did not select these seven learners because she wished to have an adequate sample size so her findings could be applied to other classroom teachers. Rather, Debbi selected these seven learners because they were struggling, and she cared deeply about finding some ways to help them become more capable readers. Finally, Debbi didn't consciously and deliberatively isolate what might be considered her treatment variable (the reading of fractured fairy tale plays) from all other intervening variables that might play a role in her struggling students' fluency development (like Debbi's approach to the teaching of phonics and intonation). Rather, Debbi integrated everything she knew about the teaching of reading in combination with her introduction of fractured fairy tale plays to target these seven learners' success as readers. Debbi approached her research not as a scientist who wished to discover the best way to teach all children to read but as a teacher who cared passionately for seven individuals in her own classroom, with the hope of discovering some insights that might help her reach these struggling readers. Debbi's research, as is the case with all teacher research, was designed to focus *inward* on informing her own classroom teaching, rather than *outward* on proving that a particular strategy would be effective for others.

Keeping the notion of the inward versus outward significance of teacher research in mind, an important question emerges: "Is there any worth in Debbi's research for other teachers?" The answer to this question is a resounding, "Yes!" The worth of Debbi's (or any individual's teacher research) for other teachers is in its transferability to their own classroom. According to Jeffrey Barnes and his colleagues (2007), qualitative researchers define transferability as

> a process performed by readers of research. Readers note the specifics of the research situation and compare them to the specifics of

an environment or situation with which they are familiar. If there are enough similarities between the two situations, readers may be able to infer that the results of the research would be the same or similar in their own situation. In other words, they "transfer" the results of a study to another context. To do this effectively, readers need to know as much as possible about the original research situation in order to determine whether it is similar to their own. Therefore, researchers must supply a highly detailed description of their research situation and methods. (n.p.)

Another important component of assessing the transferability of other teachers' action research to your own classroom is considering the quality of that teacher's research, a process easier said than done. Teacher researchers need to understand the quality of the study in order to determine for themselves whether the knowledge shared in the form of findings would be potentially useful in their own classroom.

HOW DO I GO ABOUT ASSESSING TEACHER-RESEARCH QUALITY AND WHY IS IT SO DIFFICULT TO DO?

While a plethora of books, journal articles, and websites address the importance of engaging in action research and provide detailed instructions on how to do it, surprisingly, there has been relatively little discussion on how to assess action research quality. The reason for the lack of discussion on teacher-research quality may be that for years, the focus has been on getting teachers started in the process, as there is clear evidence that engagement in action research can be a powerful form of teacher professional development as well as a transformative process (Zeichner, 1986, 1996, 2003; Zeichner & Liston, 1996). Teacher research has been around for quite some time, and for years, action research quality has been the proverbial elephant in the room. It seems to have mattered more that teachers were engaged in action research, and as long as engagement was present and individual teachers were personally improving, teacher-research quality, in and of itself, received less attention. Yet we believe it is important for every teacher to consider quality. Recall that in the introduction to this book we stated,

> Teacher inquiry is a vehicle that can be used by teachers to untangle some of the complexities that occur in the profession, raise teachers' voices in discussions of educational reform, and ultimately transform assumptions about the teaching profession itself. Transforming the profession is really the capstone to the teacher inquiry story.

If teacher inquiry is about transforming the simple, connect-the-dots view of teaching so prevalently held by those who set and implement policy that affects the lives of teachers and students in schools and replacing it with a worldview of teaching that is deeply intellectual and fundamentally ethical and raises teachers' voices in the discussion of educational reform, it is critical to consider the question of quality. As the quality of the action research generated by teachers increases, the knowledge generated is perceived as both valid and valuable to policymakers, the general public, and other educational practitioners. As this teacher knowledge is created and recognized, transformation of the teaching profession becomes more likely as a result of the teacher-research movement.

While it is easy to make a case for the importance of assessing teacher-research quality, it is a much more difficult task to discuss how to do it! One reason it is difficult to assess teacher-research quality is that traditional notions of what constitutes quality research (such as generalizability) might creep into discussions of quality, even though they are not applicable to teacher-research studies. This is especially likely to occur when teacher research quality assessment is done by those with limited understandings of teacher research and the ways it differs from other research traditions as discussed in Chapter 1. In fact, we believe one reason teacher-research quality has received limited attention is that discussions of teacher-research quality might deter teachers from engaging in the process to begin with if discussions of quality become biting critiques or attacks on the validity, generalizability, or reliability of an individual's research. Such critiques, steeped in traditional notions of research and the process-product paradigm, would be erroneous and nonsensical. You cannot assess research produced in one research paradigm from the viewpoint of a different paradigm. To do so would be like assessing the play of a football player using the criteria invoked to assess the performance of a ballerina. A teacher researcher becoming discouraged due to assessments of their work that used nonsensical criteria would be a travesty!

Another complication associated with determining the quality of an action research effort is the dual purposes for engaging in teacher research. For example, one purpose of teacher research is to serve as a tool for self-directed and differentiated professional development that actualizes itself in self-regulated, lifelong learners who approach their learning from an inquiry stance (Glickman, Gordon, & Ross-Gordon, 2007). Using this purpose as a framework for assessing quality, one might consider a teacher's experience with teacher research to be of quality if, as a result of her participation, she developed an inquiry stance that caused her to regularly construct wonderings and make her practice problematic. However, the second goal of teacher research as discussed by Cochran-Smith and Lytle (1991, 1999) is to contribute to the knowledge base of teaching. In order to make a valuable contribution to the knowledge base for teaching, teacher research must be credible. In teacher research, credibility refers to the compatibility between the teacher researcher's inquiry findings and the reality lived out by students and teacher each school day in that same teacher researcher's classroom. Credibility of a piece of teacher research is enhanced by such mechanisms as engaging in an inquiry for a sufficient time period relative to the wondering being asked, situating that wondering in the existing knowledge base for teaching with thoughtful reference to what is already known about the subject, and checking consistency of inquiry findings by using more than one source of data to gain insights into a wondering. In this case, using the contribution to the knowledge base for teaching as a framework for assessing quality, one might consider a teacher's experience with teacher research to be of quality if the teacher-inquirer spent sufficient time studying her question, connecting her question thoughtfully to what is already known, and using multiple data sources to understand and represent the complexity of her problem for study.

It is possible for a teacher researcher's work to be considered of quality using the professional development framework but lacking in quality using the contribution to the knowledge base for teaching framework—and vice versa. Consider a teacher who has historically approached teaching as a stagnant routine. His first pass through the cycle of inquiry as a required professional development activity in his district focused on the implementation of a commercially prepared curriculum package with no research base, and he used only standardized test scores to indicate the value of this particular commercially prepared curriculum package. As a contribution to the knowledge base for teaching, this inquiry was lacking credibility as it was based on a curriculum that was disconnected from what is known about teaching, and he relied solely on one form of data to gain insights into his wondering. However, being immersed in this cycle of inquiry with other teacher researchers led him to begin to raise questions about his own teaching and his own unquestioned implementation of mandated commercially prepared material in his classroom. A teacher who once saw teaching as "black and white" (I implement a commercially prepared curriculum in my classroom in the ways I am told to) began to see shades of gray in his teaching practice (this commercially prepared curriculum may not work the same ways with all my learners, and its effectiveness is dependent upon my ability to supplement it with other materials). While this particular inquiry contributed little to the knowledge base for teaching, it was extremely powerful in moving a teacher forward in his own teaching practice. As you can see, the fact that teacher research serves dual purposes actually makes the work of assessing quality even more complicated than traditional research.

A third reason it is difficult to assess the quality of teacher research is the relationship between inquiry stance (one's way of being as a teacher) and the products one produces as a result of actualizing that stance (a piece of teacher research). As previously mentioned, more important than any one teacher research product is the inquiry stance. It is the cultivation of such a stance in every educator that will improve our profession. While you can't assess stance (you either have it or you don't), you can assess a piece of action research produced as an actualization of that stance. In fact, given the definition of inquiry stance, a teacher who possesses an inquiry stance toward teaching would logically invite reflection on the quality of individual pieces of teacher research.

But which comes first, the adoption of an inquiry stance toward teaching or the production of teacher-research projects? The posing of this question resembles the old chicken and egg adage, "Which comes first, the chicken or the egg?" It might be logical to think that stance comes first, but we have seen many teacher researchers approach the teacher-research process first as a project they were required to complete to earn professional development points for state licensure, as a new professional development initiative their school or district implemented (veteran teachers), or as a "university thing"—an assignment they had to complete for a college course (prospective teachers). While they initially approached their work as a *project*, it was through the completion of the project that they developed *stance*. If engagement in projects can lead to stance, once again it would become a travesty if any teacher researcher became discouraged by quality assessment and subsequently abandoned teacher research.

A fourth reason it is difficult to assess the quality of teacher research is that the ways teachers encapsulate what they did and what they have learned through the process of teacher research come in many shapes and sizes. Some teachers write detailed accounts of their work, some teachers write summaries or brochures, and still others present their work orally. No matter how teacher researchers encapsulate and report on their learning, there are always limitations in time and space. Teacher researchers make decisions based on time and space allotments in regard to which portions of their teacher-inquiry journey they will emphasize and sometimes, which portions they won't even mention in a written account or an oral presentation. Therefore, assessments might be made about the quality of teacher research based on the absence of particular components of the inquiry journey that may have been present but not a part of the written or oral report.

A final reason it is difficult to assess the quality of an inquiry is because in any discussion of teacher-research quality, it is important to consider where teachers are developmentally as researchers and teachers. Does one assess quality teacher research for all from the standpoint of what to look for in an experienced teacher researcher's work or from the standpoint of what would be developmentally appropriate for whatever phase of development a teacher researcher is at? Just as one's teaching practice develops over the years through experience, so does one's research skills. You would not hold the same expectations for the classroom teaching performance of a novice teacher as you would for a 25-year veteran. Likewise, it is unrealistic to think that the first time you engage in research, you will excel at every aspect of the inquiry process. Not excelling at every aspect of the process, however, is neither a reason to negate the value of a piece of teacher research nor, more importantly, a reason *not* to engage in teacher research!

Everyone has to start somewhere, and if you take the time to assess the quality of your research you will grow as a researcher through each cycle of the inquiry process. Furthermore, if you engage in careful, thoughtful assessment of others' action research, you can make more informed decisions about the transferability of your colleagues' research to your own teaching practice. Participating in careful discussions of quality—what it is and how to achieve it—helps us all improve both teaching practice and teacher research and further understand the intimate connection between the two. In turn, these discussions move the profession of teaching forward.

In the next section of this chapter then, we offer five indicators to consider the quality of your own and others' research, as well as spark a discussion among you and your colleagues about what constitutes quality. Definitions of each quality indicator are followed by two sets of questions. The first set of questions are those you can ask yourself as you reflect on and assess your own inquiry work. The second set of questions are those you can ask yourself as you reflect on and assess the quality of work done by other teacher researchers and the ways their work might be transferable to your own teaching context. Our list of quality indicators and questions is by no means meant to be definitive or exhaustive of all potential quality indicators but to serve as a starting point to reflect on your work. As you read these indicators, keep in mind that one develops as a teacher researcher over many years and many cycles of teacher research. Rarely is any teacher researcher outstanding in all aspects of the inquiry process all the time. Less important than using these indicators to scrutinize and "grade" every aspect of your own and others' work is using these indicators as a tool to gain new insights into the teacher-research process that you can apply to your next research cycle.

WHAT ARE SOME QUALITY INDICATORS FOR TEACHER RESEARCH?

Quality Indicator 1: Context of study. Teacher researchers provide complete information about the context in which their research took place. This may include, but is not limited to, information about the school, district, classroom, students, content, and curriculum. Questions you might ask yourself when you consider the context of your study include the following:

- Have I considered all aspects of my teaching context in the design of my study?
- Did I situate my teacher research for others so they will understand my context?

Questions you might ask yourself when assessing the quality and transferability of others' inquiry context to your own classroom include the following:

- In what ways are my teaching context and this teacher researcher's context similar and different?
- Did the teacher researcher describe his or her context in enough detail so I can understand the context in which his or her wonderings emerged and the decisions he or she made throughout his or her research?
- Did the teacher researcher thoughtfully consider his or her context in the design of the inquiry?
- To what extent did this teacher researcher's work stimulate my thinking about teaching and learning in my own context (even if his or her context was dramatically different from my own)?

Quality Indicator 2: Wonderings and purpose. Teacher researchers explain the root of their questions/wonderings in detail. The explanation makes a convincing case for the wonderings' personal importance to the researcher. The stated wonderings are connected to appropriate and pertinent literature from the field. The purpose and questions/wonderings are clearly articulated, free of educational jargon, focused inward (on the teacher's own practice), and open-ended (i.e., the teacher researcher did not pose a question for which the answer was already known). Questions you might ask yourself when you consider your wonderings and purpose include the following:

- Did I describe the dilemma or tension in my teaching that led to the formation of my wonderings?
- Did I connect my own personal wonderings with existing knowledge about my topic by mentioning related literature?
- Are my wonderings clearly articulated (free of educational jargon)?
- Did my wonderings focus on me, my personal classroom practice, and on something that I can *do* rather than on trying to "fix," "change," or "prove something" to others through my research?
- Did I ask something I really didn't know?
- Did I *not* frame my wondering as a simple, dichotomous (yes/no) question so as to honor all the complexity that teaching entails?

Questions you might ask yourself when assessing the quality and transferability of others' inquiry wonderings and purpose to your own classroom include the following:

- Did the wonderings emerge from a real tension, dilemma, issue, or problem of practice the teacher researcher faced?

- In what ways does the teacher researcher's tension, dilemma, issue, or problem resonate with my own felt difficulties and real-world dilemmas?
- Did the teacher researcher share the ways the tension, dilemma, issue, or problem his or her wondering addresses and resonates with broader discussions of related issues by addressing literature from the field?
- Were the teacher researcher's wonderings clearly articulated, free of educational jargon, and open-ended?
- Did the teacher researcher's wondering focus *inward* on the teacher's own practice?
- Did the teacher researcher convince me of his or her passion for the topic?

Quality Indicator 3: Teacher-research design (data collection and data analysis). Teacher researchers collect data from multiple sources (e.g., test scores, surveys, field notes, student work, interviews, journal entries). Each data collection strategy employed is clearly explained and is a logical choice in relationship to the teacher researcher's posed questions/wonderings. Teacher researchers include detailed explanations of all procedures and a time line for data collection, as well as an explanation of how data were analyzed. Questions you might ask yourself when you consider the design of your inquiry include the following:

- Did I carefully consider all the sources of data that could potentially give me insights into my wondering when I designed my inquiry (see Exercise 2 in Chapter 4)?
- Did I use three or more data sources to gain insights into my wondering? (e.g., field notes, student work, interviews, focus groups, pictures, video, journals, blogs, student performance on tests or other assessment measures, CFG feedback, surveys)?
- Did I collect literature related to my topic as a form of data?
- Did I explain all procedures associated with my inquiry including a time line for my work and how I analyzed data?
- Was my time line consonant with the nature of my wondering (Did I spend too much or too little time collecting data)?
- Was I flexible in implementing my plan for inquiry (Did I adjust my wonderings or data collection strategies along the way if I found such adjustments were important for my learning)?

Questions to ask yourself when assessing the quality and transferability of others' inquiry design to your own classroom include the following:

- Did the teacher researcher employ multiple forms of data to gain insights into his or her wonderings (e.g., field notes, student work, interviews, focus groups, pictures, video, journals, blogs, student performance on tests or other assessment measures, CFG feedback, surveys)?

- Given the teacher researcher's wonderings, were the data collection strategies the teacher researcher selected logical choices?
- Did the teacher researcher collect literature related to his or her topic as a form of data?
- Did the teacher researcher collect data for a sufficient amount of time to gain credible insights into his or her wonderings? (For example, if the data collection period was one week, did that time frame make sense for the wonderings? Conversely, if the data collection period was an entire school year, did that time frame make sense for the wonderings?)
- Did the teacher researcher explain all procedures associated with the conduct of the inquiry?
- Did the teacher researcher describe changes or adjustments he or she made in his or her inquiry procedures that were warranted based on what he or she was learning while engaging in the process?

Quality Indicator 4: Teacher-researcher learning. Teacher researchers articulate clear, thoughtful statements about what they learned through the process. Each statement is supported, in detail, by data. If relevant, data may also be included that did not appear to fit with what the teacher researcher is claiming, with possible explanations for the discrepant data. Teacher researchers weave readings and other relevant experiences into the discussion of their findings as the readings and experiences relate to what was learned. Teacher researchers discuss not only what was learned about their topic of study but also include a personal reflection on what was learned about the process of teacher research. Questions to ask yourself when you consider the learning that resulted from your inquiry include the following:

- Did I select a strategy for illustrating my findings to others (e.g., themes, patterns, categories, metaphors, claims, vignettes) that best captures what I learned through the inquiry? (See Chapter 6, Table 6.2.)
- Did I support every statement of learning with excerpts from my data?
- Am I confident my findings, as well as my selection of a strategy to illustrate my findings, emerged from my data and my learning through this cycle of inquiry rather than by forcing my data to fit the opinions and values I had in place before beginning the inquiry?
- Did I carefully consider data that didn't fit with the themes/patterns/ claims I am making as a result of my research?
- Can I explain data that didn't fit?

- Did I weave what I know about teaching and the topic of my inquiry from my prior experiences and readings into my analysis and interpretation of data?
- Did I reflect on what I learned about the teacher research process in addition to reflecting on what I learned about my teaching practice?

Questions to ask yourself when assessing the quality and transferability of the learning reported by others as a result of engagement in inquiry include the following:

- Did the teacher researcher select a powerful way to illustrate his or her findings to me (e.g., themes, patterns, categories, metaphors, similes, claims, assertions, typologies, vignettes)?
- Did the teacher researcher support every statement of learning with excerpts from his or her data?
- Are the learning statements made by this teacher researcher directly related to the teacher researcher's data, or is there a disconnect between the teacher researcher's learning statements and the data they share?
- Does the teacher researcher share and explain data that doesn't seem to fit with his or her learning?
- Did the teacher researcher integrate knowledge from his or her own prior experiences and educational readings into his or her analysis and interpretation of his or her data?
- Does the integration of these experiences and readings enhance the learning that emerged for this teacher researcher from his or her data and analysis or are they used to force data to fit into learning statements it appears the teacher researcher held prior to even beginning his or her research?
- Does the teacher researcher reflect on what he or she learned about his or her teaching as well as what he or she learned about the process of teacher inquiry?
- To what extent do this teacher researcher's reflections resonate with my own teaching experience?
- To what extent do this teacher researcher's reflections inspire me as a teacher and inquirer?

Quality Indicator 5: Implications for practice. Teacher researchers detail examples of instructional change they have made or will consider making based on what they learned through their research. Changes in practice flow logically from the teacher researcher's statements of learning. In addition, teacher researchers discuss wonderings that might be pursued in the future based on what was learned from their current teacher research. Questions to ask yourself when you consider the implications your inquiry holds for your practice include the following:

- Did my inquiry result in action (changes I have made or plan to make in my practice based on what I learned through this inquiry)?
- Are the actions I've taken or plan to take logical outgrowths of what I've learned through my inquiry?
- Do I have a plan for further assessing, reflecting on, and/or studying the changes in practice that have resulted from my inquiry?
- Did I share new wonderings that emerged for me as a result of my inquiry?

Questions to ask yourself when assessing the quality and transferability of the implications for practice reported by others as result of inquiry include the following:

- Did the teacher researcher address action he or she has or will take to change and improve teaching practice based on what he or she has learned?
- Are the stated actions informed by the teacher researcher's learning through this cycle of inquiry?
- In what ways do this teacher researcher's actions resonate with my own teaching experience?
- How might what this teacher researcher has learned and done throughout his or her inquiry apply to my own classroom teaching?
- What actions might I take in my own classroom teaching based on what I learned from this teacher researcher?

WHAT ARE SOME WAYS TO ENHANCE INQUIRY QUALITY?

As previously mentioned, the quality of teacher research can be enhanced simply by taking the time to reflect on and discuss the quality of your work with others and apply what you learn through these discussions to your next cycle as a teacher researcher. The questions we have provided in the previous section are designed to get you started on these reflections and discussions. In addition to engaging in collaborative reflections on the quality of your teacher research with colleagues, we have found that the coaching teacher-inquirers receive throughout the process is directly related to the quality of their work (Dana & Yendol-Hoppey, 2006; Drennon & Cervero, 2002; Krell & Dana, 2012). These coaches might be colleagues in your building with many years of inquiry experience or national board teachers in your district who have made inquiry a central piece of their teaching practice. You might also solicit help from university partners who specialize in coaching the teacher-research process. Whomever you select, involving an experienced coach can greatly enhance the quality of your inquiry, as engaging in conversation with a critical friend about your wondering will deepen both the process and the knowledge constructed. If you are interested in increasing the quality of teacher inquiry that occurs in your school, district, or teacher education program through careful and thoughtful attention to the development of quality coaching, you might enjoy the companion book to this text, *The Reflective Educator's Guide to Professional Development: Coaching Inquiry-Oriented Learning Communities.*

CHAPTER 8 EXERCISES

1. Table 8.1 summarizes the five quality indicators in this chapter and the corresponding questions you can use to reflect on and assess the quality of your own work. Use this table to review your most recent piece of teacher research. What do you consider to be your strengths as a teacher-inquirer? What are some areas you wish to improve on in your next pass though the teacher inquiry cycle?

Table 8.1 Quality Indicators for Assessing Your Own Inquiry

Quality Indicator	Description	Questions to Ask Myself When Self-Assessing the Quality of My Inquiry
Context of Study	Teacher researchers provide complete information about the context in which the action research took place. This may include, but not be limited to, information about the school, district, classroom, students, content, and curriculum.	• Have I considered all aspects of my teaching context in the design of my study? • Did I situate my teacher research for others so they understand my context?
Wonderings and Purpose	Teacher researchers explain the root of their wonderings in detail. The explanation makes a convincing case for the wonderings' personal importance to the researcher. The stated wonderings are connected to appropriate and pertinent literature from the field. The purpose and questions/wonderings are	• Did I describe the dilemma or tension in my teaching that led to the formation of my wonderings? • Did I connect my own personal wonderings with existing knowledge about my topic by mentioning related literature? • Are my wonderings clearly articulated (free of educational jargon)? • Did my wonderings focus on me, my personal classroom practice,

(Continued)

(Continued)

Quality Indicator	Description	Questions to Ask Myself When Self-Assessing the Quality of My Inquiry
	clearly articulated, free of educational jargon, focused inward (on the teacher's own practice), and open-ended (i.e., the teacher researcher did not pose a question for which the answer was already known).	and something that I can *do* rather than on trying to "fix," "change," or "prove something" to others through my research? • Did I ask something I really didn't know? • Did I *not* frame my wondering as a simple, dichotomous (yes/no) question so as to honor all the complexity that teaching entails?
Teacher-Research Design (Data Collection and Data Analysis)	Teacher researchers collect data from multiple sources (e.g., test scores, surveys, field notes, student work, interviews, journal entries). Each data collection strategy employed is clearly explained and a logical choice in relationship to the teacher researcher's posed questions/wonderings. Teacher researchers include detailed explanations of all procedures and a time line for data collection, as well as an explanation of how data were analyzed.	• Did I carefully consider all the sources of data that could potentially give me insights into my wonderings when I designed my inquiry (see Exercise 4 in Chapter 1)? • Did I use three or more data sources to gain insights into my wonderings? (e.g., field notes, student work, interviews, focus groups, pictures, journals, blogs, student performance on tests or other assessment measures, CFG feedback, surveys)? • Did I collect literature related to my topic as a form of data? • Did I explain all procedures associated with my inquiry, including a time line for my work and how I analyzed data? • Was my time line consonant with the nature of my wonderings? (Did I spend too much or too little time collecting data?) • Was I flexible in implementing my plan for inquiry? (Did I adjust my wonderings or data collection strategies along the way if I found such adjustments were important for my learning?)

Quality Indicator	Description	Questions to Ask Myself When Self-Assessing the Quality of My Inquiry
Teacher-Researcher Learning	Teacher researchers articulate clear, thoughtful statements about what they learned through the process. Each statement is supported, in detail, by data. If relevant, data may also be included that did not appear to fit with what the teacher researcher is claiming, with possible explanations for the discrepant data. Teacher researchers weave readings and other relevant experiences into the discussion of their findings as the readings and experiences relate to what was learned. Teacher researchers discuss not only what was learned about their topic of study but also include a personal reflection on what was learned about the process of teacher research.	• Did I select a strategy for illustrating my findings to others (e.g., themes, patterns, categories, metaphors, claims, vignettes) that best captures what I learned through the inquiry (see Chapter 6, Table 6.2)? • Did I support every statement of learning with excerpts from my data? • Am I confident my findings, as well as my selection of a strategy to illustrate my findings, emerged from my data and my learning through this cycle of inquiry rather than forcing my data to fit the opinions and values I had in place before beginning the inquiry? • Did I carefully consider data that didn't fit with the themes/patterns/claims I am making as a result of my research? • Can I explain data that didn't fit? • Did I weave what I know about teaching and the topic of my inquiry from my prior experiences and readings into my analysis and interpretation of data? • Did I reflect on what I learned about the teacher-research process in addition to reflecting about what I learned about my teaching practice?
Implications for Practice	Teacher researchers detail examples of instructional change they have made or will consider making based	• Did my inquiry result in action (changes I have made or plan to make in my practice based on what I learned through this inquiry)?

(Continued)

(Continued)

Quality Indicator	Description	Questions to Ask Myself When Self-Assessing the Quality of My Inquiry
	on what they learned through their research. Changes in practice flow logically from the teacher researcher's statements of learning. In addition, teacher researchers discuss action that might be pursued in the future based on what was learned from their current teacher research.	• Are the actions I've taken or plan to take logical outgrowths of what I've learned through my inquiry? • Do I have a plan for further assessing, reflecting on, and/or studying the changes in practice that have resulted from my inquiry?

2. Table 8.2 summarizes the five quality indicators in this chapter and the corresponding questions you can use to reflect on and assess the quality and transferability of others' teacher research to your own classroom and teaching context. Use this table to review a piece of teacher research that you have recently read or heard presented at a faculty meeting, as a class presentation, at a teacher inquiry conference, or at any other venue where you had the opportunity to hear teacher researchers share their work.

Table 8.2 Quality Indicators for Assessing Other Teachers' Inquiry

Quality Indicator	Description	Questions to Ask When Assessing the Quality and Transferability of Teacher Research to Other Teachers' Classrooms
Context of Study	Teacher researchers provide complete information about the context in which the action research took place. This may include, but not be limited to, information about the school, district, classroom, students, content, and curriculum.	• In what ways are my teaching context and this teacher researcher's context similar and different? • Did the teacher researcher describe his or her context in enough detail so I can understand the context in which his or her wonderings emerged and the decisions he or she made throughout his or her research?

Quality Indicator	Description	Questions to Ask When Assessing the Quality and Transferability of Teacher Research to Other Teachers' Classrooms
		• Did the teacher researcher thoughtfully consider his or her context in the design of the study? • To what extent did this teacher researcher's work stimulate my thinking about teaching and learning in my own context (even if his or her context was dramatically different from my own)?
Wonderings and Purpose	Teacher researchers explain the root of their wonderings in detail. The explanation makes a convincing case for the wonderings' personal importance to the researcher. The stated wonderings are connected to appropriate and pertinent literature from the field. The purpose and questions/wonderings are clearly articulated, free of educational jargon, focused inward (on the teacher's own practice), and open-ended (i.e., the teacher researcher did not pose a question for which the answer was already known).	• Did the wonderings emerge from a real tension, dilemma, issue, or problem of practice the teacher researcher faced? • In what ways does the teacher researcher's tension, dilemma, issue, or problem resonate with my own felt difficulties and real-world dilemmas? • Did the teacher researcher share the ways the tension, dilemma, issue, or problem his or her wonderings address and resonate with broader discussions of related issues by addressing literature from the field? • Were the teacher researcher's wonderings clearly articulated, free of educational jargon, and open-ended? • Did the teacher researcher's wonderings focus inward on the teacher's own practice? • Did the teacher researcher convince me of his or her passion for the topic?

(Continued)

(Continued)

Quality Indicator	Description	Questions to Ask When Assessing the Quality and Transferability of Teacher Research to Other Teachers' Classrooms
Teacher-Research Design (Data Collection and Data Analysis)	Teacher researchers collect data from multiple sources (e.g., test scores, surveys, field notes, student work, interviews, journal entries). Each data collection strategy employed is clearly explained and is a logical choice in relationship to the teacher researcher's posed questions/wonderings. Teacher researchers include detailed explanations of all procedures and a time line for data collection, as well as an explanation of how data were analyzed.	• Did the teacher researcher employ multiple forms of data to gain insights into his or her wondering (e.g., field notes, student work, interviews, focus groups, pictures, journals, blogs, student performance on tests or other assessment measures, CFG feedback, surveys)? • Given the teacher researcher's wonderings, were the data collection strategies the teacher researcher selected logical choices? • Did the teacher researcher collect literature related to his or her topic as a form of data? • Did the teacher researcher collect data for a sufficient amount of time to gain credible insights into his or her wonderings? (If the data collection period was one week, did that time frame make sense for the wonderings? Conversely, if the data collection period was an entire school year, did that time frame make sense for the wonderings?) • Did the teacher researcher explain all procedures associated with the conduct of the inquiry? • Did the teacher researcher describe changes or adjustments he or she made in his or her inquiry procedures that were warranted based on what he or she was learning while engaging in the process?
Teacher-Researcher Learning	Teacher researchers articulate clear, thoughtful statements about what they learned through the process.	• Did the teacher researcher select a powerful way to illustrate his or her findings to me (e.g., themes, patterns, categories, metaphors, similes, claims, assertions, typologies, vignettes)?

Quality Indicator	Description	Questions to Ask When Assessing the Quality and Transferability of Teacher Research to Other Teachers' Classrooms
	Each statement is supported, in detail, by data. If relevant, data may also be included that did not appear to fit with what the teacher researcher is claiming, with possible explanations for the discrepant data. Teacher researchers weave readings and other relevant experiences into the discussion of their findings as the readings and experiences relate to what was learned. Teacher researchers discuss not only what was learned about their topic of study but also include a personal reflection on what was learned about the process of teacher research.	• Did the teacher researcher support every statement of learning with excerpts from his or her data? • Are the learning statements made by this teacher researcher directly related to the teacher researcher's data, or is there a disconnect between the teacher researcher's learning statements and the data they share? • Does the teacher researcher share and explain data that doesn't seem to fit with his or her learning? • Did the teacher researcher integrate knowledge from his or her own prior experiences and educational readings into his or her analysis and interpretation of his or her data? • Does the integration of these experiences and readings enhance the learning that emerged for this teacher researcher from his or her data and analysis or are they used to force data to fit into learning statements it appears the teacher researcher held prior to even beginning his or her research? • Does the teacher researcher reflect on what he or she learned about his or her teaching as well as what he or she learned about the process of teacher inquiry? • To what extent do this teacher researcher's reflections resonate with my own teaching experience? • To what extent do this teacher researcher's reflections inspire me as a teacher and inquirer?

(Continued)

(Continued)

Quality Indicator	Description	Questions to Ask When Assessing the Quality and Transferability of Teacher Research to Other Teachers' Classrooms
Implications for Practice	Teacher researchers detail examples of instructional change they have made or will consider making based on what they learned through their research. Changes in practice flow logically from the teacher researcher's statements of learning. In addition, teacher researchers discuss action that might be pursued in the future based on what was learned from their current teacher research.	• Did the teacher researcher address action they have taken or will take to change and improve teaching practice based on what they have learned? • Are the stated actions informed by the teacher researcher's learning through this cycle of inquiry? • In what ways do this teacher researcher's actions resonate with my own teaching experience? • How might what this teacher researcher has learned and done throughout his or her inquiry apply to my own classroom teaching? • What actions might I take in my own classroom teaching based on what I learned from this teacher researcher?

3. Discuss the five quality indicators presented in the chapter with teacher-inquirer colleagues.

- Which of the quality indicators do you agree and disagree with and why?
- What are some additional quality indicators you would add to this list?
- How can you create a mechanism for providing honest feedback to colleagues on their inquiries that both honors and celebrates their work and provides areas for future growth and development as teacher researchers?
- How can you ensure that discussions with colleagues about enhancing the quality of their own as well as your own teacher inquiry in future cycles will not negate the value of the research you all have produced?

9

The Beginning at the End of Your Journey

Making Your Inquiry Public

Back in Chapter 2, you began your inquiry journey by finding and defining your first wondering. Since then, you have navigated components of the inquiry process—collaboration, data collection, ethical considerations, data analysis, and writing up and assessing the quality of your work. You are nearing the end of your journey, but there are still a few last steps that must be taken to make your journey complete. These last steps involve making your inquiry public through the sharing of your work with others.

WHY IS IT IMPORTANT TO SHARE MY WORK WITH OTHERS?

To illustrate the importance of sharing your work with others, imagine that as you start the last leg of your journey, you notice a large, stagnant pond and are enticed to create some type of movement or change in the water. As you near the edge, you notice that numerous large stones surround the pond. You reach down, pick up a stone, and toss it as far out into the center of the pond as your strength allows you. Lying beside the pond, the stone had no chance of impacting the water. But once tossed in, the stone not only disturbs the stillness of the water in the immediate vicinity of where it landed but also creates ripples of water that emanate out from the stone's landing place and eventually reach the perimeter of the pond.

An unshared teacher inquiry is like the stone lying beside the pond. Unless that inquiry is tossed into the professional conversation and dialogue that contributes to the knowledge base for teaching, the inquiry has little chance of creating change. However, once tossed in, the inquiry disturbs the status quo of educational practices, creating a ripple effect, beginning with the teacher himself or herself and his or her immediate vicinity (the students and his or her classroom) and emanating out to a school, a district, a state, and eventually reaching and contributing to the transformation of the perimeter of all practice—the profession of teaching itself.

Hence, it is critical that you "get into the pond" and share your inquiry for yourself, for your students, for other teachers, and for the profession. For you, the process of preparing your findings to share with others helps you to clarify your own thinking about your work. In addition to clarifying your own thinking, in the actual sharing of your work, you give other professionals access to your thinking so they can question, discuss, debate, and relate. This process helps you and your colleagues push and extend your thinking about practice as well.

Clarifying, pushing, and extending thinking are not the only benefits of sharing for you and your colleagues. Fellow professionals also benefit from the knowledge you created. For example, veteran teacher researcher George Dempsie's passion for using puppets as a form of pedagogy with young children led him to study and publish the results of this practice (Dempsie, 1997, 2000). In his own district, he has inspired puppetry as pedagogy in dozens of teachers, across 11 elementary buildings. In addition, as a mentor-teacher in a professional development school, he has shared his research with interns and inspired a large percentage of these new teachers to use puppets as a way to gain access into children's thinking. His presentations at conferences and publications allow his work to spread outside his immediate vicinity (classroom, school, and district) as well.

Sharing your inquiry with other professionals can change the very ways your students experience schooling. For example, one student teacher we know completed an inquiry on a second-grade child who was having great difficulty fitting into the structure of schooling but was not receiving any services because she did not qualify in traditional ways. The student teacher's inquiry illuminated many critical insights into the child that traditional forms of assessment would not have generated. Becoming an advocate for this child, the student teacher and her cooperating teacher shared the results of her inquiry with other specialists and the principal. Eventually, a full-time paraprofessional was hired to work individually with this child within the regular classroom each school day. In a year's time, the child made great strides forward in her academic and social development.

Another example of impacting students and colleagues through sharing your inquiry with others comes from Angela Jackson, a second-grade teacher at Woodson Elementary School in Jacksonville, Florida. Angela was one of the first teachers at her school to try inquiry as a mechanism for professional development. After completing one inquiry cycle, Angela found the process of teacher inquiry so powerful for her own professional learning that she wondered how she might translate this way of learning into a pedagogical approach she would use with her children. Using *teacher* inquiry to study the process of integrating *student* inquiry into instruction, Angela's classroom was transformed the next school year. When she shared what she learned about engaging students in the process of inquiry at a faculty meeting, other teachers as well as the principal and vice principal were so intrigued with the idea that the school set out to engage all students in inquiry the following school year. In May, every Woodson Elementary student shared an inquiry into a different learning topic of his or her own choosing at a student inquiry showcase, attended by parents and other visitors from across the district. A culture of inquiry for teachers *and* students quickly emerged at Woodson Elementary School, and within a few short years, *every* teacher and *every* student in the building engaged in inquiry *every* school year. Themes for teachers' engagement in inquiry, such as inquiring into the Common Core State Standards, provided a focus for this high-need, high-poverty school where 99% of the students receive a free lunch. As more and more teachers and students engaged in inquiry at Woodson over time, their school was transformed! Five years after receiving a failing grade from their state, Carter G. Woodson students made 92 learning gain points on their Florida Comprehensive Assessment Test, earning a school letter grade of "A" and being recognized as one of the highest-performing schools in the state. With the motto "Woodson: A Prescription for Inquiring Minds" buoying their efforts, this elementary school had reformed the way school worked for its students through collaboration, innovation, high expectations for every student, and the process of teacher inquiry. Read more about Woodson's success story in *Inquiring Into the Common Core* (Dana, Burns, & Wolkenhauer, 2013).

We have provided just three specific examples here to illustrate the power and, therefore, necessity of sharing inquiry. Some inquiries inspire small, local change. Some inspire large, sweeping change. All change, large or small, is significant in that the changes occurring are emanating from those best positioned to make a difference in education and those that for years have been kept from making that difference—teachers themselves.

Kincheloe (1991) writes about the ways teachers have been kept from making that difference using a comparison between teachers and peasants within a third world culture with hierarchical power structures, scarce resources, and traditional values:

> Like their third world counterparts, teachers are preoccupied with daily survival—time for reflection and analysis seems remote and even quite fatuous given the crisis management atmosphere and the immediate attention survival necessitates. In such a climate those who would suggest that more time and resources be delegated to reflective and growth-inducing pursuits are viewed as impractical visionaries devoid of common sense. Thus, the status quo is perpetuated, the endless cycle of underdevelopment rolls on with its peasant culture of low morale and teachers as "reactors" to daily emergencies. (p. 12)

By getting into the pond and sharing your inquiry, as a teacher, you contribute to breaking the cycle just described. You contribute to educational reform: "The plethora of small changes made by critical teacher researchers around the world in individual classrooms may bring about far more authentic educational reform than the grandiose policies formulated in state or national capitals" (Kincheloe, 1991, p. 14).

By getting into the pond and sharing your inquiry, you contribute to changing the ways some people outside of teaching view teachers and their practice and try to change education from the outside in. In the sharing of your inquiry, you contribute to reforming the profession of teaching—from the inside out! You become a teacher leader, a professional who engages in "experimentation and examination of more powerful learning activities with and for students, in the service of enhanced student productions and performances of knowledge and understanding. Based on this leadership with and of students, teacher leaders invite other teachers to similar engagements with students in the learning process" (Sergiovanni & Starratt, 1998, p. 149).

Teacher leaders slide their classroom doors open to collaborate with other teachers; discuss common problems; share approaches to various learning situations; explore ways to overcome the structural constraints of limited time, space, resources, and restrictive policies; and/or investigate motivational strategies to bring students to a deeper engagement with their learning. Teacher inquiry is a pathway to teacher leadership. The relationship between teacher inquiry and teacher leadership is further discussed in the following boxed inset.

TEACHER LEADERSHIP AND INQUIRY

Nearly 25 years ago, Roland Barth stated that "teachers harbor extraordinary leadership capabilities, and their leadership is a major untapped resource for improving our nation's schools (Barth, 1990, p. 124). In recognition of this fact, the importance of teacher leadership has been elevated in educational dialogue and conversation during the past quarter century (Barth, 2001; Crowther, 2009; Danielson, 2006; York-Barr & Duke, 2004), with both national standards (www.teacherleaderstandards.org) and many graduate degree programs in teacher leadership springing up throughout the nation (Leonard, Petta, & Porter, 2012; Ross et al., 2011).

Although teacher leadership has enjoyed a great deal of attention in the educational literature and in graduate programs at universities, the term remains ill-defined. For example, Wasley (1992) defines teacher leadership as "influencing and engaging colleagues toward improved practice" (p. 21). Whereas Crowther (1997) defines teacher leadership as

> an ethical stance that is based on views of both a better world and the power of teaching to shape meaning systems. It manifests in actions that involve the wider community in the long term. It reaches its potential in contexts where system and school structures are facilitative and supportive. (p. 15)

More recently, Charlotte Danielson (2006) defines teacher leadership as those who continue to teach while influencing practices of other teachers in other classrooms.

Regardless of the definition you hold for teacher leadership, according to Katzenmeyer and Moller (2001),

> When given opportunities to lead, teachers can influence school reform efforts. Waking this sleeping giant of teacher leadership has unlimited potential in making a real difference in the pace and depth of school change. (p. 102)

One way to awaken the teacher leader sleeping giant within you is by engaging in the process of inquiry described in this book and channeling what you learn through the process into leadership efforts within your school, district, state, and the profession at large.

Within the school and district, teacher leaders use both the *results from* and *process of* teacher inquiry to plan targeted professional development in areas of need. Teachers selecting this leadership option will examine their teacher research and determine where their findings and conclusions suggest new ideas for professional development in their context. For example, at Woodson Elementary School, teacher Angela Jackson found promise in translating inquiry as an approach to teacher professional learning into a pedagogical approach to working with her second-grade students. The results from her study ignited an interest in inquiry as a pedagogical approach to working with children at her school, and professional development opportunities for teachers to explore inquiry as an approach to instruction were

(Continued)

(Continued)

planned and implemented. The results of Angela's inquiry spurred professional development opportunities for teachers at her school. Inversely, the process of inquiry was later used at this school to structure professional development for all teachers on the implementation of the Common Core State Standards. Early release Wednesdays, a day when students were dismissed from school earlier than normal to provide teacher professional development time, were used for teachers to come together and formulate wonderings about what the Common Core would mean to their practice and support each other in their investigations into the standards. Teachers in the building organized, facilitated, and managed these meetings, demonstrating one actualization of the teacher leadership role.

Within the school and district and oftentimes moving beyond to the state level, teacher leaders use the process of teacher inquiry to engage in policy and advocacy work. Teachers selecting this leadership option do so by considering how their teacher research can be used to create meaningful policy directives and how these directives can move policy discussion at the school level and beyond. In this extension of inquiry, teachers take the findings from their teacher research and turn them into a policy brief. Sometimes the brief might illustrate the ways well-intentioned policy initiatives have had ill-intentioned effects on teachers and the students they teach. The brief, which can be shared with decision makers at the school level and beyond, is designed to provide relevant parties with an understanding of the importance of the teacher research findings, an explanation of how these findings can affect policy, and strategies for implementation of related policy. Many examples of teachers leading by using the process of inquiry to impact policy can be found in the text *Taking Action With Teacher Research* (Meyers & Rust, 2003).

Within the profession at large, teacher leaders use the process of teacher inquiry to contribute to the professional knowledge base for teaching. This means teachers intentionally focus on making their professional knowledge become a part of the research-based literature and, with this intention from the outset of their studies, go through all procedures and processes related to the ethics of conducting research (such as obtaining Institutional Review Board approval when inquiry is done in association with a university). Teachers selecting this leadership option transform their inquiry into a scholarly article that can inform the knowledge base and be used to guide the research of others. The article includes all the components normally found in scholarly work, presents findings in multiple forms to promote understanding, seeks to provide future directions for research, and is constructed with an understanding of the anticipated avenue for publication. Examples of teachers leading by contributing to the knowledge base for teaching can be found in articles published in such journals as *Networks: An Online Journal for Teacher Research*, *Educational Action Research*, *Action Research*, and *Voices of Practitioners*.

WHAT ARE SOME WAYS
I MIGHT SHARE MY WORK?

There are many structures in place that offer you opportunities to share your teacher inquiry. If you have written up your work, you have not only clarified your thinking but have produced a product that can easily be shared with others in multiple ways. First, you might begin simply by sharing your written work with local colleagues, your principal, or other professionals, asking them for some feedback. This sharing could potentially lead to the formation of a study group to discuss your particular inquiry and related topics. Another way to share your written work is to submit it to one of the many journals designed with a teacher-researcher audience in mind, such as *Action Research, Educational Action Research,* and *Voices of Practitioners.* Finally, you can share your written work online by exploring one of the many action-research websites, listservs, and online journals such as *Networks: An Online Journal for Teacher Research* (http://journals.library.wisc.edu/index.php/networks) and *Inquiry in Education* (http://digitalcommons.nl.edu/ie).

If you were not sold on writing in Chapter 7, you can select other mechanisms to share learning from an inquiry. These alternative mechanisms also engage teacher-inquirers in the process of clarifying thinking in a fashion similar to writing. Posters (see Figure 9.1), iMovies, PowerPoint presentations, and podcasts are powerful ways to share an inquiry that either complements or take the place of producing a formal write-up. For example, some of the PowerPoint slides from a presentation made by Debbi Hubbell of her inquiry into the reading of fractured fairy tale plays with fourth-grade struggling readers appear in Figure 9.2. While it is difficult to glean detail about a presentation by just looking at someone's slide and not

Figure 9.1   Inquiry Poster

Figure 9.2   PowerPoint Slides From Debbi's Presentation

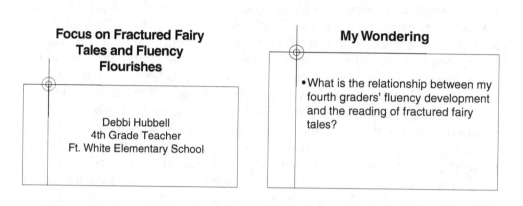

Focus on Fractured Fairy Tales and Fluency Flourishes

Debbi Hubbell
4th Grade Teacher
Ft. White Elementary School

My Wondering

- What is the relationship between my fourth graders' fluency development and the reading of fractured fairy tales?

My Instructional Plan

- **Day One:** Students chose parts, Debbi read the play to the group, then students practiced silently
- **Day Two:** Students practiced silently, then aloud with the group to Debbi; Debbi followed with short individual conferences
- **Day Three:** Students practiced silently, then aloud with the group to Debbi
- **Day Four:** Students practiced silently, then presented aloud with the group to the class

Data Collection

- DIBELS
- Observation of Students—Anecdotal Notes
- Student Artifacts—"Dear Mrs. Hubbell" letters

My Data Analysis Plan

- Charted DIBELS data
- Read through Observation Notes and Student Artifacts multiple times asking questions such as:
  What was happening?
  What have I learned about myself as a teacher?
  What have I learned about children?
  What are the implications of my findings for my teaching?
- Discussed analysis with teaching colleagues

DIBELS Test Results

	10/18	12/1	2/10	2/21	4/6
J	48	53	55	60	73
B	81	98	114	105	164
C	90	98	95	100	130
Ja	64	70	92	85	119
T	93	96	88	97	121
S	94	91	86	78	113
M	84	101	99	107	127

Three Themes:

- Enjoyment/Enthusiasm
- Students perceive academic benefits
- Positive social interactions

Enjoyment/Enthusiasm...

Dear Mrs. Hubbell, I would like to do more fractured fairy tales becaus the fairy tales bring more happiness to the school day and more laughter to the morning and the evening and we also learn a lesson from the tales. For instance we learned from one of the plays that you don't have to be perfect to marry prince that lesson was from spider-ella.

Academic Benefits...

Dear Mrs. Hubble, I realy liked doing the Fractured fairy tales because they teach you a lesson. For example, the Cheta and the sloth play tought you to start slow and save your energy for faster, when you get to the finish line. I also like them because they help you read more fluently, and with expression.

Dear Mrs. Hubbell I really did like it and I would realy want you to do more action fairy tales. And the last fairy tale we did I learned lots of few words that I didn't know. So it helped build my vocabulary. And it helps you become more of a fluent reader.

Positive social interactions...

Dear Mis Hubbell
I like the plays we did in class. And I like to be in the plays to. I all so like to entel tame the class. From being in the plays I learnd to try yore best at every thing. and do not be embarest.

Action

- Develop school/districtwide fluency objectives
- Diffentiate homework for 60wpm kids vs.180 wpm kids
- Make listening centers more effective
- Connect to struggling readers in secondary school

For More Information:

Please contact me at
debbihubbell@yahoo.com

SOURCE: Used with permission of Debbi Hubbell.

actually hearing the talk, note how Debbi's slides (and her presentation itself) followed the same four critical features of the teacher inquiry write-up we introduced in Chapter 7: (1) providing background information, (2) sharing the design of the inquiry (procedures, data collection, and data analysis), (3) stating the learning and supporting the statements with data, and (4) providing concluding thoughts. In whatever way you choose to share your work (a write-up, an oral presentation, PowerPoint slides, an iMovie, a podcast, an inquiry poster, or some combination of these mechanisms for sharing your learning), these four critical features are helpful to structure the ways you share what you learned. If you choose to share your work as an oral presentation, you may find Chapter 5 in the text *Digging Deeper Into Action Research* (Dana, 2013) a useful guide for developing and fine-tuning an oral presentation of your work.

Many teacher-inquirers use write-ups, PowerPoint slides, iMovies, podcasts, and/or posters to share their work orally in informal and more formal ways. Informally, some groups of teacher-inquirers organize a gathering outside of the school structure (e.g., an afterschool meeting at a coffee shop) to discuss their work. Or, if you are enrolled in an undergraduate or graduate class in which teacher inquiry is a focus, you may culminate the semester with a special meeting (perhaps a potluck dinner) where all share the results of their inquiry endeavors.

Within the school structure, formal sharing by teacher-inquirers is often accomplished through dedicating special portions of faculty meetings to inquiry or totally reconceptualizing faculty meetings to allow space for the ongoing sharing of inquiry (Dana, 1994, 1995). Some districts also devote entire inservice days to teacher inquiry, where colleagues gather to share their work. If you are not currently in a context where within-school structures for the sharing of inquiry like those described earlier are in place, you may begin building these structures simply by offering to talk for a few minutes about your work at a faculty meeting. Much of our own research has focused on building an inquiry culture (see, e.g., Dana, 1994, 1995, 2001; Dana & Silva, 2001, 2002; Silva & Dana, 1999). As a result of our research, we have learned that building a culture of inquiry takes time and is best started slowly, as some of your current administrators and colleagues (if you are a veteran teacher) or future administrators and colleagues (if you are a prospective teacher) may be reluctant to embrace inquiry and the changes it necessitates. While building an inquiry culture is a slow process, it has to start somewhere, and it can start with you. Be patient and persevere.

Finally, many teacher researchers present their work at conferences. There are numerous national forums that showcase presentations by teacher-inquirers. Perhaps the largest and most well known is the American Educational Research Association (AERA). The professionals who engage in teacher inquiry and are members of this organization typically assemble in special interest groups such as Teachers as Researchers or Professional Development Schools.

While we encourage you to become part of a national network such as AERA, the reality in almost every school district is that conference travel money for teachers is small or nonexistent. Many teachers receive limited support for conference endeavors and must pay out of their own pockets to attend and present. For this reason, the cost of national travel is often prohibitive for many teachers, especially on a yearly basis.

You can still experience the exhilaration that comes from presenting your work formally to an audience by connecting to conferences that occur in your vicinity. Most national organizations, such as AERA, Association for Supervision and Curriculum Development (ASCD), National Staff Development Council (NSDC), National Council for Teachers of Mathematics (NCTM), National Council for the Social Studies (NCSS), National Science Teachers Association (NSTA), National Council for Teachers of English (NCTE), National Association for the Education of Young Children (NAEYC), and Association of Teacher Educators (ATE), have state affiliates that hold conferences at least once a year. In addition, if you are a prospective teacher, most of these organizations offer very reasonable membership rates for students, so it is an excellent time to investigate professional groups that can serve as local outlets for the sharing of your inquiry, as well as a stimulus for continuing to inquire into your practice throughout your career. Finally, in addition to the journals dedicated solely to action research described previously, many of these state affiliate organizations also publish journals that offer another outlet for your written work (see, e.g., Dana, Gimbert, & Silva, 1999).

A final possibility is designing and holding your own teacher-inquiry conference. While this may sound like an overwhelming undertaking, it can be accomplished relatively easily by starting small and drawing on some sound organizational abilities. To show the range and variety possible, we describe two structures we have used to create our own conferences. The first structure uses posters and is conversational. The second structure uses presented papers and follows a more traditional conference format.

The first structure was designed as a culmination to a class on teacher inquiry with just 13 members in the class. We held the final class during the evening in the all-purpose room of a local school (7:00 p.m.–9:00 p.m.), where class members set up posters in two shifts (7:00 p.m.–7:30 p.m. and 8:00 p.m.–8:30 p.m.) that captured the essence of their inquiries. Each member of the class was responsible for inviting at least one other colleague or family member, and we also posted information about the conference in local schools and at the university. We created a program for the evening that contained the titles and abstracts of each class member's work, and the schedule for the evening conference was as follows:

7:00–7:30 p.m. Round 1 of poster presentations (six posters set up)—Conference participants visit each poster and presenters discuss their inquiries and answer questions through conversation.

7:30–8:00 p.m. Refreshments served; Round 1 posters taken down; Round 2 posters set up.

8:00–8:30 p.m. Round 2 of poster presentations (seven posters set up)—Conference participants visit each poster and presenters discuss their inquiries and answer questions through conversation.

8:30–9:00 p.m. Participants gather for discussion and reflection about teacher inquiry.

The second structure was designed as a culmination to a professional development school year where mentors and interns shared the results of inquiries conducted in their classrooms that year (Dana, 1999). We designated the last Saturday in April as the annual Professional Development School Teacher Inquiry Conference. Two weeks prior to this conference, we asked all mentors and interns who had engaged in inquiry to e-mail us titles and brief abstracts of their work. We assigned each of the inquiry abstracts received to one of five 20-minute sessions to occur concurrently throughout the morning in neighboring classrooms at one of the professional development school sites. We invited teachers, administrators, faculty from the school district and university, and the family members of all presenters. Next, we created a conference program to allow all participants to view the presentation offerings and choose which sessions they wished to attend. After three concurrent sessions, we allotted a 30-minute time slot for Bagel Brunch, offering refreshments such as coffee, juice, doughnuts, and, of course, bagels. After two more sessions, the conference ended just after the noon hour with recognition of all the presenters and those who supported their work and brief reflections on the inquiry process. A portion of the 2002 conference program appears in Figure 9.3.

Remember our advice about starting small? The first conference program we organized during the pilot year of the PDS in 1999 contained a total of 13 intern presentations and one mentor-teacher presentation from two elementary professional development school sites. There were two or three selections offered during each concurrent session, and approximately 50 people attended the conference. Just four years later, this same conference had grown to showcase the inquiries of 41 interns, 15 mentor-teachers, 6 teachers who were not currently mentoring an intern, and 4 librarians from six elementary schools, two middle schools, and the district's high school. Approximately 200 attendees chose from 10 or 11 presentations during each concurrent session. Even after we left this context to take new positions and spread the good news of inquiry in other places, this conference has continued to grow each year, demonstrating that a culture of inquiry had been built and institutionalized at this location. (For more information about building an inquiry culture, please see Dana et al., 2001; Dana, Silva & Snow-Gerono, 2002; and Snow, Dana, & Silva, 2001).

In a similar fashion, at our next institution (University of Florida), we organized an annual program similar to that which we organized in our work with the State College Area School District—Pennsylvania State University Elementary Professional Development School Program. We named this program the Teaching, Inquiry, and Innovation Showcase and gave it a very similar format to the PDS inquiry conference previously described. The purpose of this annual event was threefold: (1) to

Figure 9.3   Inquiry Conference Program

The State College Area School District—Pennsylvania State University
Professional Development School Teacher Inquiry Conference
April 27, 2002
Mt. Nittany Middle School

| 9:00 a.m. | **Welcome and Orientation** |
| *Auditorium* | |

| 9:15–9:35 a.m. | **Session I** |

Room 156   **Encouraging Lifelong Learners: Intrinsic Motivation in the Classroom**

Melissa Cinquini, Intern
Park Forest Elementary School
cinquini@psu.edu

How can we encourage students to become lifelong learners? This inquiry began with an assessment of students' current motivational responses to completing school work. The teacher then used these responses to explore how an activity rooted in guiding and supporting intrinsic motivation affected the learners in this classroom.

Room 154   **Phonemic Awareness: A Key to Kindergarten**

Darcie Hampton, Mentor
Matternville Elementary School
drh13@scasd.pa.k12.us

Beth Schickel, Intern
Matternville Elementary School
schickel@psu.edu

A veteran teacher and intern look at the learning and teaching of phonemic awareness. As teachers in a kindergarten classroom we noticed that students' sense of phonemic awareness varied a great deal. As a result of this, we wanted to see the effects of supplemental phonemic awareness activities with students who are struggling.

Room 152   **Effective Use of the Opening Routine**

Sara Evensen Tilles, Intern
Ferguson Township Elementary School
set132@psu.edu

A Professional Development School intern examines the use of various strategies during opening activities. How can all subject areas be integrated and reinforced during this time? How can students be motivated to participate?

Room 146   **Developing Differentiated Instruction Strategies and Motivational Strategies to Meet the Individual Needs of a Math Learner**

Stacee Banko, Intern
Park Forest Elementary School
smb295@psu.edu

I believe that it is crucial that students are motivated and excited to learn in every situation. This means that I must be willing to look at my own teaching styles and see where new strategies can be implemented as well as encouraged. My inquiry project focuses on an individual learner who was "slipping between the cracks" before I understood the different teaching strategies I could adopt to help him become a successful, motivated learner.

(Continued)

Figure 9.3 (Continued)

Room 144 Examining Different Types of Assessment and Evaluating Which Assessment Students Value the Most

Jamie Clouse, Intern
High School North
twirlygirl183@aol.com

There are numerous approaches to assessment, but it is crucial to choose the best type of assessment based on the assignment. Too often students believe that the only real way to measure their success is with a letter grade. I would like to explore various types of assessment to get a firmer grasp on which types of assessment are most supportive of a learning environment.

Room 256 **Building Confidence in Reading**

Jackie Mintmier, Intern
Ferguson Township Elementary School
jxm530@psu.edu

Through research and exploring two students' beliefs and thinking about reading, I tried to find ways that would help to increase the students' confidence and help them develop a positive self-image of themselves as readers.

Room 254 **Effective Parent Communication: What Does it Look Like?**

Candy Bryan, Teacher
Ferguson Township Elementary School
cjb14@scasd.k12.pa.us

Kelly Reilley-Kaminiski, Mentor
Ferguson Township Elementary School
kar15@scasd.k12.pa.us

Two elementary school teachers research effective parent communication tools that reflect the current needs within each classroom. Based on parent feedback, they implemented changes to their practices and compared the needs of the parents between first and third year students

Room 252 The Puzzle of Two Children: How to Motivate Two New and Challenging Students in My Classroom

Kelli Hollada, Intern
Radio Park Elementary School
keh164@psu.edu

In an attempt to discover how to best serve the students in my second grade class, I searched for ways to help motivate two boys who were experiencing difficulties as learners in my classroom.

Room 246 **Responding to Conflict in a First-Grade Classroom**

Meghan Marshall, Intern
Radio Park Elementary School
mlm335@psu.edu

An intern explores the conflicts in her first-grade classroom. What is causing our classroom, especially one group of girls, to have so much conflict? How can I better respond to these conflicts to encourage students to be independent problem solvers?

Room 244 **Between a Rock and a Hard Place: The Search to Find a Meaningful and Practical Way to Assess Student Writing**

Sabrina Ehmke, Intern
Mount Nittany Middle School
sae129@psu.edu

My inquiry involves the struggle I face as a teacher when it comes to evaluating student writing. The experience of writing, which seems to me inherently a subjective one, is more often than not assigned a point or grade value as an indicator of achievement. In the process of regulating writing to a quantitative variable, I wonder whether such a forced attempt at objectivity does in fact not only hinder students as writers, but also devalue what we as teachers hope to promote in terms of the act of writing itself.

Room 242 **Mathematical Rubrics-Meeting the Standards**

Brenda Khayat, Mentor
Park Forest Elementary
bgk11@scasd.k12.pa.us

My goal was to improve the written side of problem solving for fifth graders. The belief is that students can problem solve, but the challenge is for them to show it in their written explanations.

celebrate the practitioner who, through the processes of inquiry, has contributed to improving schools from within; (2) to enable practicing teachers and administrators across North Central Florida and from different programs and affiliations to network with each other; and (3) to connect prospective and practicing teachers through this forum, enabling prospective teachers to be socialized into the profession as inquirers and practicing teachers to shape the next generation of those entering the teaching profession. At this event, veteran teachers from various districts across Florida who had engaged in teacher inquiry gathered to share

Figure 9.4 Debbi Hubbell presents her inquiry at the fourth annual Teaching, Inquiry, and Innovation Showcase at the University of Florida's P. K. Yonge Developmental Research School.

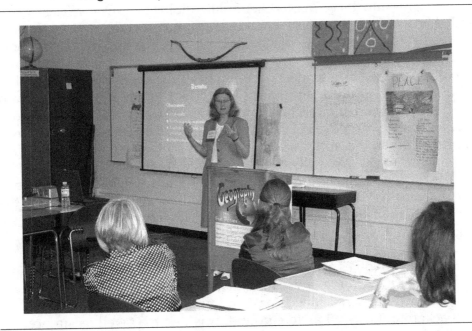

SOURCE: Used with permission of Debbi Hubbell.

their work. Prospective teachers who had completed teacher inquiry into an individual child in their preintern field experience placements presented their inquiry in a five-minute time segment at the start of each veteran teacher's presentation. The prospective teachers subsequently introduced the veteran teacher and served as presider for that session, keeping time and assisting the veteran teacher in any way needed. At our first showcase in 2005, we were thrilled to host 80 practicing teachers presenting their work and 112 preinterns who gave five-minute mini-presentations on their inquiries at the start of each teacher's session. Over 200 people attended the inaugural showcase, enabling us to start where we had left off in our work at Penn State. Just three years later, over 180 teachers and 150 preinterns presented their work at our annual event, and the event was attended by over 400 people! In three years' time, our showcase more than doubled in size, and, inspired by this annual event, similar showcases are being organized and held at other locations across our state, with some inquiry showcases in large districts such as Pinellas County Schools and Miami-Dade Public Schools nearing 1,000 participants! Now serving as a department chair at the University of South Florida, Diane has organized an inquiry showcase for the entire College of Education that honors one alumnus each year who has continued to engage in the process of inquiry postgraduation with the USF Teacher Researcher Alumni Award.

The growth of these showcases attests to the power teacher inquiry holds for teacher professional growth and brings us full circle to where we began this book. In the preface to this text we stated that "we hope to provide insights into the power teacher inquiry holds to transform classrooms and schools to places where knowledge about teaching and learning is generated from and used by those closest to the children—classroom teachers." We hope that as you end this text, you have enjoyed your journey through the basic tenets of the inquiry process, the ultimate goal of which is *not* to produce an inquiry project but to adopt a stance toward your teaching and the teaching profession characterized by continuous problematizing of practice, studying of practice, and leading change efforts based on the outcomes of such study. This is the ultimate journey on which we hope you will embark.

We believe no other author captures the nature of this ultimate journey as eloquently as William Ayers (1989) in the following quote we used at the very opening of this book. Coming full circle, we close our book, as we began it:

> Teaching involves a search for meaning in the world. Teaching is a life project, a calling, a vocation that is an organizing center of all other activities. Teaching is past and future as well as present, it is background as well as foreground, it is depth as well as surface. Teaching is pain and humor, joy and anger, dreariness and epiphany. Teaching is world building, it is architecture and design, it is purpose and moral enterprise. Teaching is a way of being in the world that breaks through the boundaries of the traditional job and in the process redefines all life and teaching itself. (p. 130)

Through embarking on the inquiry journey, you break boundaries. You redefine life. You redefine teaching itself. Bon voyage!

References

Acheson, K. A., & Gall, M. D. (1997). *Techniques in the clinical supervision of teachers: Preservice and inservice applications.* New York: Longman.

Albrecht, K., & Harrell, S. (2007). Bridging the gap: Making the transition from intervention math to general math. In N. F. Dana & D. C. Delane (Eds.), *Improving Florida schools through teacher inquiry: Selections from the 2006 Teaching, Inquiry, and Innovation Showcase* (pp. 40–44). Gainesville: University of Florida, Center for School Improvement.

Allington, R. L. (2006). *What really matters for struggling readers: Designing research-based programs* (2nd ed.). Boston: Pearson Education.

Almquist, C. (2000, April). *Science tables in first grade.* Paper presented at the second annual State College Area School District—Pennsylvania State University Teacher Inquiry Conference, State College, PA.

Ariew, S., & Powers, A. (2012). *Standing on the shoulders of giants: How to begin the literature review.* Graduate school presentation, University of South Florida, Tampa.

Aronowitz, S., & Giroux, H. (1985). *Education under siege.* New York: New World Foundation.

Avery, C. (1993). *. . . And with a light touch: Learning about reading, writing, and teaching with first graders.* Portsmouth, NH: Heinemann.

Ayers, W. (1989). *The good preschool teacher: Six teachers reflect on their lives.* New York: Teachers College Press.

Barnes, J., Conrad, K., Demont-Heinrich, C., Graziano, M., Kowalski, D., Neufeld, J., et al. (2007). *Generalizability and transferability.* Fort Collins: Colorado State University Department of English. Retrieved April 30, 2007, from http://writing.colostate.edu/guides/research/gentrans

Barth, R. (1990). *Improving schools from within: Parents, teachers, and principals can make a difference.* San Francisco: Jossey-Bass.

Barth, R. (2001). Principal centered professional development. *Theory Into Practice, 25*(3), 156–160.

Bauwens, J., & Hourcade, J. (1995). *Cooperative teaching: Rebuilding the schoolhouse for all students.* Austin, TX: PRO-ED.

Bernhardt, V. (2004). *Data analysis for continuous school improvement.* Larchmont, NY: Eye on Education.

Beyer, T. (2007, April). *Reading habits of high school seniors.* Paper presented at the third annual University of Florida Teaching, Inquiry, and Innovation Showcase, Gainesville, FL.

Bigelow, B., & Peterson, B. (1998). *Rethinking Columbus: The next 500 years*. Milwaukee, WI: Rethinking Schools LTD.

Boudett, K. P., City, W. A., Murnane, R. J. (2005). *Data wise: A step-by-step guide to using assessment results to improve teaching and learning*. Cambridge, MA: Harvard Education Press.

Boyd, T. A. (1961). *Prophet of progress: Selections from the speeches of Charles F. Kettering*. New York: E. P. Dutton.

Brindley, R., & Crocco, C. (2009). *Empowering the voice of the teacher researcher: Achieving success through a culture of inquiry*. New York: Rowman & Littlefield.

Brown, P. (2010). Teacher research and university institutional review boards. *Journal of Early Childhood Teacher Education, 31*, 276–283.

Bryan, C., & Reilly-Kaminski, K. (2002, April). *Effective parent communication: What does it look like?* Paper presented at the fourth annual State College Area School District—Pennsylvania State University Teacher Inquiry Conference, State College, PA.

Burgin, S. (2007a). A demo-a-day in high school chemistry. In N. F. Dana & D. C. Delane (Eds.), *Improving Florida schools through teacher inquiry: Selections from the 2006 Teaching, Inquiry, and Innovation Showcase* (pp. 126–135). Gainesville: University of Florida, Center for School Improvement.

Burgin, S. (2007b, April). *Student perceptions of teacher help outside of class*. Paper presented at the third annual University of Florida Teaching, Inquiry, and Innovation Showcase, Gainesville, FL.

Calkins, L. M. (1986). *The art of teaching writing*. Portsmouth, NH: Heinemann.

Calkins, L., Ehrenworth, M., & Lehman, C. (2012). *Pathways to the common core: Accelerating achievement*. Portsmouth, NH: Heinemann.

Caro-Bruce, C., Flessner, R., Klehr, M., & Zeichner, K. (2007). *Creating equitable classrooms through action research*. Thousand Oaks, CA: Corwin.

Carr, W., & Kemmis, S. (1986). *Becoming critical: Knowing through action research*. Geelong, Victoria, Australia: Deakin University Press.

Christensen, K. (2013). *Using collaborative writing to help English language learners actualize the Common Core State Standards*. Unpublished doctoral dissertation, University of Florida, Gainesville.

Clark, C. (1995). *Thoughtful teaching*. New York: Teachers College Press.

Cloutier, D., Lilley, B., Phillips, D., Weber, B., & Sanderson, D. (1987). *A guide to program evaluation and reporting*. Orono: University of Maine Cooperative Extension Service.

Cochran-Smith, M. (1991). Learning to teach against the grain. *Harvard Educational Review, 61*(3), 279–310.

Cochran-Smith, M., & Lytle, S. L. (1993). *Inside/outside: Teacher research and knowledge*. New York: Teachers College Press.

Cochran-Smith, M., & Lytle, S. L. (1999). The teacher research movement: A decade later. *Educational Researcher, 28*(7), 15–25.

Cochran-Smith, M., & Lytle, S. L. (2001). Beyond certainty: Taking an inquiry stance on practice. In A. Lieberman & L. Miller (Eds.), *Teachers caught in the action: Professional development that matters* (pp. 45–58). New York: Teachers College Press.

Cochran-Smith, M., & Lytle, S. L. (2006). Troubling images of teaching in No Child Left Behind. *Harvard Educational Review, 76*(4), 668–697.

Cochran-Smith, M., & Lytle, S. L. (2009). *Inquiry as stance: Practitioner research for the next generation*. New York: Teachers College Press.

Cook, G. (2004). Grade inflation reaches new heights. *American School Board Journal, 191*(6), 8.

Creswell, J. W. (2008). *Research design: Qualitative, quantitative, and mixed methods approaches* (2nd ed.). Thousand Oaks, CA: Sage.

Creswell, J. W. (2012). *Qualitative inquiry and research design.* Thousand Oaks, CA: Sage.

Crowther, F. (1997). The William Walker oration, 1996: Unsung heroes: The leaders in our classrooms. *Journal of Educational Administration, 3591,* 5–17.

Crowther, F. (2009). *Developing teacher leaders: How teacher leadership enhances school success.* Thousand Oaks, CA: Corwin.

Dana, N. F. (1994). Building partnerships to effect educational change: School culture and the finding of teacher voice. In M. J. O'Hair & S. J. Odell (Eds.), *Partnerships in education: Teacher education yearbook II* (pp. 11–26). New York: Harcourt Brace College.

Dana, N. F. (1995). Action research, school change, and the silencing of teacher voice. *Action in Teacher Education, 16*(4), 59–70.

Dana, N. F. (1999). *The professional development school story: Assessing the impact of year one (1998–99) of the State College Area School District—Pennsylvania State University Elementary Professional Development Schools.* Research report submitted to The State College Area School District Board of Directors.

Dana, N. F. (2001, April). *Inquiry in the PDS: The thread that ties the content areas together.* Paper presented at the annual meeting of the American Educational Research Association, Seattle, WA.

Dana, N. F. (2013). *Digging deeper into action research: A teacher inquirer's field guide.* Thousand Oaks, CA: Corwin.

Dana, N. F., & Baker, J. (Eds.). (2006). *Improving Florida schools through teacher inquiry: Selections from the 2005 Teaching, Inquiry, and Innovation Showcase.* Monograph published by the Center for School Improvement and North East Florida Educational Consortium.

Dana, N. F., Burns, J. B., & Wolkenhauer, R. (2013). *Inquiring into the common core.* Thousand Oaks, CA: Corwin.

Dana, N. F., & Delane, D. C. (Eds.). (2007). *Improving Florida schools through teacher inquiry: Selections from the 2006 Teaching, Inquiry, and Innovation Showcase.* Monograph published by the Center for School Improvement and North East Florida Educational Consortium.

Dana, N. F., Gimbert, B., & Silva, D. Y. (1999). Teacher inquiry: Staff development for the 21st century. *Pennsylvania Educational Leadership, 18*(2), 6–12.

Dana, N. F., & Silva, D. Y. (2001). Student teachers as researchers: Developing an inquiry stance towards teaching. In J. D. Rainer & E. M. Guyton (Eds.), *Research on the effects of teacher education on teacher performance* (pp. 91–104). Dubuque, IA: Kendall/Hunt.

Dana, N. F., & Silva, D. Y. (2002). Building an inquiry oriented PDS: Inquiry as a part of mentor teacher work. In I. N. Guadarrama, J. Nath, & J. Ramsey (Eds.), *Forging alliances in community and thought: Research in professional development schools* (pp. 87–104). Greenwich, CT: Information Age.

Dana, N. F., Silva, D. Y., Gimbert, B., Nolan, J., Zembal-Saul, C., Tzur, R., et al. (2001). Developing new understandings of PDS work: Better problems, better questions. *Action in Teacher Education, 22*(4), 15–27.

Dana, N. F., Silva, D. Y., & Snow-Gerono, J. (2002). Building a culture of inquiry in a professional development school. *Teacher Education and Practice, 15*(4), 71–89.

Dana, N. F., Smith, J., & Yendol-Hoppey, D. (2011). Teacher research in the PDS: How do we define quality? In J. L. Nath, I. N. Guadarrama, & J. Ramsey (Eds.), *Investigating university-school partnerships* (pp. 137–152). Greenwich, CT: Information Age.

Dana, N. F., Thomas, C., & Boynton, S. (2011). *Inquiry: A districtwide approach to staff and student learning.* Thousand Oaks, CA: Corwin.

Dana, N. F., & Yendol-Hoppey, D. (2006, April). *Facilitating the inquiry of others.* Paper presented at the second annual Teaching, Inquiry, and Innovation Showcase, Gainesville, FL.

Dana, N. F., & Yendol-Hoppey, D. (2008a). *The reflective educator's guide to professional development: Coaching inquiry-oriented learning communities.* Thousand Oaks, CA: Corwin.

Dana, N. F., & Yendol-Hoppey, D. (2008b). Resisting crash diet staff development. *Kappa Delta Pi Record, 44*(2), 66–71.

Dana, N. F., Yendol-Hoppey, D., & Snow-Gerono, J. L. (2006). Deconstructing inquiry in the professional development school: Exploring the domains and contents of teachers' questions. *Action on Teacher Education, 27*(4), 59–71.

Dana, N. F., & Yendol-Silva, D. (2003). *The reflective educator's guide to classroom research.* Thousand Oaks, CA: Corwin.

Danielson, C. (2006). *Teacher leadership that strengthens professional practice.* Alexandria, VA: ASCD.

Darling-Hammond, L. (1994). Developing professional development schools: Early lessons, challenge, and promise. In L. Darling-Hammond (Ed.), *Professional development schools: Schools for developing a profession* (pp. 1–27). New York: Teachers College Press.

Darling-Hammond, L. (2007). The story of Gloria is a future vision of the new teacher. *Journal of Staff Development, 28*(3), 25–26.

Dawson, K., & Dana, N. F. (2007). When curriculum-based, technology enhanced field experiences and teacher inquiry coalesce: An opportunity for conceptual change? *British Journal of Educational Technology, 38*(4), 656–667.

Delane, D., Dana, N. F., & Steward, M. (2010). *The story of May and her inquiry journey: Creating a positive behavior support system in a seventh grade science classroom.* Unpublished manuscript.

Dempsie, G. (1997). Using puppets in a primary classroom: A teacher-researcher's findings. *Teaching and Learning: The Journal of Natural Inquiry, 11*(3), 5–13.

Dempsie, G. (2000). Can I love you? A child's adventure with puppets and play. *The Journal of the Imagination in Language Learning, 5,* 28–36.

Derman-Sparks, L. (1989). *Anti-bias curriculum: Tools for empowering young children.* Washington, DC: National Association for the Education of Young Children.

Dewey, J. (1933). *Democracy and education.* New York: Free Company.

Drennon, C. E., & Cervero, R. M. (2002). The politics of facilitation: Negotiating power and politics in practitioner inquiry groups. *Adult Education Quarterly, 52,* 193–209.

Drexler, W., Dawson, K., & Ferdig, R. (2007). Collaborative blogging as a means to develop elementary expository writing skills. *Electronic Journal for the Integration of Technology in Education, 16,* 140–160.

DuFour, R., & DuFour, B. (2007). What might be: Open the door to a better future. *Journal of Staff Development, 28*(3), 27–28.

Dunkle, C. A. (2012). *Leading the common core state standards: From common sense to common practice.* Thousand Oaks, CA: Corwin.

Easton, L. B. (2004). *Powerful designs for professional learning.* Oxford, OH: National Staff Development Council.

Elliot, J. (1988). Educational research and outsider-insider relations. *Qualitative Studies in Education, 1*(2), 155–166.

Elmore, R. F. (2007). Let's act like professionals. *Journal of Staff Development, 28*(3), 31–32.

Escue, C. (2006, April). *Why can't we all get along? If cooperative learning is such a great teaching strategy, why is it so painful at times?* Paper presented at the second annual University of Florida Teaching, Inquiry, and Innovation Showcase, Gainesville, FL.

Fashola, O. S. (Ed.). (2005). *Educating African American males: Voices from the field.* Thousand Oaks, CA: Corwin.

Fielding, R., & Nair, P. (2005). *The language of school design: Design patterns for 21st century schools.* Minneapolis, MN: DesignShare.

Frank, M. (1979). *If you're trying to teach kids how to write, you've gotta have this book!* Nashville, TN: Incentive.

Friend, M., & Cook, L. (2000). *Interactions: Collaboration skills for school professionals* (3rd ed.). New York: Longman.

Fullan, M. (2007). Change the terms for teacher learning. *Journal of Staff Development, 28*(3), 35–36.

Fullan, M. (2009). Positive pressure. *Springer International Handbooks of Education, 23*(1), 119–130.

Garman, Q. (1997, Fall). The slap heard 'round the room. *Partnership News (Newsletter of the Pennsylvania State University College of Education),* 1–4.

Glaser, B. (1978). *Theoretical sensitivity: Advances in the methodology of grounded theory.* Mill Valley, CA: Sociology Press.

Glickman, C. D., Gordon, S. P., & Ross-Gordon, J. M. (2007). *Super vision and instructional leadership* (7th ed.). Boston: Allyn & Bacon.

Glogowski, K., & Sessums, C. D. (2007). *Personal learning environments: Exploring professional development in a networked world.* Paper presented at the meeting of Web Heads in Action Online Conference 2007. Retrieved October 31, 2007, from http://www.webheadsinaction. org/node/168

Goldhammer, R. (1969). *Clinical supervision: Special methods for the supervision of teachers.* New York: Holt, Rinehart & Winston.

Greene, M. (1986). Reflections and passion in teaching. *Journal of Curriculum and Supervision, 2*(1), 68–81.

Hall, J. (1998). *Organizing wonder: Making inquiry science work in the elementary school.* Portsmouth, NH: Heinemann.

Hall, T. (2002). *Differentiated instruction.* Wakefield, MA: National Center on Accessing the General Curriculum. Retrieved November 11, 2008, from http://www.cast .org/publications/ncac/ncac_diffinstruc.html

Hampton, D., & Schickel, B. (2002, April). *Phonemic awareness: A key to kindergarten.* Paper presented at the fourth annual State College Area School District—Pennsylvania State University Teacher Inquiry Conference, State College, PA.

Hill, A. P. (2013). *Understanding and enacting self-regulated learning with students receiving tier 3 instruction in reading: A practitioner inquiry approach.* Unpublished doctoral dissertation, University of Florida, Gainesville.

Hord, S. (2007). Learn in community with others. *Journal of Staff Development, 28*(3), 39–40.

Hosfeld, A. (2000, April). *Implementing anti-bias curriculum: Addressing the needs and constraints of an elementary classroom.* Paper presented at the second annual State College Area School District—Pennsylvania State University Teacher Inquiry Conference, State College, PA.

Hubbard, R. S., & Power, B. M. (1993). *The art of classroom inquiry: A handbook for teacher researchers.* Portsmouth, NH: Heinemann.

Hubbard, R. S., & Power, B. M. (1999). *Living the questions: A guide for teacher researchers.* York, ME: Stenhouse.

Hubbell, D. (2006). Focus on fractured fairy tales and fluency flourishes. In N. F. Dana & J. Baker (Eds.), *Improving Florida schools through teacher inquiry: Selections from the 2005 Teaching, Inquiry, and Innovation Showcase* (pp. 5–8). Gainesville: University of Florida, Center for School Improvement.

Hubbell, D. (2007). *What is teacher inquiry?* Retrieved November 11, 2007, from http://csi.uflearn.org/node/188

Hughes, J. (2007). *Define teacher inquiry.* Retrieved November 11, 2007, from http://csi.uflearn.org/node/188

Jacobs, F. (1992). *The Tainos: The people who welcomed Columbus.* New York: G. P. Putman.

Jones, A., & Reed, D. (2000, April). *Rethinking Columbus.* Paper presented at the second annual State College Area School District—Pennsylvania State University Teacher Inquiry Conference, State College, PA.

Katzenmeyer, M., & Moller, G. (2001). *Awakening the sleeping giant: Helping teachers develop as leaders* (2nd ed.). Thousand Oaks, CA: Corwin.

Kincheloe, J. (1991). *Teachers as researchers: Qualitative inquiry as a path to empowerment.* New York: Falmer.

Krell, D. E., & Dana, N. F. (2012). Facilitating action research: A study of coaches, their experiences, and their reflections on leading teachers in the process of practitioner inquiry. *Professional Development in Education, 38*(5), 827–844.

Koziak, M., & Abruzzo, S. (2000, April). *Effective parent-teacher communication: Enhancing the teaching partnership between home and school.* Paper presented at the second annual State College Area School District—Pennsylvania State University Teacher Inquiry Conference, State College, PA.

Kreinbihl, J. (2007). *What is inquiry?* Retrieved November 11, 2007, from http://csi.uflearn.org/node/189

Kur, J. (2000, April). *Dinosaurs in the primary classroom: From facts and crafts to inquiry.* Paper presented at the second annual State College Area School District—Pennsylvania State University Teacher Inquiry Conference, State College, PA.

Lang, J. (2007). *Final paper submitted to EDE 6325: Guided Teacher Inquiry.* University of Florida, Gainesville.

Langrall, C. W. (Ed.). (2006). *Teachers engaged in research: Inquiry in mathematics classrooms, grades 3–5.* Charlotte, NC: Information Age.

Lassonde, C. A., Ritchie, G. V., & Fox, R. K. (2008). How teacher research can become your way of being. In C. A. S. Lassonde & S. E. Israel (Eds.), *Teachers taking action: A comprehensive guide to teacher research.* Newark, DE: International Reading Association.

Leonard, J., Petta, K., & Porter, C. (2012) A fresh look at graduate programs in teacher leadership in the United States. *Professional Development in Education, 38*(2), 189–204, doi:10.1080/19415257.2012.657826

Lesesne, T. S. (2003). *Making the match: The right book for the right reader at the right time*. Portland, ME: Stenhouse.

Lessem, D. (1991, May 19). The great dinosaur rip-off. *New York Times*.

Lewis, C., Perry, R., & Hurd, J. (2004). A deeper look at lesson study. *Educational Leadership, 61*(5), 18.

Lieberman, A., & Wood, D. R. (2002). The National Writing Project. *Educational Leadership, 59*(6), 40–43.

Loewen, J. (1995). *Lies my teacher told me: Everything your American history textbook got wrong*. New York: New Press.

Lortie, D. C. (1975). *School teacher: A sociological study*. Chicago: University of Chicago Press.

Love, N. (2004). Taking data to new depths. *Journal of Staff Development, 25*(4), 22–26.

Lunsford, S. (1998). *Literature-based mini-lessons to teach writing*. New York: Scholastic Professional Books.

MacDonald, M. (2007). Grade inflation, grade deflation—What can data tell me? In N. F. Dana & D. C. Delane (Eds.), *Improving Florida schools through teacher inquiry: Selections from the 2006 Teaching, Inquiry, and Innovation Showcase* (pp. 51–68). Gainesville: University of Florida: Center for School Improvement.

Malaggese, L. (2001, April). *What is a fair share? And other fractional adventures in a first grade classroom*. Paper presented at the third annual State College Area School District—Pennsylvania State University Teacher Inquiry Conference, State College, PA.

Marzano, R. J. (2007). *The art and science of teaching: A comprehensive framework for effective instruction*. Alexandria, VA: ASCD.

Masingila, J. O. (2006). *Teacher engaged in research: Inquiry into mathematics classrooms, grades 6–8*. Greenwich, CT: Information Age.

McCarty, C., & Poehner, P. (2002, April). *Peer coaching in an elementary classroom*. Paper presented at the fourth annual State College Area School District—Pennsylvania State University Teacher Inquiry Conference, State College, PA.

McLeod, S. (2006). *Essential elements of data-driven PLCs*. Retrieved April 30, 2007, from http://www.scottmcleod.net/dddm_resources

Meegan, G. (2007). *Paper submitted for EDE 6325: Guided Teacher Inquiry*. University of Florida, Gainesville.

Meyers, E., & Rust, F. (Eds.). (2003). *Taking action with teacher research*. Portsmouth, NH: Heinemann.

Mills, G. E. (2014). *Action research: A guide for the teacher researcher* (5th ed.). Saddle River, NJ: Pearson Education.

Mitchell, K. (2000, April). *How do airplanes fly? (How do I become a more effective science teacher?)* Paper presented at the second annual State College Area School District—Pennsylvania State University Teacher Inquiry Conference, State College, PA.

Munsart, C. A. (1993). *Investigating science with dinosaurs*. Englewood, CO: Teacher Ideas Press.

National Center of Student Progress Monitoring. (2007). *Student progress monitoring*. Retrieved April 30, 2007, from http://www. studentprogress.org/default.asp

National Council for Accreditation of Teacher Education. (2010, November). *Transforming teacher education through clinical practice: A national strategy to prepare effective teachers*. Washington, DC: Blue Ribbon Panel on Clinical Preparation and Partnerships for Improved Student Learning.

National Education Association. (2013). *Code of ethics*. Retrieved September 19, 2013, from www.nea.org/home/30442.htm

National Governors Association Center for Best Practices & Council of Chief State School Officers. (2012a). *Common core state standards initiative: About the standards*. Retrieved from http://www.corestandards.org/about-the-standards

National Governors Association Center for Best Practices & Council of Chief State School Officers. (2012b). *Common core state standards initiative: English language arts standards—Introduction—Key design consideration*. Retrieved from http://www.corestandards.org/ELA-Literacy/introduction/key-design-consideration

National Parent and Teachers Association (PTA). (1997). *National standards for parent/family involvement programs* (booklet). Available at http://www.pta.org

National School Reform Faculty. (2007). *Frequently asked questions*. Retrieved November 2007, from www.nsrfharmony .org/faq.html#1

Niebauer, H. (1997, Fall). Learning, not control. *Partnership News (Newsletter of the Pennsylvania State University College of Education)*, 10–11.

Nolan, J. F., & Huber, T. (1989, Winter). Nurturing the reflective practitioner through instructional supervision: A review of the literature. *Journal of Curriculum and Supervision, 4*(2), 126–145.

Nolen, A. L., & Putten, V. (2007). Action research in education: Addressing gaps in ethical principles and practices. *Educational Researcher, 36*(7), 401–407.

Olsen, L. (2003, May 21). Study relates cautionary tale of misusing data. *Education Week, 22*(37), 12.

Paris, G., & Paris, A. (2001). Classroom applications of research on self-regulated learning. *Educational Psychologist, 36*(2), 89–101.

Patton, M. Q. (2002). *Qualitative research & evaluation methods* (3rd ed.). Thousand Oaks, CA: Sage.

Perry, G., Henderson, B., & Meier, D. R. (2012). *Our inquiry, our practice: Undertaking, supporting, and learning from early childhood teacher research(ers)*. Washington, DC: National Association for the Education of Young Children.

Perry, N. (1998). Young children's self-regulated learning and contexts that support it. *Journal of Educational Psychology, 90*(4), 715–729.

Peters, B., & Romig, G. (2001, April). *Let's talk about science*. Paper presented at the third annual State College Area School District—Pennsylvania State University Teacher Inquiry Conference, State College, PA.

Pritchard, I. A. (2002). Travelers and trolls: Practitioner research and institutional review boards. *Educational Research, 31*(3), 3–13.

Quindlen, A. (1997). *Happily ever after*. New York: Random House.

Ramirez, M. (2007). Differentiating instruction in math in the primary grades. In N. F. Dana & D. C. Delane (Eds.), *Improving Florida schools through teacher inquiry: Selections from the 2006 Teaching, Inquiry, and Innovation Showcase* (pp. 100–106). Gainesville: University of Florida, Center for School Improvement.

Richardson, W. (2006). *Blogs, wikis, podcasts and other powerful Web tools for classrooms*. Thousand Oaks, CA: Corwin.

Richert, A. E. (1997). Teaching teachers for the challenge of change. In J. Loughran & T. Russell (Eds.), *Teaching about teaching: Purpose, passion, and pedagogy in teacher education* (pp. 73–94). Washington, DC: Falmer.

Roberts, R., & Elliot, L. (2002, April). *Taking a look at inquiry through inquiry*. Paper presented at the fourth annual State College Area School District—Pennsylvania State University Teacher Inquiry Conference, State College, PA.

Ross, D., Adams, A., Bondy, E., Dana, N., Dodman, S., & Swain, C. (2011). Preparing teacher leaders: Perceptions of the impact of a cohort-based, job-embedded, blended teacher leadership program. *Teaching and Teacher Education, 27*(8), 1213–1222.

Rotz, L., Kur, J., Robert, M., & Heitzmann, M. (2002, April). *Getting smarter with Smart boards: A collaborative project.* Paper presented at the fourth annual State College Area School District—Pennsylvania State University Teacher Inquiry Conference, State College, PA.

Routman, R. (2002). *Conversations: Strategies for teaching, learning, and evaluating.* Portsmouth, NH: Heinemann.

Ruddock, J., & Hopkins, D. (Eds.). (1985). Research as a basis for teaching: Readings from the work of Lawrence Stenhouse. London: Heinemann.

Russell, J. L. (2002, April). *Once upon a writer's workshop: Using children's literature to inspire dazzling, complete stories.* Paper presented at the fourth annual State College Area School District—Pennsylvania State University Teacher Inquiry Conference, State College, PA.

Rust, R., & Meyers, E. (2006). The bright side: Teacher research in the context of educational reform and policy-making. *Teaching and Teaching: Theory and Practice, 12*(1), 69–86.

Ruth, A. (1999, May). *The kindergarten writing center: Providing opportunities for an ESL student's language growth and development.* Paper presented at the first annual State College Area School District—Pennsylvania State University Teacher Inquiry Conference, State College, PA.

Ruth, A. (2001, April). *Two journeys of exploration.* Paper presented at the third annual State College Area School District—Pennsylvania State University Teacher Inquiry Conference, State College, PA.

Ruth, A. (2002, April). *Wanted: A new approach to using the minutes between 8:30 and 9:00 a.m. in my classroom.* Paper presented at the fourth annual State College Area School District—Pennsylvania State University Teacher Inquiry Conference, State College, PA.

Schlechty, P. C. (2007). Move staff development into the digital world. *Journal of Staff Development, 28*(3), 41–42.

Schon, D. A. (1983). *The reflective practitioner.* San Francisco: Jossey-Bass.

Schon, D. A. (1987). *Educating the reflective practitioner.* San Francisco: Jossey-Bass.

Schwandt, T. A. (1997). *Qualitative inquiry: A dictionary of terms.* Thousand Oaks, CA: Sage.

Seligman, D. (2002). The grade-inflation swindle. *Forbes, 169*(6), 94.

Sergiovanni, T. J., & Starratt, R. J. (1998). *Supervision: A redefinition.* New York: McGraw-Hill.

Sherman, R. R., & Webb, R. B. (1997). *Qualitative research in education: Focus and methods.* Philadelphia: Falmer.

Shulman, L. (1986). Knowledge and teaching: Foundations of the new reform. *Harvard Educational Review, 57*(1), 1–22.

Silva, D. Y., & Dana, N. F. (1999, February). *Cultivating inquiry within a professional development school.* Presentation at the annual meeting of the American Association of Colleges for Teacher Education, Washington, DC.

Silva, D. Y., & Dana, N. F. (2001). Collaborative supervision in the professional development school. *Journal of Curriculum and Supervision, 16*(4), 305–321.

Smith, L. M. (1990). Ethics in qualitative field research: An individual perspective. In E. W. Eisner & A. P. Peshkin (Eds.), *Qualitative inquiry in education: The continuing debate* (pp. 258–276). New York: Teachers College Press.

Smith, S. Z., & Smith, M. E. (Eds.). (2006). *Teachers engaged in research: Inquiry in mathematics classrooms, grades Pre-K–2.* Charlotte, NC: Information Age.

Snow, J. L., Dana, N. F., & Silva, D. Y. (2001). Where are they now? Former PDS interns emerge as first year teacher leaders. *The Professional Educator, 24*(1), 35–48.

Somekh, B., & Zeichner, K. (2009). Action research for educational reform: Remodeling action research theories and practices in local contexts. *Educational Action Research, 17*(1), 5–21.

Sousa, D., & Tomlinson, C. A. (2010). *Differentiation and brain: How neuroscience supports the learner-friendly classroom.* Alexandria, VA: ASCD.

Stiles, P. (1999). *Reflective journal.* Unpublished manuscript.

Sunner, N. (1999, May). *Questioning.* Paper presented at the first annual State College Area School District—Pennsylvania State University Teacher Inquiry Conference, State College, PA.

Tatum, A. W. (2005). *Teaching reading to black adolescent males: Closing the achievement gap.* Portland, ME: Stenhouse.

Thate, J. (2007a). *Thoughts on the kick-off.* Retrieved November 11, 2007, from http://csi.uflearn.org/node/172#comments

Thate, J. (2007b, April). *Can culturally relevant literature change attitudes towards reading?* Paper presented at the third annual University of Florida Teaching, Inquiry, and Innovation Showcase, Gainesville, FL.

Thorne, S. (2000). Data analysis in qualitative research. *Evidence-Based Nursing, 3,* 68–70.

Thulin, J. (1999, May). *Meaningful melodies: Reading to the beat of a different drummer.* Paper presented at the first annual State College Area School District—Pennsylvania State University Teacher Inquiry Conference, State College, PA.

Tomlinson, C. A. (1999). *The differentiated classroom: Responding to the needs of all learners.* Alexandria, VA: ASCD.

Tomlinson, C. A. (2001). *How to differentiate instruction in mixed-ability classrooms* (2nd ed.). Alexandria, VA: ASCD.

Tomlinson, C. A., & Imbeau, M. (2010). *Leading and managing a differentiated classroom.* Alexandria, VA: ASCD.

van Ingen, S. (2013). *Preparing teachers to apply research to mathematics teaching: Using design-based research to define and assess the process of evidence-based practice.* (Doctoral dissertation). Retrieved from ProQuest Dissertations and Theses (Accession Order No. 1425355200).

Van Zoest, L. R. (Ed.). (2006). *Teachers engaged in research: Inquiry in mathematics classrooms, grades 9–12.* Charlotte, NC: Information Age.

Wasley, P. A. (1992). Working together: Teacher leadership and collaboration. In C. Livingston (Ed.), *Teacher leaders: Evolving roles* (pp. 21–55). Washington, DC: National Education Association.

Weller, K. (2007, March). *Adapting lessons from the NCAA Web site to differentiate instruction for my middle school students.* Presentation at the P. K. Yonge Developmental Research School March Seventh Grade Team Meeting, Gainesville, FL.

Wildavsky, B. (2000). At least they have high self esteem. *U.S. News and World Report, 128*(5), 50.

Wilson, S. M., Floden, R. E., & Ferrini-Mundy, J. (2001). *Teacher preparation research: Current knowledge, gaps, recommendations.* A research report prepared for the U.S. Department of Education and the Office for Education Research and Improvement. University of Washington: Center for the Study of Teaching and Policy.

Wolcott, H. F. (1990). *Writing up qualitative research.* Newbury Park, CA: Sage.

Wolcott, H. F. (2008). *Writing up qualitative research* (3rd ed.). Thousand Oaks, CA: Sage.

Wolcott, H. F. (1994). *Transforming qualitative data: Description, analysis, and interpretation.* Thousand Oaks, CA: Sage.

Wolk, S. (2008). School as inquiry. *Kappan, 90*(2), 115–122.

Wright, J. (2007). *RTI toolkit: A practical guide for schools.* Retrieved from http:// www.jimwrightonline.com/php/rti/rti_wire.php

Yendol-Hoppey, D., & Dana, N. F. (2008). Inquiry-oriented mentoring in the professional development school: The case of Claudia. In I. N. Guadarrama, J. Nath, & J. Ramsey (Eds.), *Collaboration in leadership and learning: Research in professional development schools, volume 3* (pp. 251–274). Greenwich, CT: Information Age.

York-Barr, J., & Duke, K. (2004). What do we know about teacher leadership? Findings from two decades of scholarship. *Review of Educational Research, 74*(3), 255–316.

Zeichner, K. (1986). Preparing reflective teachers: An overview of instructional strategies which have been employed in preservice teacher education. *International Journal of Educational Research, 7*(5), 565–575.

Zeichner, K. (1996). Teachers as reflective practitioners and the democratization of school reform. In K. Zeichner, S. Melnick, & M. L. Gomez (Eds.), *Currents of reform in preservice teacher education* (pp. 199–214). New York: Teacher College Press.

Zeichner, K. (2003). Teacher research as professional development for P–12 educators in the USA. *Educational Action Research, 2*(2), 301–326.

Zeichner, K. M., & Liston, D. P. (1996). *Reflective teaching: An introduction.* Mahwah, NJ: Lawrence Erlbaum.

Zimmerman, B. J. (2000). Attaining self-regulation: A social cognitive perspective. In M. Boekaerts, P. Pintrich, & M. Ziedner (Eds.), *Handbook on self-regulation,* (pp. 13–39). Orlando, FL: Academic Press.

Index

Figures and tables are indicated by *f* or *t* following the page number.

CORWIN

A SAGE Company

The Corwin logo—a raven striding across an open book—represents the union of courage and learning. Corwin is committed to improving education for all learners by publishing books and other professional development resources for those serving the field of PreK–12 education. By providing practical, hands-on materials, Corwin continues to carry out the promise of its motto: **"Helping Educators Do Their Work Better."**